8.10 (Title II) ERS 5-66 (Hemley)

STUDIES OF
GOOD AND EVIL

A SERIES OF ESSAYS UPON PROBLEMS
OF PHILOSOPHY AND OF LIFE

BY

JOSIAH ROYCE

ARCHON BOOKS
HAMDEN, CONNECTICUT
1964

INTRODUCTION.

THE essays which constitute the present volume, despite the variety of their topics and of the occasions under which they were prepared, have an unity which is already indicated in the title, but which may well be more explicitly set forth in this introduction.

As a teacher of philosophy, the author of the papers here collected has several times given expression, in former books, to theories upon fundamental metaphysical issues.* These theories belong to a type not unfamiliar in the present speculation, namely, to the type of post-Kantian idealism. But the philosophical idealist is interested not only in stating his fundamental convictions, but also in applying them to more concrete problems, especially to relatively practical problems. If idealism means anything, it means a theory of the universe which simply must not be divorced from empirical considerations, or from the business of life. It is not, as many have falsely supposed, a theory of the world founded merely upon *a priori* speculation, and developed solely in the closet. It is, and in its best historical representatives always has been, an effort to inter-

---

* Reference may be made to The Religious Aspect of Philosophy (Boston, 1855), to The Spirit of Modern Philosophy (Boston, 1892), and to the author's most mature statement of the argument for idealism in The Conception of God (New York, 1897).

iii

pret the facts of life. The present is hardly the place to summarize the grounds upon which an idealistic interpretation of the world depends. In a very brief summary, these grounds have been indicated in one of the essays of the prevent volume, namely, the sixth, entitled The Implications of Self-Consciousness. But to many readers fundamental metaphysical arguments are sure to be less enlightening than studies of more familiar issues in the light of philosophical considerations. To such readers, as well as to more technical philosophical students, the present essays are an appeal.

I have thus indicated, to readers who may not already know, the general philosophical position which these papers in common undertake to illustrate. Yet I can not wish to leave upon the reader's mind the impression that he is dealing merely with the predetermined product of the thought of a particular school. Idealistic philosophizing is, from the nature of the case, subject to wide individual variations. Without any effort to make extravagant claims for philosophical originality, any life-long student of this region of inquiry finds it very natural to be aware that in trying to contribute to the subject he has not merely been reporting the opinions of other people or giving in his adherence to a traditional doctrine. I have always insisted that my own idealism does not make me in any sense worthy of being called a follower, say, of Hegel, although of the importance of Hegel's thought I am well aware, and although, on occasion, in former publications, I have given expression to the obligations which, in common with other students, I feel towards Hegel's doctrine. In many respects I must insist that I have been quite as strongly influenced by Schopenhauer or by Fichte as by Hegel; nor can any student of recent idealism be unaware that his strongest obligations are, after all, to the general tendencies of contemporary speculation. In any case, if it is not one's duty to be wholly original, it is certainly one's natural purpose, and as far as possible, one's obligation, to be, in philosophical matters, relatively independent, both as regards the manner in which one reaches one's conclusions, and as regards the kind of insight that one seeks to impart to one's readers. In common, therefore, with other philosophical students, I am not unwilling to have my own opinions judged by and for themselves. Accordingly, I have hoped that a collection of papers like the present, containing various, and necessarily individual applications of doctrine to special problems, may serve to indicate in what sense the philosophical theses that I have to maintain possess a genuinely individual character.

I have called these papers Studies of Good and Evil. The title is in its nature wide. It commits the essays contained in this volume merely to one common character. They are all, directly or indirectly, contributions to the comprehension of the ethical aspects of the universe. The papers are of very various relations to technical philosophical issues. Four of them are essays in literary and philosophical criticism. One is directly concerned with the effect of the "Knowledge of Good and Evil" upon the character of the individual man. One is a contribution to the metaphysical "Problem of Evil" in its most general sense. Five, while dealing with metaphysical and psychological problems connected with the nature and relationships of our human type of consciousness, are somewhat more indirect contributions to the ethical interpretation of our place in the universe. One is an historical study of a concrete conflict between good and evil tendencies in early California life.

In publishing papers most of which are the product of accidental calls, and were originally adjusted to various occasions, one runs a certain risk of giving the impression not merely of miscellaneous contents, but of minor inconsistencies in statement and in the point of view. Yet to attempt by artificial devices to bring such papers into a purely external unity by erasing all signs of the original occasions to which they were adapted may in its turn remove the very character that I have most desired to preserve in the present volume. It is here simply not a philosophical system as such, nor even a systematic applied ethics, nor yet a rigidly connected series of discourses concerning good and evil that I have desired explicitly to present to the reader. I have merely wished to show how a certain philosophical theory, whose more systematic statement I have in part already given elsewhere, may be applied to the study now of this and now of that issue relating to good and evil. I have deliberately chosen, therefore, in general not to erase the marks of the origin of the individual papers. Several were lectures, and appear in the text as such. Two or three were contributions to periodical literature specially called out by particular occasions. All may serve to show a certain philosophical doctrine at work, and endeavoring not to remain an abstract theory, but to busy itself about the issues of life.

The series begins with a paper entitled The Problem of Job. This was originally the result of a call from a ministerial convention. It was later published in The New World. It deals in a most general, and I hope not at all an evasive way, with the metaphysical and religious " Problem of Evil." It presupposes, and does not endeavor either to justify or with any elaboration to explain, the idealistic theory of the nature of reality. Both my form of this theory, and my general application thereof to the problem of evil, were first set forth in The Religious Aspect of Philosophy. In my later work, The Spirit of Modern Philosophy, published in 1892, the closing chapter is devoted to a similar application of idealism to the problem of evil. The present discussion does not therefore stand alone. The theory of evil here in question brings me perhaps into a somewhat more intimate relation with characteristic statements presented and defended by Hegel, than is the case in some of my other philosophical theses. Yet, in the present essay on the problem of Job, special attention is given to the psychological basis upon which every metaphysical generalization concerning the nature and justification of evil may be, I think, properly said to be founded. Still, the reader who chooses to compare with this paper the papers in the former books mentioned, may be able to form a clearer judgment both of the meaning, and of the ground of the theory here presented than would be possible from this discussion alone.

If the theory of evil here in question is at all well founded, one of the most convincing practical solutions of the problem of evil must be presented wherever we find a good man triumphantly struggling with a profound problem of evil in his own life. Hence as the second paper of the present volume, I have ventured to set a psychological study of a personal experience of John Bunyan—an experience known to us as narrated by himself. This personal experience of Bunyan has been, as I think, despite all the elaborate biographical study that has been given to the poet's career, still too much neglected. In the present analysis, I have made use of certain concepts that have now become familiar in modern psychiatrical literature. Yet I do not believe that a psychological analysis of such experiences as these in any wise hinders our interpretation of their ethical or, for that matter, of their poetical meaning. Bunyan felt himself to be struggling with the "Tempter," with the Demon in personal presence. We have now the power to recognize, much more exactly than Bunyan could do, the nervous nature of this enemy. Yet in a deeper ethical meaning, the "demon's" presence is none the less a genuine fact when you have interpreted the psychological causation of the process in more modern forms. For Bunyan himself, the problem was indeed one of moral struggle, and when he won, and when, as he says, he brought of the "spoils of battle" and offered them in the temple of the Lord for the help of his suffering brethren, he gave us an instance of a concrete solution of the problem of evil whose philosophical significance is not made less by the fact that Bunyan's theology is no longer acceptable in Bunyan's form. This paper was originally written for the American Psychological Association, and appeared in the Psychological Review.

The third paper in the volume—that on Tennyson and Pessimism—appeared in a college student's journal, The Harvard Monthly. Published as it was a considerable number of years ago, this essay is obviously unsatisfactory if viewed as a characterization of the genius of Tennyson, who is now so much better known to us through his published biography. Yet to my mind as I wrote it the principal interest of the paper lay in its theory of the relation between good and evil. The poem which forms the text of the discussion had in my mind a merely illustrative value.

The fourth paper of the volume discusses another general aspect of the relations between good and evil. Here the original occasion of the paper was somewhat polemic. An essay by Professor George Simmel of Berlin, published in the International Journal of Ethics, provoked some criticism, and I was asked to take part in the controversy; but the purely objective significance of the issue served in the end to keep the merely polemic aspect rather in the background. The idealistic theory of the meaning of evil here gets again presented, but this time in reference to the delicate ethical question as to how far "the knowledge of evil" contributes to moral perfection. I hope that this paper, taken in connection with the foregoing, may serve to give the reader a general survey of the principal applications of the whole doctrine.

These more direct studies of good and evil prepare the

way for a metaphysical issue, namely, that of the ethical interpretation of reality, both human and extra-human. This book makes of course no effort to contribute more than fragments to the stupendous philosophical undertaking thus suggested. What fragments belong here are easily characterized. From our modern point of view, the ethical interpretation of the universe is hindered by two especially serious difficulties. It is hindered, in the first place, by the general presuppositions of modern naturalism. In the second place it is hampered by our incomplete appreciation of the meaning and the essential limitations of the human type of consciousness. But a study either of naturalism or of the nature of human consciousness, must necessarily lead one into very theoretical regions, where the ethical problems themselves are, for the time being, in the background. Yet, since our consciousness is the basis of all the good and evil that we human beings know, and since our relations with Nature form a most problematic aspect of life, both theoretical and practical, I have supposed that the essays from the fifth to the ninth in the present volume might serve to contribute in a genuine way to the issues suggested by my title. The fifth essay states, in the form of a critical paper suggested by a well-known lecture of Huxley, the problem with regard to the general relation between natural law and the demands of ethics. This paper appeared in the International Journal of Ethics. The sixth essay states the general case for an idealistic interpretation of the universe in its relations to self-consciousness. This paper originally appeared in the New World. The question what finite consciousness with all its burdens of good and evil may under these circumstances be and mean, is then treated first in some psychological particulars in the seventh essay, on the Anomalies of Self-Consciousness, and then in connection with cosmological problems, in the eighth essay, on the Relation between Human Consciousness and Nature. The theory of evolution indicated in the latter part of this essay is one to which I am expecting to give a more detailed statement in forthcoming books. These papers were originally printed in the Psychological Review, and in the Philosophical Review.

The theory of the social basis of self-consciousness, which is common to the seventh and to the eighth essays, is a theory which has many points in common with the views already published by Professor Baldwin in his well-known works on Mental Development in the Child and in the Race. Professor Baldwin, in his own papers on this subject, has frequently referred in the kindest way to my own work, whether published or unpublished. In return, I can only express both my sense of my general agreement, as to the social theory of self-consciousness, with Professor Baldwin, and my cordial recognition of his priority both in statement, and in publication, with respect to a number of the most important features of this theory. Students of social phenomena may find some interest both in the purely psychological aspects of this theory of finite self-consciousness and in my own suggested cosmological extensions of the theory. Such students of general idealism as find the theory of absolute self-consciousness too abstract and seemingly too *a priori* to win their easy assent, may also be interested in seeing by what means at least one student of idealism endeavors to bridge the gulf that at the outset seems to separate any psychological theory of consciousness from any idealistic theory of reality. As a fact, I myself can find no hostility between the psychological interpretation of consciousness and the philosophical interpretation of reality in terms of consciousness. The differences between the two are founded, in part, upon the empirical nature of the psychological material as contrasted with the general logical nature of the arguments for idealism ; and, in part, upon the difference in the point of view between a psychological and a philosophical study. But a difference in point of view certainly does mean hostility in doctrine. And every interpretation of experience involves at once a recognition of the facts of experience, and a consideration of their general logical meaning. Sooner or later psychology and philosophy must join hands afresh; and the more closely, in view of the fact that of late, for many minds, they have seemed to part company. It belongs to the future to suggest many of the ways in which this ultimate reconciliation will take place. I think it is the right of any philosophical student who feels also, as I do, an interest in empirical psychology, to undertake a suggestion, however fragmentary, of the union to be brought about, and to base this suggestion even upon the facts already accessible.

The ninth essay, originally contributed to the Harvard Monthly, is here given as a supplementary statement concerning certain general aspects of the nature of human consciousness. It is intended to bring a little more clearly to light a point whose philosophical and psychological significance seem to me to have been overlooked, namely, the fact that what gives us the most difficult aspect of the world-problem, and what most impresses upon us the tragedy of good and evil, as well as what, on the other hand, gives our human psychology its specific character, is the purely arbitrary fact of the "Limitation of Span" which characterizes the human type of consciousness. My own thesis is that the mere removal of this one limitation would in and of itself involve a lifting of the veil that is proverbially said to "hide" the reality. For reality, according to my idealism, is simply the Whole of what one actually means from the finite point of view. This "whole of what one means," viewed as a concrete whole, viewed as a significant and self-possessed unity of conscious life, is, for this idealism, the Real World. It is also the Divine Life. Therein the problem of evil is seen as solved. The limitations which exclude us, in our

character as human beings, from the concrete possession of
this ultimate solution, are not limitations that are to be interpreted as involving any ultimate separation between us
and the reality. The " separation " exists in truth only as a
certain characteristic *limitation of conscious span*, whereby our own finite meaning does not become perfectly clear
to us, and our own conscious processes are not themselves,
to their own very depths, presented to our fleeting finite
moments of consciousness. In order to grasp the nature of
reality, it would therefore not be necessary to be something
else than what we are, but only to be the Whole of what we
now in substance and essence already are. From grasping
this wholeness of our own meaning we are hindered, at any
moment, by the mere narrowness of the moment's view of
its own sense, and not by any gulf which separates us from
real Things in Themselves. The arguments for such a doctrine need of course their own room. But the application of
the doctrine both to the theoretical problems of human self-
consciousness, and to the practical problem of evil, may be
made clearer by means of the group of essays now in question.

The book closes with a return to decidedly more special
issues. Two philosophers are made the topics of a critical
study and portrayal; and in both cases the portrayal takes
up more space than the criticism. I have endeavored to
make the criticism itself rather immanent than external.
In addition, one historical incident, in itself extremely insignificant, but, in its illustrative character, as interesting as
many another fragment of human life, is made the topic of
a discussion whose length has to be frankly explained by
the personal and local interests that guided the author in
preparing this study. But all these three concluding studies
have in common their obvious relation to good and evil.
All three of them are instances of the way in which I
should try to express the idealistic spirit. Idealism has

meaning only in case you can judge whatever facts and
experience you please, or whatever varieties of philosophical opinion you may take into account, in the light of
idealistic insight. Of these three concluding essays the
first, or, in the order of the papers in this volume, the tenth,
discusses Meister Eckhart, the German mystic, a figure who
has been comparatively neglected by those students of philosophy who have written in English. From a scholarly
point of view I distinctly feel the limitations of this portrayal. Meister Eckhart has been the topic of some important recent researches, since the discovery of his Latin tracts ;
and these researches in some respects modify the views of
his historical position which were formerly maintained. I
have not been able to take explicit account of these most
recent investigations. On the other hand, I have endeavored to limit what I had to say of Eckhart's historical relations to what may be considered, on the whole, fairly sure,
without entering upon more doubtful considerations. The
general theoretical interest of a paper of this sort lies in the
intimate relations which must always exist between philosophical idealism and traditional mysticism. These intimate
relations I fully admit. Their practical as well as their theoretical interest I wholly recognize, and yet I am very sure
that one is unfair to the modern idealist who characterizes
his doctrine as identical with the mysticism even of an Eckhart. The actual contrast between the idealistic and the
mystic point of view I have several times discussed, notably
in the concluding essays of the book called The Spirit of
Modern Philosophy, and in passing, in some passages in the
third essay of the present volume. The practical danger
of seeking one's relation to the absolute in wholly remote
realms, apart from concrete human experience, is not only
insisted upon in the earlier papers of the present volume, but
is also further illustrated by such concrete cases as are discussed in the essay that, in this volume, immediately follows

the paper upon Meister Eckhart. And once more, the theoretical solution of the problem is to be sought, as I take it, in considerations bearing upon the form of human consciousness. That in some respects our own consciousness would have to be transformed before its relations to reality became directly clear, is of course precisely the idealistic thesis. On the other hand, this transformation must not mean, as the mystics desired it to mean, an ignoring of what there is positive, rational, significant, about the human type of consciousness itself ; just as the practical solution of the struggle with evil can not lie in such a virtue as that which Eckhart made central, namely, the virtue which he called "Departedness" of soul—*Abgescheidenheit.* The whole discussion of the concrete problem of evil, as given in the earlier essays of the present volume, ought to make clear to any fair-minded reader the genuine contrast between the central insights of idealism and the characteristic assertions of the mystic. On the other hand, it is unquestionable that the mystic and the idealist have much in common, namely, precisely what the idealist would call the truth of the mystical doctrine ; and there can be no doubt of the enormous historical importance of mysticism in keeping alive the sense of the intimacy of our human relation to the divine Reality. Nor can any portrayal of mysticism be fair which is not intimate and sympathetic. Nor yet can any criticism of mysticism be fair which goes far beyond the immanent criticism that mysticism, once fully portrayed, passes upon itself. I have endeavored to let Meister Eckhart, as practical adviser of his disciples and hearers, himself state the case of the good and evil of the present life, and I feel that hardly a word need be added to transform this practical outcome of his own doctrine into that willingness to accept finitude even while seeing in finite life an infinite meaning —a willingness which is to my mind the very essence of the idealistic spirit.

Immediately after this characterization of the mediæval mystic, I have permitted my study of California local history to follow as the eleventh paper. I can conceive of no better way to express the intimate relation of every fragment with the whole, in the universe as idealism conceives it, than just some such way as this ; and if any reader, after fairly reading the papers of the present volume, wonders why this particular constellation of papers was chosen, I fear that I shall have written for him quite in vain.

A series of philosophical essays may well close with the characterization of a philosopher, and I offer as my twelfth paper, although not without some hesitation, my contribution to the estimate of a recent French philosopher, J. M. Guyau. Here again the subject of the essay has been too infrequently presented to English readers. Here again one has a doctrine affiliated with modern idealism, yet by no means identical with such idealism, as I myself should endeavor to represent, and here again one has a distinctly ethical philosophy, with whose discussion these studies of the problem of good and evil may well close. The similarity between the "sociological" theory of the finite world in Guyau's latest book, and my own variety of this same theory, as stated in the eighth essay of the present volume, is plain, and is one reason the more for printing this final paper.

A few further notes concerning the origin and special occasions of the various papers of this volume will be found in connection with each. The papers on Meister Eckhart and on Guyau appear here for the first time in print. The account of the Squatter Riot of 1850 in Sacramento was published in the Overland Monthly, in 1885.

CONTENTS.

xvii

2

STUDIES OF GOOD AND EVIL.

I.

THE PROBLEM OF JOB.

IN speaking of the problem of Job, the present writer comes to the subject as a layman in theology, and as one ignorant of Hebrew scholarship. In referring to the original core of the Book of Job he follows, in a general way, the advice of Professor C. H. Toy ; and concerning the text of the poem he is guided by the translation of Dr. Gilbert. What this paper has to attempt is neither criticism of the book, nor philological exposition of its obscurities, but a brief study of the central problem of the poem from the point of view of a student of philosophy.

The problem of our book is the personal problem of its hero, Job himself. Discarding, for the first, as of possibly separate authorship, the Prologue, the Epilogue and the addresses of Elihu and of the Lord, one may as well come at once to the point of view of Job, as expressed in his speeches to his friends. Here is stated the problem of which none of the later additions in our poem offer any intelligible solution. In the exposition of this problem the original author develops all his poetical skill, and records thoughts that can never grow old. This is the portion of our book which is most frequently quoted. and which best expresses the genuine experience of suffering humanity. Here, then, the philosophical as well as the human interest of our poem centres.

1

I.

Job's world, as he sees it, is organized in a fashion extremely familiar to us all. The main ideas of this cosmology are easy to be reviewed. The very simplicity of the scheme of the universe here involved serves to bring into clearer view the mystery and horror of the problem that besets Job himself. The world, for Job, is the work of a being who, in the very nature of the case, ought to be intelligible (since he is wise), and friendly to the righteous, since, according to tradition, and by virtue of his divine wisdom itself, this God must know the value of a righteous man. But—here is the mystery—this God, as his works get known through our human experiences of evil, appears to us not friendly, but hopelessly foreign and hostile in his plans and his doings. The more, too, we study his ways with man, the less intelligible seems his nature. Tradition has dwelt upon his righteousness, has called him merciful, has magnified his love towards his servants, has described his justice in bringing to naught the wicked. One has learned to trust all these things, to conceive God in these terms, and to expect all this righteous government from him. Moreover, tradition joins with the pious observation of nature in assuring us of the omnipotence of God. Job himself pathetically insists that he never doubts, for an instant, God's power to do whatever in heaven or earth he may please to do. Nothing hinders God. No blind faith thwarts him. Sheol is naked before him. The abyss has no covering. The earth hangs over chaos because he orders it to do so. His power shatters the monsters and pierces the dragons. He can, then, do with evil precisely what he does with Rahab or with the shades, with the clouds or with the light or with the sea, namely, exactly what he chooses. Moreover, since he knows everything, and since the actual value of a righteous man is, for Job, an unquestionable and objective fact, God cannot fail to know this real worth of righteousness in his servants, as well as the real hatefulness and mischief of the wicked. God knows worth, and cannot be blind to it, since it is as real a fact as heaven and earth themselves.

Yet despite all these unquestioned facts, this God, who can do just what he chooses, "deprives of right" the righteous man, in Job's own case, and "vexes his soul," becomes towards him as a "tyrant," "persecutes" him "with strong hand," "dissolves" him "into storm," makes him a "byword" for outcasts, "casts" him "into the mire," renders him "a brother to jackals," deprives him of the poor joy of his "one day as a hireling," of the little delight that might come to him as a man before he descends hopelessly to the dark world of the shades, "watches over" him by day to oppress, by night to "terrify" him "with dreams and with visions"—in brief, acts as his enemy, "tears" him "in anger," "gnashes upon" him "with his teeth." All these are the expressions of Job himself. On the other hand, as, with equal wonder and horror the righteous Job reports, God on occasion does just the reverse of all this to the notoriously and deliberately wicked, who "grow old," "wax mighty in power," "see their offspring established," and their homes "secure from fear." If one turns from this view of God's especially unjust dealings with righteous and with wicked individuals to a general survey of his providential government of the world, one sees vast processes going on, as ingenious as they are merciless, as full of hints of a majestic wisdom as they are of indifference to every individual right.

> A mountain that falleth is shattered,
> And a rock is removed from its place;
> The waters do wear away stones,
> Its floods sweep the earth's dust away;
> And the hope of frail man thou destroyest.
> Thou subdu'st him for aye, and he goes;
> Marring his face thou rejectest him.

Here is a mere outline of the divine government as Job sees it. To express himself thus is for Job no momentary outburst of passion. Long days and nights he has brooded over these bitter facts of experience, before he has spoken at all. Unweariedly, in presence of his friends' objections, he reiterates his charges. He has the right of the sufferer to speak, and he uses it. He reports the facts that he sees. Of the paradox involved in all this he can make nothing. What is clear to him, however, is that this paradox is a matter for reasoning, not for blind authority. God ought to meet him face to face, and have the matter out in plain words. Job fears not to face his judge, or to demand his answer from God. God knows that Job has done nothing to deserve this fury. The question at issue between maker and creature is therefore one that demands a direct statement and a clear decision. "Why, since you can do precisely as you choose, and since you know, as all-knower, the value of a righteous servant, do you choose, as enemy, to persecute the righteous with this fury and persistence of hate ?" Here is the problem.

The human interest of the issue thus so clearly stated by Job lies, of course, in the universality of just such experiences of undeserved ill here upon earth. What Job saw of evil we can see ourselves to-day whenever we choose. Witness Armenia. Witness the tornadoes and the earthquakes. Less interesting to us is the thesis mentioned by Job's friends, in the antiquated form in which they state it, although to be sure, a similar thesis, in altered forms, is prevalent among us still. And of dramatic significance only is the earnestness with which Job defends his own personal righteousness. So naïve a self-assurance as is his is not in accordance with our modern conscience, and it is seldom indeed that our day would see any man sincerely using this phraseology of Job regarding his own consciousness of rectitude. But what is to-day as fresh and real to us as it was to our poet is the fact

that all about us, say in every child born with an unearned
heredity of misery, or in every pang of the oppressed, or in
every arbitrary coming of ill fortune, some form of innocence is beset with an evil that the sufferer has not deserved.
Job wins dramatic sympathy as an extreme, but for the purpose all the more typical, case of this universal experience
of unearned ill fortune. In every such case we therefore
still have the interest that Job had in demanding the solution of this central problem of evil. Herein, I need not say,
lies the permanent significance of the problem of Job,—a
problem that wholly outlasts any ancient Jewish controversy as to the question whether the divine justice always
does or does not act as Job's friends, in their devotion to
tradition, declare that it acts. Here, then, is the point
where our poem touches a question, not merely of an older
religion, but of philosophy, and of all time.

II.

The general problem of evil has received, as is well
known, a great deal of attention from the philosophers.
Few of them, at least in European thought, have been as
fearless in stating the issue as was the original author of
Job. The solutions offered have, however, been very numerous. For our purposes they may be reduced to a few.

First, then, one may escape Job's paradox by declining
altogether to view the world in teleological terms. Evils,
such as death, disease, tempests, enemies, fires, are not, so
one may declare, the works of God or of Satan, but are natural phenomena. Natural, too, are the phenomena of our
desires, of our pains, sorrows and failures. No divine purpose rules or overrules any of these things. That happens
to us, at any time, which must happen, in view of our natural limitations and of our ignorance. The way to better
things is to understand nature better than we now do. For
this view—a view often maintained in our day—there is no

problem of evil, in Job's sense, at all.   Evil there indeed is,
but the only rational problems are those of natural laws.   I
need not here further consider this method, not of solving
but of abolishing the problem before us, since my intent is,
in this paper, to suggest the possibility of some genuinely
teleological answer to Job's question.   I mention this first
view only to recognize, historically, its existence.

In the second place, one may deal with our problem by
attempting any one, or a number, of those familiar and
popular compromises between the belief in a world of natural law and the belief in a teleological order, which are
all, as compromises, reducible to the assertion that the presence of evil in the creation is a relatively insignificant, and
an inevitable, incident of a plan that produces sentient creatures subject to law.   Writers who expound such compromises have to point out that, since a burnt child dreads the
fire, pain is, on the whole, useful as a warning.   Evil is a
transient discipline, whereby finite creatures learn their place
in the system of things.   Again, a sentient world cannot get
on without some experience of suffering, since sentience
means tenderness.   Take away pain (so one still again often
insists), take away pain, and we should not learn our share
of natural truth.   Pain is the pedagogue to teach us natural
science.   The contagious diseases, for instance, are useful in
so far as they lead us in the end to study Bacteriology, and
thus to get an insight into the life of certain beautiful creatures of God whose presence in the world we should otherwise blindly overlook !   Moreover (to pass to still another
variation of this sort of explanation), created beings obviously grow from less to more.   First the lower, then the
higher.   Otherwise there could be no Evolution.   And were
there no evolution, how much of edifying natural science
we should miss !   But if one is evolved, if one grows from
less to more, there must be something to mark the stages of
growth.   Now evil is useful to mark the lower stages of

evolution. If you are to be, first an infant, then a man, or first a savage, then a civilized being, there must be evils attendant upon the earlier stages of your life—evils that make growth welcome and conscious. Thus, were there no colic and croup, were there no tumbles and crying-spells in infancy, there would be no sufficient incentives to loving parents to hasten the growing robustness of their children, and no motives to impel the children to long to grow big! Just so, cannibalism is valuable as a mark of a lower grade of evolution. Had there been no cannibalism we should realize less joyously than we do what a respectable thing it is to have become civilized! In brief, evil is, as it were, the dirt of the natural order, whose value is that, when you wash it off, you thereby learn the charm of the bath of evolution.

The foregoing are mere hints of familiar methods of playing about the edges of our problem, as children play barefoot in the shallowest reaches of the foam of the sea. In our poem, as Professor Toy expounds it, the speeches ascribed to Elihu contain the most hints of some such way of defining evil, as a merely transient incident of the discipline of the individual. With many writers explanations of this sort fill much space. They are even not without their proper place in popular discussion. But they have no interest for whoever has once come into the presence of Job's problem as it is in itself. A moment's thought reminds us of their superficiality. Pain is useful as a warning of danger. If we did not suffer, we should burn our hands off. Yes, but this explanation of one evil presupposes another, and a still unexplained and greater evil, namely, the existence of the danger of which we need to be thus warned. No doubt it is well that the past sufferings of the Armenians should teach the survivors, say the defenseless women and children, to have a wholesome fear in future of Turks. Does that explain, however, the need for the exist-

ence, or for the murderous doings of the Turks? If I can
only reach a given goal by passing over a given road, say
of evolution, it may be well for me to consent to the toil-
some journey. Does that explain why I was created so far
from my goal? Discipline, toil, penalty, surgery, are all
explicable as means to ends, if only it be presupposed that
there exists, and that there is quite otherwise explicable, the
necessity for the situations which involve such fearful ex-
penses. One justifies the surgery, but not the disease; the
toil, but not the existence of the need for the toil; the penalty, but not the situation which has made the penalty necessary, when one points out that evil is in so many cases
medicinal or disciplinary or prophylactic—an incident of
imperfect stages of evolution, or the price of a distant good
attained through misery. All such explanations, I insist,
trade upon borrowed capital. But God, by hypothesis, is
no borrower. He produces his own capital of ends and
means. Every evil is explained on the foregoing plan only
by presupposing at least an equal, and often a greater and a
preëxistent evil, namely, the very state of things which renders the first evil the only physically possible way of reaching a given goal. But what Job wants his judge to explain
is not that evil A is a physical means of warding off some
other greater evil B, in this cruel world where the waters
wear away even the stones, and where hopes of man are so
much frailer than the stones; but why a God who can do
whatever he wishes chooses situations where such a heaped-
up mass of evil means become what we should call physical
necessities to the ends now physically possible.

No real explanation of the presence of evil can succeed
which declares evil to be a merely physical necessity for
one who desires, in this present world, to reach a given goal.
Job's business is not with physical accidents, but with the
God who chose to make this present nature; and an answer
to Job must show that evil is not a physical but a logical

necessity—something whose non-existence would simply contradict the very essence, the very perfection of God's own nature and power. This talk of medicinal and disciplinary evil, perfectly fair when applied to our poor fate-bound human surgeons, judges, jailors, or teachers, becomes cruelly, even cynically trivial when applied to explain the ways of a God who is to choose, not only the physical means to an end, but the very *Physis* itself in which path and goal are to exist together. I confess, as a layman, that whenever, at a funeral, in the company of mourners who are immediately facing Job's own personal problem, and who are sometimes, to say the least, wide enough awake to desire not to be stayed with relative comforts, but to ask that terrible and uttermost question of God himself, and to require the direct answer—that whenever, I say, in such company I have to listen to these half-way answers, to these superficial plashes in the wavelets at the water's edge of sorrow, while the black, unfathomed ocean of finite evil spreads out before our wide-opened eyes—well, at such times this trivial speech about useful burns and salutary medicines makes me, and I fancy others, simply and wearily heartsick. Some words are due to children at school, to peevish patients in the sickroom who need a little temporary quieting. But quite other speech is due to men and women when they are wakened to the higher reason of Job by the fierce anguish of our mortal life's ultimate facts. They deserve either our simple silence, or, if we are ready to speak, the speech of people who ourselves inquire as Job inquired.

III.

A third method of dealing with our problem is in essence identical with the course which, in a very antiquated form, the friends of Job adopt. This method takes its best known expression in the doctrine that the presence of evil in the world is explained by the fact that the value of free will in moral agents logically involves, and so explains and justifies, the divine permission of the evil deeds of those finite beings who freely choose to sin, as well as the inevitable fruits of the sins. God creates agents with free will. He does so because the existence of such agents has of itself an infinite worth. Were there no free agents, the highest good could not be. But such agents, because they are free, can offend. The divine justice of necessity pursues such offenses with attendant evils. These evils, the result of sin, must, logically speaking, be permitted to exist, if God once creates the agents who have free will, and himself remains, as he must logically do, a just God. How much ill thus results depends upon the choice of the free agents, not upon God, who wills to have only good chosen, but of necessity must leave his free creatures to their own devices, so far as concerns their power to sin.

This view has the advantage of undertaking to regard evil as a logically necessary part of a perfect moral order, and not as a mere incident of an imperfectly adjusted physical mechanism. So dignified a doctrine, by virtue of its long history and its high theological reputation, needs here no extended exposition. I assume it as familiar, and pass at once to its difficulties. It has its share of truth. There is, I doubt not, moral free will in the universe. But the presence of evil in the world simply cannot be explained by free will alone. This is easy to show. One who maintains this view asserts, in substance, "All real evils are the results of the acts of free and finite moral agents." These agents may be angels or men. If there is evil in the city, the Lord has *not* done it, except in so far as his justice has acted in readjusting wrongs already done. Such ill is due to the deeds of his creatures. But hereupon one asks at once, in presence of any ill, "Who did this?" Job's friends answer: "The sufferer himself; his deed wrought his own undoing. God punishes only the sinner. Every one suffers for his own wrongdoing. Your ill is the result of your crime."

But Job, and all his defenders of innocence, must at once reply : "Empirically speaking, this is obviously, in our visible world, simply not true. The sufferer may suffer innocently. The ill is often undeserved. The fathers sin ; the child, diseased from birth, degraded, or a born wretch, may pay the penalty. The Turk or the active rebel sins. Armenia's helpless women and babes cry in vain unto God for help."

Hereupon the reply comes, although not indeed from Job's friends: "Alas! it is so. Sin means suffering; but the innocent may suffer *for* the guilty. This, to be sure, is God's way. One cannot help it. It is so." But therewith the whole effort to explain evil as a logically necessary result of free will and of divine justice alone is simply abandoned. The unearned ills are not justly due to the free will that indeed partly caused them, but to God who declines to protect the innocent. God owes the Turk and the rebel their due. He also owes to his innocent creatures, the babes and the women, his shelter. He owes to the sinning father his penalty, but to the son, born in our visible world a lost soul from the womb, God owes the shelter of his almighty wing, and no penalty. Thus Job's cry is once more in place. The ways of God are not thus justified.

But the partisan of free will as the true explanation of ill may reiterate his view in a new form. He may insist that we see but a fragment. Perhaps the soul born here as if lost, or the wretch doomed to pangs now unearned, sinned of old, in some previous state of existence. Perhaps Karma is to blame. You expiate to-day the sins of your own former existences. Thus the Hindoos varied the theme of our familiar doctrine. This is what Hindoo friends might have said to Job. Well, admit even that, if you like ; and what then follows ? Admit that here or in former ages the free deed of every present sufferer earned as its penalty every ill, physical or moral, that appears as besetting just this sufferer to-day. Admit that, and what logically follows ? It follows, so I must insist, that the moral world itself, which this free-will theory of the source of evil, thus abstractly stated, was to save, is destroyed in its very heart and centre.

For consider. A suffers ill. B sees A suffering. Can B, the onlooker, help his suffering neighbor, A ? Can he comfort him in any true way ? No, a miserable comforter must B prove, like Job's friends, so long as B, believing in our present hypothesis, clings strictly to the logic of this abstract free-will explanation of the origin of evil. To A he says : " Well, you suffer for your own ill-doing. I therefore simply cannot relieve you. This is God's world of justice. If I tried to hinder God's justice from working in your case, I should at best only postpone your evil day. It would come, for God is just. You are hungry, thirsty, naked, sick, in prison. What can I do about it ? All this is your own deed come back to you. God himself, although justly punishing, is not the author of this evil. You are the sole originator of the ill." " Ah ! " so A may cry out, " but can you not give me light, insight, instruction, sympathy ? Can you not at least teach me to become good ? " " No," B must reply, if he is a logical believer in the sole efficacy of the private free will of each finite agent as the one source, under the divine justice, of that agent's ill : " No, if you deserved light or any other comfort, God, being just, would enlighten you himself, even if I absolutely refused. But if you do not deserve light, I should preach to you in vain, for God's justice would harden your heart against any such good fortune as I could offer you from without, even if I spoke with the tongues of men and of angels. Your free will is yours. No deed of mine could give you a good free will, for what I gave you from without would not be *your* free will at all. Nor can any one but you cause your free

will to be this or that. A great gulf is fixed between us.
You and I, as sovereign free agents, live in God's holy world
in sin-tight compartments and in evil-tight compartments
too. I cannot hurt you, nor you me. You are damned for
your own sins, while all that I can do is to look out for my
own salvation." This, I say, is the logically inevitable result of asserting that every ill, physical or moral, that can
happen to any agent, is solely the result of that agent's own
free will acting under the government of the divine justice.
The only possible consequence would indeed be that we
live, every soul of us, in separate, as it were absolutely fire-
proof, free-will compartments, so that real coöperation as to
good and ill is excluded. What more cynical denial of the
reality of any sort of moral world could be imagined than
is involved in this horrible thesis, which no sane partisan of
the abstract and traditional free-will explanation of the
source of evil will to-day maintain, precisely because no
such partisan really knows or can know what his doctrine
logically means, while still continuing to maintain it. Yet
whenever one asserts with pious obscurity, that "No harm
can come to the righteous," one in fact implies, with logical
necessity, just this cynical consequence.

IV.

There remains a fourth doctrine as to our problem.
This doctrine is in essence the thesis of philosophical idealism, a thesis which I myself feel bound to maintain, and, so
far as space here permits, to explain. The theoretical basis
of this view, the philosophical reasons for the notion of the
divine nature which it implies, I cannot here explain.
That is another argument. But I desire to indicate how the
view in question deals with Job's problem.

This view first frankly admits that Job's problem is,
upon Job's presuppositions, simply and absolutely insolu-
ble. Grant Job's own presupposition that God is a being

other than this world, that he is its external creator and ruler, and then all solutions fail. God is then either cruel or helpless, as regards all real finite ill of the sort that Job endures. Job, moreover, is right in demanding a reasonable answer to his question. The only possible answer is, however, one that undertakes to develop what I hold to be the immortal soul of the doctrine of the divine atonement. The answer to Job is: God is not in ultimate essence another being than yourself. He is the Absolute Being. You truly are one with God, part of his life. He is the very soul of your soul. And so, here is the first truth: When you suffer, *your sufferings are God's sufferings*, not his external work, not his external penalty, not the fruit of his neglect, but identically his own personal woe. In you God himself suffers, precisely as you do, and has all your concern in overcoming this grief.

The true question then is: Why does God thus suffer? The sole possible, necessary, and sufficient answer is, Because without suffering, without ill, without woe, evil, tragedy, God's life could not be perfected. This grief is not a physical means to an external end. It is a logically necessary and eternal constituent of the divine life. It is logically necessary that the Captain of your salvation should be perfect through suffering. No outer nature compels him. He chooses this because he chooses his own perfect selfhood. He is perfect. His world is the best possible world. Yet all its finite regions know not only of joy but of defeat and sorrow, for thus alone, in the completeness of his eternity, can God in his wholeness be triumphantly perfect.

This, I say, is my thesis. In the absolute oneness of God with the sufferer, in the concept of the suffering and therefore triumphant God, lies the logical solution of the problem of evil. The doctrine of philosophical idealism is, as regards its purely theoretical aspects, a fairly familiar metaphysical theory at the present time. One may, then, presuppose here

as known the fact that, for reasons which I have not now to
expound, the idealist maintains that there is in the universe
but one perfectly real being, namely, the Absolute, that the
Absolute is self-conscious, and that his world is essentially
in its wholeness the fulfillment *in actu* of an all-perfect
ideal. We ourselves exist as fragments of the absolute life,
or better, as partial functions in the unity of the absolute
and conscious process of the world. On the other hand, our
existence and our individuality are not illusory, but are
what they are in an organic unity with the whole life
of the Absolute Being. This doctrine once presupposed,
our present task is to inquire what case idealism can
make for the thesis just indicated as its answer to Job's
problem.

In endeavoring to grapple with the theoretical problem
of the place of evil in a world that, on the whole, is to be
conceived, not only as good, but as perfect, there is happily
one essentially decisive consideration concerning good and
evil which falls directly within the scope of our own human
experience, and which concerns matters at once familiar
and momentous as well as too much neglected in philosophy. When we use such words as good, evil, perfect, we
easily deceive ourselves by the merely abstract meanings
which we associate with each of the terms taken apart from
the other. We forget the experiences from which the words
have been abstracted. To these experiences we must return
whenever we want really to comprehend the words. If we
take the mere words, in their abstraction, it is easy to say,
for instance, that if life has any evil in it at all, it must
needs not be so perfect as life would be were there no evil
in it whatever. Just so, speaking abstractly, it is easy to
say that, in estimating life, one has to set the good over
against the evil, and to compare their respective sums. It
is easy to declare that, since we hate evil, wherever and just
so far as we recognize it, our sole human interest in the

3

world must be furthered by the removal of evil from the world. And thus viewing the case, one readily comes to say that if God views as not only good but perfect a world in which we find so much evil, the divine point of view must be very foreign to ours, so that Job's rebellious pessimism seems well in order, and Prometheus appears to defy the world-ruler in a genuinely humane spirit. Shocked, however, by the apparent impiety of this result, some teachers, considering divine matters, still misled by the same one-sided use of words, have opposed one falsely abstract view by another, and have strangely asserted that the solution must be in proclaiming that since God's world, the real world, in order to be perfect, must be without evil, what we men call evil must be a mere illusion—a mirage of the human point of view—a dark vision which God, who sees all truth, sees not at all. To God, so this view asserts, the eternal world in its wholeness is not only perfect, but has merely the perfection of an utterly transparent crystal, unstained by any color of ill. Only mortal error imagines that there is any evil. There is no evil but only good in the real world, and that is why God finds the world perfect, whatever mortals dream.

Now neither of these abstract views is my view. I consider them both the result of a thoughtless trust in abstract words. I regard evil as a distinctly real fact, a fact just as real as the most helpless and hopeless sufferer finds it to be when he is in pain. Furthermore, I hold that God's point of view is not foreign to ours. I hold that God willingly, freely, and consciously suffers in us when we suffer, and that our grief is his. And despite all this I maintain that the world from God's point of view fulfills the divine ideal and is perfect. And I hold that when we abandon the one-sided abstract ideas which the words good, evil, and perfect suggest, and when we go back to the concrete experiences upon which these very words are founded, we can see, even within the limits of our own experience, facts which make these very paradoxes perfectly intelligible, and even commonplace.

As for that essentially pernicious view, nowadays somewhat current amongst a certain class of gentle but inconsequent people—the view that all evil is *merely* an illusion and that there is no such thing in God's world—I can say of it only in passing that it is often advanced as an idealistic view, but that, in my opinion, it is false idealism. Good idealism it is to regard all finite experience as an appearance, a hint, often a very poor hint, of deeper truth. Good idealism it is to admit that man can err about truth that lies beyond his finite range of experience. And very good idealism it is to assert that all truth, and so all finite experience, exists in and for the mind of God, and nowhere outside of or apart from God. But it is not good idealism to assert that any facts which fall within the range of finite experience are, even while they are experienced, mere illusions. God's truth is inclusive, not exclusive. What you experience God experiences. The difference lies only in this, that God sees in unity what you see in fragments. For the rest, if one said, " The source and seat of evil is only the error of mortal mind," one would but have changed the name of one's problem. If the evil were but the error, the error would still be the evil, and altering the name would not have diminished the horror of the evil of this finite world.

V.

But I hasten from the false idealism to the true ; from the abstractions to the enlightening insights of our life. As a fact, idealism does not say : The finite world is, as such, a mere illusion. A sound idealism says, whatever we experience is a fragment, and, as far as it goes, a genuine fragment of the truth of the divine mind. With this principle before us, let us consider directly our own experiences of

good and of evil, to see whether they are as abstractly opposed to each other as the mere words often suggest.   We
must begin with the elementary and even trivial facts.   We
shall soon come to something deeper.

By good, as we mortals experience it, we mean something
that, when it comes or is expected, we actively welcome, try
to attain or keep, and regard with content.   By evil in general, as it is in our experience, we mean whatever we find in
any sense repugnant and intolerable.   I use the words repugnant and intolerable because I wish to indicate that
words for evil frequently, like the words for good, directly
refer to our actions as such.   Commonly and rightly, when
we speak of evil, we make reference to acts of resistance, of
struggle, of shrinking, of flight, of removal of ourselves
from a source of mischief—acts which not only follow upon
the experience of evil, but which serve to define in a useful
fashion what we mean by evil.   The opposing acts of pursuit and of welcome define what we mean by good.   By the
evil which we experience we mean precisely whatever we
regard as something to be gotten rid of, shrunken from, put
out of sight, of hearing, or of memory, eschewed, expelled,
assailed, or otherwise directly or indirectly resisted.   By
good we mean whatever we regard as something to be wel-
comed, pursued, won, grasped, held, persisted in, preserved.
And we show all this in our acts in presence of any grade of
good or evil, sensuous, æsthetic, ideal, moral.   To shun, to
flee, to resist, to destroy, these are our primary attitudes
towards ill; the opposing acts are our primary attitudes
towards the good ; and whether you regard us as animals or
as moralists, whether it is a sweet taste, a poem, a virtue, or
God that we look to as good, and whether it is a burn or a
temptation, an outward physical foe, or a stealthy, inward,
ideal enemy, that we regard as evil.   In all our organs of
voluntary movement, in all our deeds, in a turn of the eye,
in a sigh, a groan, in a hostile gesture, in an act of silent

contempt, we can show in endlessly varied ways the same general attitude of repugnance.

But man is a very complex creature. He has many organs. He performs many acts at once, and he experiences his performance of these acts in one highly complex life of consciousness. As the next feature of his life we all observe that he can at the same time shun one object and grasp at another. In this way he can have at once present to him a consciousness of good and a consciousness of ill. But so far in our account these sorts of experience appear merely as facts side by side. Man loves, and he *also* hates, loves this, and hates that, assumes an attitude of repugnance towards one object, while he welcomes another. So far the usual theory follows man's life, and calls it an experience of good and ill as mingled but exclusively and abstractly opposed facts. For such a view the final question as to the worth of a man's life is merely the question whether there are more intense acts of satisfaction and of welcome than of repugnance and disdain in his conscious life.

But this is by no means an adequate notion of the complexity of man's life, even as an animal. If every conscious act of hindrance, of thwarting, of repugnance, means just in so far an awareness of some evil, it is noteworthy that men can have and can show just such tendencies, not only towards external experiences, but towards their own acts. That is, men can be seen trying to thwart and to hinder even their own acts themselves, at the very moment when they note the occurrence of these acts. One can consciously have an impulse to do something, and at that very moment a conscious disposition to hinder or to thwart as an evil that very impulse. If, on the other hand, every conscious act of attainment, of pursuit, of reinforcement, involves the awareness of some good, it is equally obvious that one can show by one's acts a disposition to reinforce or to emphasize or to increase, not only the externally present gifts of for-

tune, but also one's own deeds, in so far as one observes
them.   And in our complex lives it is common enough to
find ourselves actually trying to reinforce and to insist upon
a situation which involves for us, even at the moment of its
occurrence, a great deal of repugnance.   In such cases we
often act as if we felt the very thwarting of our own primary impulses to be so much of a conscious good that we persist in pursuing and reinforcing the very situation in which
this thwarting and hindering of our own impulses is sure to
arise.

In brief, as phenomena of this kind show, man is a being
who can to a very great extent find a sort of secondary satisfaction in the very act of thwarting his own desires, and
thus of assuring for the time his own dissatisfactions.   On
the other hand, man can to an indefinite degree find himself dissatisfied with his satisfactions and disposed to thwart,
not merely his external enemies, but his own inmost impulses themselves.   But I now affirm that in all such cases
you cannot simply say that man is preferring the less of
two evils, or the greater of two goods, as if the good and the
evil stood merely side by side in his experience.   On the
contrary, in such cases, man is not merely setting his acts
or his estimates of good and evil side by side and taking the
sum of each ; but he is making his own relatively primary
acts, impulses, desires, the objects of all sorts of secondary
impulses, desires, and reflective observations.   His whole
inner state is one of tension ; and he is either making a secondary experience of evil out of his estimate of a primary
experience of good, as is the case when he at once finds
himself disposed to pursue a given good and to thwart this
pursuit as being an evil pursuit ; or else he is making a secondary experience of good out of his primary experience of
evil, as when he is primarily dissatisfied with his situation,
but yet secondarily regards this very dissatisfaction as itself
a desirable state.   In this way man comes not only to love

some things and also to hate other things, he comes to love
his own hates and to hate his own loves in an endlessly
complex hierarchy of superposed interests in his own interests.

Now it is easy to say that such states of inner tension,
where our conscious lives are full of a warfare of the self
with itself, are contradictory or absurd states. But it is easy
to say this only when you dwell on the words and fail to
observe the facts of experience. As a fact, not only our
lowest but our highest states of activity are the ones which
are fullest of this crossing, conflict, and complex interrela-
tion of loves and hates, of attractions and repugnances. As
a merely physiological fact, we begin no muscular act without at the same time initiating acts which involve the in-
nervation of opposing sets of muscles, and these opposing
sets of muscles hinder each other's freedom. Every sort of
control of movement means the conflicting play of opposed
muscular impulses. We do nothing simple, and we will no
complex act without willing what involves a certain measure of opposition between the impulses or partial acts which
go to make up the whole act. If one passes from single acts
to long series of acts, one finds only the more obviously this
interweaving of repugnance and of acceptance, of pursuit
and of flight, upon which every complex type of conduct
depends.

One could easily at this point spend time by dwelling
upon numerous and relatively trivial instances of this interweaving of conflicting motives as it appears in all our life.
I prefer to pass such instances over with a mere mention.
There is, for instance, the whole marvelous consciousness of
play, in its benign and in its evil forms. In any game that
fascinates, one loves victory and shuns defeat, and yet as a
loyal supporter of the game scorns anything that makes
victory certain in advance ; thus as a lover of fair play preferring to risk the defeat that he all the while shuns, and

partly thwarting the very love of victory that from moment to moment fires his hopes. There are, again, the numerous cases in which we prefer to go to places where we are sure to be in a considerable measure dissatisfied ; to engage, for instance, in social functions that absorbingly fascinate us despite or even in view of the very fact that, as long as they continue, they keep us in a state of tension which makes us, amongst other things, long to have the whole occasion over. Taking a wider view, one may observe that the greater part of the freest products of the activity of civilization, in ceremonies, in formalities, in the long social drama of flight, of pursuit, of repartee, of contest and of courtesy, involve an elaborate and systematic delaying and hindering of elemental human desires, which we continually outwit, postpone and thwart, even while we nourish them. When students of human nature assert that hunger and love rule the social world, they recognize that the elemental in human nature is trained by civilization into the service of the highest demands of the Spirit. But such students have to recognize that the elemental rules the higher world only in so far as the elemental is not only cultivated, but endlessly thwarted, delayed, outwitted, like a constitutional monarch, who is said to be a sovereign, but who, while he rules, must not govern.

But I pass from such instances, which in all their universality are still, I admit, philosophically speaking, trivial, because they depend upon the accidents of human nature. I pass from these instances to point out what must be the law, not only of human nature, but of every broader form of life as well. I maintain that this organization of life by virtue of the tension of manifold impulses and interests is not a mere accident of our imperfect human nature, but must be a type of the organization of every rational life. There are good and bad states of tension, there are conflicts that can only be justified when resolved into some higher

form of harmony. But I insist that, in general, the only
harmony that can exist in the realm of the spirit is the harmony that we possess when we thwart the present but more
elemental impulse for the sake of the higher unity of experience ; as when we rejoice in the endurance of the tragedies
of life, because they show us the depth of life, or when we
know that it is better to have loved and lost than never to
have loved at all, or when we possess a virtue in the moment of victory over the tempter. And the reason why
this is true lies in the fact that the more one's experience
fulfills ideals, the more that experience presents to one, not
of ignorance, but of triumphantly wealthy acquaintance
with the facts of manifold, varied and tragic life, full of
tension and thereby of unity. Now this is an universal and
not merely human law. It is not those innocent of evil
who are fullest of the life of God, but those who in their
own case have experienced the triumph over evil. It is not
those naturally ignorant of fear, or those who, like Siegfried, have never shivered, who possess the genuine experience of courage : but the brave are those who have fears,
but control their fears. Such know the genuine virtues of
the hero. Were it otherwise, only the stupid could be perfect heroes.

To be sure it is quite false to say, as the foolish do, that
the object of life is merely that we may " know life " as an
irrational chaos of experiences of good and of evil. But
knowing the good in life is a matter which concerns the
form, rather than the mere content of life. One who knows
life wisely knows indeed much of the content of life ; but
he knows the good of life in so far as, in the unity of his
experience, he finds the evil of his experience not abolished,
but subordinated, and in so far relatively thwarted by a
control which annuls its triumph even while experiencing
its existence.

VI.

Generalizing the lesson of experience we may then say: It is logically impossible that a complete knower of truth should fail to know, to experience, to have present to his insight, the fact of actually existing evil. On the other hand, it is equally impossible for one to know a higher good than comes from the subordination of evil to good in a total experience. When one first loving, in an elemental way, whatever you please, himself hinders, delays, thwarts his elemental interest in the interest of some larger whole of experience, he not only knows more fact, but he possesses a higher good than would or could be present to one who was aware neither of the elemental impulse, nor of the thwarting of it in the tension of a richer life. The knowing of the good, in the higher sense, depends upon contemplating the overcoming and subordination of a less significant impulse, which survives even in order that it should be subordinated. Now this law, this form of the knowledge of the good, applies as well to the existence of moral as to that of sensuous ill. If moral evil were simply destroyed and wiped away from the external world, the knowledge of moral goodness would also be destroyed. For the love of moral good is the thwarting of lower loves for the sake of the higher organization. What is needed, then, for the definition of the divine knowledge of a world that in its wholeness is perfect, is not a divine knowledge that shall ignore, wipe out and utterly make naught the existence of any ill, whether physical or moral, but a divine knowledge to which shall be present that love of the world as a whole which is fulfilled in the endurance of physical ill, in the subordination of moral ill, in the thwarting of impulses which survive even when subordinated, in the acceptance of repugnances which are still eternal, in the triumph over an enemy that endures even through its eternal defeat, and in the discovery that the endless tension of the finite world is included in the contemplative consciousness of the repose and harmony of eternity. To view God's nature thus is to view his nature as the whole idealistic theory views him, not as the Infinite One beyond the finite imperfections, but as the being whose unity determines the very constitution, the lack, the tension, and relative disharmony of the finite world.

The existence of evil, then, is not only consistent with the perfection of the universe, but is necessary for the very existence of that perfection. This is what we see when we no longer permit ourselves to be deceived by the abstract meanings of the words good and evil into thinking that these two opponents exist merely as mutually exclusive facts side by side in experience, but when we go back to the facts of life and perceive that all relatively higher good, in the trivial as in the more truly spiritual realm, is known only in so far as, from some higher reflective point of view, we accept as good the thwarting of an existent interest that is even thereby declared to be a relative ill, and love a tension of various impulses which even thereby involves, as the object of our love, the existence of what gives us aversion or grief. Now if the love of God is more inclusive than the love of man, even as the divine world of experience is richer than the human world, we can simply set no human limit to the intensity of conflict, to the tragedies of existence, to the pangs of finitude, to the degree of moral ill, which in the end is included in the life that God not only loves, but finds the fulfillment of the perfect ideal. If peace means satisfaction, acceptance of the whole of an experience as good, and if even we, in our weakness, can frequently find rest in the very presence of conflict and of tension, in the very endurance of ill in a good cause, in the hero's triumph over temptation, or in the mourner's tearless refusal to accept the lower comforts of forgetfulness, or to wish that the lost one's preciousness had been less painfully revealed by death—well, if even we know our little share of this harmony in the midst of the wrecks and disorders of life, what limit shall we set to the divine power to face this world of his own sorrows, and to find peace in the victory over all its ills.

But in this last expression I have pronounced the word that serves to link this theory as to the place of evil in a good world with the practical problem of every sufferer. Job's rebellion came from the thought that God, as a sovereign, is far off, and that, for his pleasure, his creature suffers. Our own theory comes to the mourner with the assurance: "Your suffering, just as it is in you, is God's suffering. No chasm divides you from God. He is not remote from you even in his eternity. He is here. His eternity means merely the completeness of his experience. But that completeness is inclusive. Your sorrow is one of the included facts." I do not say: "God sympathizes with you from without, would spare you if he could, pities you with helpless external pity merely as a father pities his children." I say: "God here sorrows, not *with* but *in* your sorrow. Your grief is identically his grief, and what you know as your loss, God knows as his loss, just in and through the very moment when you grieve."

But hereupon the sufferer perchance responds: "If this is God's loss, could he not have prevented it? To him are present in unity all the worlds; and yet he must lack just this for which I grieve." I respond: "He suffers here that he may triumph. For the triumph of the wise is no easy thing. Their lives are not light, but sorrowful. Yet they rejoice in their sorrow, not, to be sure, because it is mere experience, but because, for them, it becomes part of a strenuous whole of life. They wander and find their home even in wandering. They long, and attain through their very love of longing. Peace they find in triumphant warfare. Contentment they have most of all in endurance. Sovereignty they win in endless service. The eternal world contains Gethsemane."

Yet the mourner may still insist: "If my sorrow is God's, his triumph is not mine. Mine is the woe. His is the peace." But my theory is a philosophy. It proposes to be coherent. I must persist: "It is your fault that you are thus sundered from God's triumph. His experience in its wholeness cannot now be yours, for you just as you—this individual—are now but a fragment, and see his truth as through a glass darkly. But if you see his truth at all, through even the dimmest light of a glimmering reason, remember, that truth is in fact your own truth, your own fulfillment, the whole from which your life cannot be divorced, the reality that you mean even when you most doubt, the desire of your heart even when you are most blind, the perfection that you unconsciously strove for even when you were an infant, the complete Self apart from whom you mean nothing, the very life that gives your life the only value which it can have. In thought, if not in the fulfillment of thought, in aim if not in attainment of aim, in aspiration if not in the presence of the revealed fact, you can view God's triumph and peace as your triumph and peace. Your defeat will be no less real than it is, nor will you falsely call your evil a mere illusion. But you will see not only the grief but the truth, your truth, your rescue, your triumph."

Well, to what ill-fortune does not just such reasoning apply? I insist: our conclusion is essentially universal. It discounts any evil that experience may contain. All the horrors of the natural order, all the concealments of the divine plan by our natural ignorance, find their general relation to the unity of the divine experience indicated in advance by this account of the problem of evil.

"Yes," one may continue, "ill-fortune you have discovered, but how about moral evil? What if the sinner

now triumphantly retorts: 'Aha! So my will is God's
will. All then is well with me.'" I reply: What I have
said disposes of moral ill precisely as definitely as of physical ill. What the evil will is to the good man, whose goodness depends upon its existence, but also upon the thwarting and the condemnation of its aim, just such is the sinner's
will to the divine plan. God's will, we say to the sinner, is
your will. Yes, but it is your will thwarted, scorned, overcome, defeated. In the eternal world you are seen, possessed, present, but your damnation is also seen including
and thwarting you. Your apparent victory in this world
stands simply for the vigor of your impulses. God wills
you not to triumph. And that is the use of you in the
world—the use of evil generally—to be hated but endured,
to be triumphed over through the very fact of your presence,
to be willed down even in the very life of which you are a
part.

But to the serious moral agent we say: What you mean
when you say that evil in this temporal world ought not to
exist, and ought to be suppressed, is simply what God means
by seeing that evil ought to be and is endlessly thwarted, endured, but subordinated. In the natural world you are the
minister of God's triumph. Your deed is his. You can
never clean the world of evil; but you can subordinate evil.
The justification of the presence in the world of the morally
evil becomes apparent to us mortals only in so far as this
evil is overcome and condemned. It exists only that it may
be cast down. Courage, then, for God works in you. In
the order of time you embody in outer acts what is for him
the truth of his eternity.

THE CASE OF JOHN BUNYAN.

THE casuistry of the numerous forms of insistent mental processes of a pathological character has of late years become very extensive. The names and sub-classes of these morbidly insistent kinds of feeling, thought, or volition have occasionally been multiplied beyond any reason, until, in view of the endless "*manias*" and "*phobias*" that some writers have been disposed to dignify with special titles, I myself have sometimes wondered whether it would not be wise for some one, in the interests of good sense, to try to check this process by defining, as a peculiarly dangerous type of insistent impulses, a "new mental disorder," to be described as the "mania" for multiplying words ending in *mania* or in *phobia*. Meanwhile, despite this inconvenience, and despite numerous hasty speculations upon the whole subject, there can be no doubt that the theoretical interest of these morbidly insistent mental processes is great, and that the pathological secret and the genuine natural classification of these disorders will be such as well to repay the trouble of the most minute study of cases, if only that secret ever comes to be made out, and that natural classification is ever set up. And while we wait for further light, the careful preliminary scrutiny of cases is indeed the only course open to students of psychology.

The present paper is but a very modest contribution to the casuistry of the morbidly insistent mental processes. I

have no new *phobia* or *mania* to define, and in any case I
speak only as student of psychology. The medical reader
might be able to see much more in the documents to which
I here wish to attract his attention than I am able to see.
My task is simply one of summary and report. The case to
which I wish to call attention is meanwhile one of peculiar
interest, namely, that of the author of the Pilgrim's Progress. The principal document concerned is John Bunyan's
remarkable confession, entitled Grace Abounding to the
Chief of Sinners, an autobiographical statement which
Bunyan wrote and published, as the title-page tells us, "for
the support of the weak and tempted people of God." This
little book is, from the literary point of view, of very high
interest, ranking, as I suppose, amongst all the author's
works, second only to the great Pilgrim's Progress itself.
As a record of human experience, the Grace Abounding
will never lose its charm, both for lovers of religious biography, and for admirers of honesty, of sincerity, and of simple pathos. Nothing that can be said as to the psychological
significance of the author's recorded experiences will ever
detract from the worth of the book, even when viewed just
as the author viewed it, as a "support" for the "weak and
tempted." Bunyan, as we shall see, had at one time a decidedly heavy and morbid burden to bear. But, like many
another nervous sufferer of the "strong type" (Koch's
starker Typus), Bunyan carried this burden with heroic
perseverance, and in the end won the mastery over it by a
most instructive kind of self-discipline. In view of this
fact, a clearer recognition of the nature of the burden,
from the psychological point of view, rather helps than
hinders our admiration for the author's genius, and our respect for his unconquerable manhood. It is this sort of
case, in fact, that renders the study of the nervous disorders
so frequently associated with genius, a pursuit adapted, in
very many instances, not to cheapen our sense of the dig-

nity of genius, but to heighten our reverence for the strength that could contend, as some men of genius have done, with their disorders, and that could conquer the nervous "Apollyon" on his own chosen battle-ground.

But an estimate of Bunyan's genius belongs not here. I venture only to say that I write as an especially profound admirer of this wonderful and untaught artist, whose homely style shows in almost every line the born master, whose simple realism in portraying human character as he saw it amongst the live men about him often puts to shame the ingenuity of scores of cunning literary craftsmen in these our own most realistic days, and whose few highest flights of poetic imagination, such as the closing scenes of the first part of the Pilgrim's Progress, belong without question in the really loftiest regions of art. Range of invention, self-control in production, perfect objectivity in the portrayal of human life—these are leading traits in the work of this man ; and these things, as well as others that we shall later see, forever forbid our classing Bunyan, taken as a whole, amongst the weaklings. It is perfectly consistent with this fact, however, when we find this admirable man and artist living, for a bitter and instructive period of his early years, a life of stern conflict with a nervous foe of a fairly recognizable and, under the circumstances, decidedly grave type. How, unaided and ignorant, he won the victory, is in itself an interesting tale. And, for the rest, the case tends to throw light on the interesting problem as to how far the presence of elaborate insistent mental processes of a morbid type is of itself a sufficient indication of the depth of the "degeneracy" of constitution of the subject who is for a time burdened with them.* That Bunyan's malady must

---

* The frequent association of the morbidly insistent processes with the nervously "degenerate" type is a commonplace in the literature of the subject, and a few years since it was, I believe, an almost if not quite universal

4

have had a certain constitutional basis will, I suppose, appear decidedly probable to most readers of the following summary. Yet it will be hard to question the fact that, quite apart from his special creative abilities, Bunyan's general constitution—his extraordinary and persistent power of work, his long endurance of very serious mental and physical hardships, his reasonably lengthy life of sixty years (ended by an acute disease, due to an exposure), his apparently even temper and self-possession in later years, his sustained influence over men as leader, adviser, and preacher—when taken altogether, must give us an idea of his inherited organization that will, in any event, stand in a fairly strong contrast to the impression that the temporary nervous disorder of his early manhood, if it were taken alone, would leave upon our minds.

But a deeper estimate of such things I must leave to more competent judges. I have here only to present the facts.

I.

John Bunyan was born November 30, 1628, and died August 31, 1688. The principal known facts of his life which bear in any way upon the question of his health and constitution, apart from the narrative in the Grace Abounding, are as follows: * Bunyan was a native of the

---

dogma that considerable masses of insistent fears, impulses, or thoughts occurred only as part of the "stigmata" of degeneracy. The possibility of the development of even elaborate systems of such insistent impulses upon a basis of wholly acquired neurasthenia was maintained by Dr. Cowles, in his well-known paper on Insistent and Fixed Ideas in the American Journal of Psychology (vol. i. p. 222 *sq.*), and has also been asserted by others.

* I use, for the most part, the principal recent biography, that of John Brown (2d edition, London, 1886)—an elaborate and extremely patient research into every discoverable detail relating to Bunyan's family and fortunes. Other recent accounts are those of Venables (in the "Great Writers" series, London, 1888) and of Froude (in the "English Men of Letters"

little village of Elstow, near Bedford. His family can be traced in Bedfordshire as far back as 1200. In the sixteenth century, an ancestor of Bunyan, and the wife of this ancestor, appear in court records as brewers and bakers. Thomas Bunyan, his grandfather, was "a small village trader." Difficulties in the courts are the occasion of some of the records preserved of these ancestors, but the difficulties named are petty, e. g., minor violations of excise laws, disrespect to churchwardens, and perhaps religious nonconformity.* Bunyan's father was notoriously, like Bunyan himself, a "tinker" or "brasier," probably, says Brown, "neither better nor worse than the rest of the craftsmen of the hammer and the forge." Tinkers had, to be sure, in that time and place, a reputation as rather hard drinkers; but on the other hand they wandered much on foot, and so lived freely out of doors. Bunyan's father lived until 1676, dying at seventy-three years of age. The poet's mother was of a poor but very honest and thrifty family; she died when John Bunyan himself had reached the age of fifteen. Little more is known of the family before we reach our poet himself. He was not an only child. One sister is known to have died early. One brother is known to have lived until 1695.

Of John Bunyan's childhood history we shall see a little soon. In youth he was apparently, until after the time of his marriage, of pretty lusty health. The "wicked" early life of which he speaks so severely in his Grace Abounding proves, on the whole, to have been, physically speaking, a wholesome life, during all the time preceding his marriage and his conversion. Alcoholic excesses and unchastity are, in the opinion of all his modern biographers, nearly or quite

---

series). The ground has thus been very thoroughly gone over, for all literary purposes, in recent years.

* Brown, pp. 27–31.

excluded by what we most certainly know of him at this time. At about sixteen years of age Bunyan was enrolled in the army, probably on the Parliamentary side, and remained some two years in service, but apparently without any physical ill effects. He married at twenty years of age, both himself and his wife being very poor. He now followed his trade as tinker. Within the next four years fall, first his conversion, and then the experiences of which we are principally to speak in what follows. In these years, furthermore, falls also the birth of his first child, a daughter who was very early blind. In 1653, after he had passed through these principal experiences, he joined the church in Bedford. In 1654 his second child was born, also a daughter. In 1655 he began that career as preacher which he continued thenceforward, so far as he was permitted to do so, until the end. In 1660 he was imprisoned in the county jail at Bedford, for violating the law by acting as an irregular preacher ; and there he remained, in a confinement which varied in its degrees of strictness, for some twelve years. The physical strain of this imprisonment must have been great, and the mental anxieties involved were of the severest, as we learn from his own account ; yet Bunyan plainly experienced no return of his previous mental troubles with anything like their old force. He was now often weak in body and depressed in mind, but never long despairing. He busied himself both in preaching to his fellow-prisoners and in writing. He was released in 1672. For three years thereafter he was at liberty. In 1675-6 he suffered a second imprisonment, during which it was, according to recent research, that he wrote the Pilgrim's Progress.* Thenceforth he continued working as writer and preacher to the end. The list of his works contains "sixty pieces," says his first bibliographer, "and he was sixty years of age." One stand-

---

* Brown, p. 254 ; Venables, p. 151.

ard edition occupies four volumes octavo. His works are, of course, largely theological. They are certainly laborious productions, even apart from the genius involved; for this man was never trained to write.

As to his health otherwise, we know that after 1653 there was a time in his early life when, as he says, "I was much inclining to a consumption, wherewith, about the Spring, I was suddenly and violently seized with much weakness in my outward man, insomuch that I thought I could not live." Other times, still later, he mentions, when he was "very ill and weak"; and he notes great depression of spirits as characteristic of his state at all such times.* Brown † holds, concerning Bunyan, that "at any time he was far from strong" as to physical health. But when one considers his remarkable activity both as writer and preacher, and the long and severe strains to which he had been subject before he reached sixty years of age, and when one remembers also the possibly hypochondriac nature of the disorders of which his own account, as just cited, speaks, it seems hard, after all, to form any exact opinion as to the actual degree of the physical weakness of his constitution. One is disposed to set the work done and the external sufferings endured over against the rather meagre record of later illnesses in his life. "His friend," says Brown (a friend, namely, who wrote an account of Bunyan), "tells us that though he was only sixty he was worn out with sufferings, age, and often teaching." One remembers hereupon that a persecuted genius who had written "sixty pieces" without having received any sort of early scholarly training, and who had passed more than twelve years in unjust imprisonment, and all

---

* "The Tempter did beset me strongly (for I find he is much for assaulting the soul when it begins to approach towards the grave, then is his opportunity)."—Grace Abounding (Clarendon Press Ed.), p. 375.

† *Op. cit.*, p. 390.

his life in struggle, had a right to be somewhat worn at sixty.

He died of "a violent fever," or, as others say, of "the sweating distemper," after having been exposed to "heavy rains and drenched to the skin" while on a preaching journey. Bunyan was twice married. He had in all three daughters and three sons. His first child, born during the time of his early disorder—a daughter—was, as observed above, blind, and died before him. Descendants of another of his daughters are the only descendants of Bunyan still known to survive. The later history of the family is incomplete, but, as reported by Brown, contains nothing of any note for our present purpose—no record, namely, of remarkable disease or ability.

Of Bunyan's outward seeming, in his later years, we have two good accounts by contemporaries. One runs thus:

"As for his person, he was tall of stature, strong-boned, though not corpulent, somewhat of a ruddy face, with sparkling eyes ; . . . his hair reddish, but in his latter days time had sprinkled it with gray ; his nose well set, but not declining or bending, and his mouth moderately large ; his forehead something high, and his habit always plain and modest. He appeared in countenance to be of a stern and rough temper, but in his conversation mild and affable, not given to loquacity or much discourse in company, unless some urgent occasion required it ; observing never to boast of himself or his parts, but rather to seem low in his own eyes and submit himself to the judgment of others. . . . He had a sharp quick eye, accomplished with an excellent discerning of persons, being of good judgment and quick wit."

The other account speaks of his countenance as "grave and sedate," and of a sort to "strike something of awe into them that had nothing of the fear of God." The writer adds that his memory was "tenacious, it being customary with him to commit his sermons to writing after he had preached them." Bunyan's executive ability in church management and discipline is also noted in this account. As to his eloquence as a preacher, all accounts agree. This great "dreamer," then, was also, in his later years, a man of decided practical power, dignified in bearing, accustomed to control other men.

II.

So much, then, for the man as a whole. As to the experiences of his early manhood, recorded in the Grace Abounding, biographers in general have felt their perplexing intensity and abnormity, but have been accustomed either to refer them once for all to Bunyan's theological associations and ideas, or else to conceive them as indeed somehow pathological, but then to define their abnormal nature with the utmost looseness and confusedness.*

Patent, then, as are the reported experiences, beautifully as Bunyan confesses them, transparently as he unveils himself, one still has to go almost alone in trying to portray their actual connections; for biographer after biographer

---

* Macaulay, for instance, in his Miscellanies, declares that, at a certain point, Bunyan's mind began to be " fearfully disordered "; but he then proceeds, with a very undiscriminating analysis of the data, to define Bunyan's mental symptoms so that, if this analysis were sound, they would make up a case of what we should now define as " hallucinatory delirium." This Bunyan's disorder very certainly was not, in any fashion whatever. Taine, who, as psychologist, should have seen more clearly, is, in his way (in the account of Bunyan in the English Literature), almost equally confused as to Bunyan's true temperament and condition, and even imagines the calm and self-possessed art of Pilgrim's Progress to be the outcome of the " inflamed brain " whose sufferings are depicted in the Grace Abounding. But the Bunyan of 1650 was not yet the Bunyan of the Pilgrim's Progress of 1675. Venables and Brown, well as they summarize the salient facts, fail to see their psychological significance. Froude also appears to go wholly astray in this respect.

has passed these connections by with blindfold eyes. Yet the story, read in its psychological aspect, is as follows :

As a child Bunyan showed some of the familiar signs of the sensitive brain. He is not at all concerned, in his Autobiography, to gossip as to any minor matters. He tells us almost nothing of the externals of his life. He is wholly concerned in setting forth what God has done for his soul. He feels it worth while, however, to describe to us, in beginning the narration of his spiritual conflicts, certain of his early mental experiences. In childhood, so we learn, his "cursing, swearing, lying, and blaspheming" were very marked faults. To quote his own words : "So settled and rooted was I in these things, that they became as a second Nature to me. The which, as I have with soberness considered since, did so offend the Lord, that even in my Childhood He did scare and affright me with fearful Dreams, and did terrify me with dreadful Visions. For often after I had spent this and the other day in sin, I have in my Bed been greatly afflicted, while asleep, with the apprehensions of Devils and wicked Spirits, who still, as I then thought, laboured to draw me away with them, of which I could never be rid." To these persistent nocturnal terrors there were added still other and evidently often waking troubles, "thoughts of the Day of Judgment," which gave him fears and "distressed" his "soul," "both night and day," so that "I was often much cast down and afflicted . . . yet could I not let go my sins." These experiences came "when I was but a child, nine or ten years old." "Yea," he adds, "I was also then so overcome with despair of life and heaven, that I should often wish either that there had been no Hell, *or that I had been a Devil*—supposing they were only Tormentors ; that if it must needs be that I went thither, I might be rather a Tormentor, than tormented myself." Of such early sufferings we have several accounts besides the foregoing summary statements.

Childhood experiences of this sort have to be estimated as important in direct proportion to their depth and in inverse proportion to their dependence upon the suggestions to which a given child is subjected. These dreams were, plainly, in some instances, very elaborate and detailed. Bunyan's later youthful ignorance, so freely confessed, concerning all theological matters indicates, however, that these fears and this despair were no part of any very coherent system of childish thoughts on religious topics. The content of his "terrible dreams" was of course derived from what he heard at church and elsewhere; but a sufficient basis, in these suggested ideas, for such marked trouble, seems very improbable. That the nocturnal terrors and the despair were in part primary symptoms of nervous irritability, one can thus hardly doubt. As to the depth of the experiences themselves, the very fact of Bunyan's careful report of them is, under the circumstances, convincing. For his Autobiography is, as has just been noted, extremely reticent as to all matters that he does not consider essential parts of the tale of God's dealings with his soul.

In youth, at what seems to have been the healthiest period of his life, these dreams left him, and were "soon forgot . . . as if they never had been." And now began the wilful and sinful time which Bunyan later so unsparingly condemns. That his sins did not include unchastity or drunkenness seems, as aforesaid, clear to all his recent biographers, and for good reasons too, into which I need not here enter. Bunyan was now a very active and daring lad, who, in his almost complete ignorance, as Froude and others have observed, had no other way of expressing his genius than by "inventing lies to amuse his companions, and swearing they were true" (Froude's expression), and by showing extraordinary ingenuity as the chief swearer and wild talker of the village, so that even "very loose and ungodly" wretches, as Bunyan tells us, were shocked by the flood of bad language in which this still unconscious poet was moved to voice his latent powers. These offenses, and the still worse crime of playing tip-cat on Sundays, abide later in Bunyan's memory as evidences of the depth of his lost condition during these days. Meanwhile, despite the vulgarity of his surroundings, and the restless waywardness of his life, Bunyan would otherwise appear to have been, on the whole, an exceptionally pure-minded youth. His early education, obtained in a local school, was extremely meagre.

His boyish marriage must have involved serious responsibilities. He and his young wife had at first not "so much household stuff as a Dish or Spoon" between them. But the wife, "whose Father was counted godly," had, as her inheritance from this now dead father, two religious books, which Bunyan read with her, yet, so far as he was concerned, without "conviction." But ere long these books and his wife's speech "did beget within me some desires to religion," and for a while Bunyan attended church busily, "still retaining my wicked life," but already feeling some doubtful concern as to his own salvation, and much admiration for the formal side of church worship. A sermon against Sabbath-breaking brought him his first "conviction." After service and dinner, that day, when his full stomach had made him already cheerfully forget his transient remorse, he went, as usually on Sunday afternoons, to play his game of cat. But having struck the cat one blow from the hole, "just as I was about to strike it a second time, a Voice did suddenly dart from Heaven into my Soul, which said, *Wilt thou leave thy sins and go to Heaven, or have thy sins and go to Hell?* At this," he goes on, "I was put to an exceeding maze. Wherefore, leaving my Cat upon the ground, I looked up to Heaven, and was as if I had, with the Eyes of my understanding, seen the Lord

Jesus looking down upon me, as being very hotly displeased with me, and as if he did severely threaten me." The result of this sudden internal vision, of which he said nothing to his comrades, was an immediate sense of his general sinfulness, and an overwhelming despair, which kept him standing " in the midst of my Play, before all that were then present," until, with a swift dialectic characteristic of all his later experiences, he had reasoned out the conclusion that it was now too late, since he had sinned so much, and that the only hope was to go back to sin, and take his fill of present sweets. " I can but be damned, and if I must be so, I had as good be damned for many sins as damned for few." He thereupon went on with the game, and in the immediately subsequent days swore, played, and " went on in sin with great greediness of mind."

The automatic internal vision, seen with " the eyes of the understanding," but seen more or less suddenly, with extraordinary detail and with strong emotional accompaniment, appears henceforth as a frequent incident in Bunyan's inner life, and later became, of course, the main source of his peculiar artistic power. He was plainly always a good visualizer. But this automatic organization of his images was an added characteristic of the man, and an invaluable one. This "power of vision " remained, as the Pilgrim's Progress itself shows, late in life; and without it our "dreamer's " genius could not be conceived. In his times of depression these visions, in later days, took on the shading of his mood; but in themselves they were of course signs, not of depression, but of poetic power. Apart from other and serious causes of disturbance they plainly never approached near to any hallucinatory degree; and Bunyan always describes them so as to distinguish them clearly from hallucinations, even when his condition, as described, is one of great agitation.

Shortly after this time the reproof of a neighbor again

startled Bunyan from his reckless ways, and he resolved to begin in earnest the work of reform. The result was a period of a year (or probably somewhat less), during which he undertook nothing less than a systematic course of conscientious self-suppression. He " left" his swearing at once, and in a way that astonished himself. He gave up his games as vain practices; after a long struggle he even abandoned dancing. He read the Bible ; he lived a life of reform that astonished his neighbors; " for this my conversion was as great as for Tom of Bethlem to become a sober man." Inhibition of all outwardly suspicious deeds became the one rule of his life. He still wholly lacked what he later regarded as true piety, and he indulged in some spiritual pride in view of the approbation of his neighbors ; but he cultivated a painful scrupulosity. We can well conceive how the material cares that beset this very poor but now married youth, and this sudden change from a careless life, of numerous relaxations, to an existence wherein every act was a matter of scruple, and wherein the opinions of all his neighbors were now so much taken into account, must have involved a considerable strain. The immediate consequences were characteristic of the whole case.

III.

" Now you must know," says Bunyan, " that before this I had taken much delight in Ringing,* but my *Conscience* beginning to be tender, I thought such practice was but vain, and therefore forced myself to leave it, yet my mind hankered. Wherefore I should go to the Steeple-house, and look on it, though I durst not ring. . . . But quickly after, I began to think, *How if one of the Bells should*

---

* I. e., of course, in ringing the chimes of the village church. Venables has skilfully pointed out, in various passages of Bunyan's writings, how deep a train of associations this practice later involved for the poet.

fall? Then I chose to stand under a main Beam, that lay overthwart the Steeple, from side to side, thinking there I might stand sure. But then I should think again, Should the Bell fall with a swing, it might first hit the wall, and then rebounding upon me, might kill me for all this Beam. This made me stand in the Steeple-door; and now, thought I, I am safe enough; for, if a Bell should then fall I can slip out behind these thick Walls, and so be preserved notwithstanding. So after this I would yet go to see them ring, but would not go further than the Steeple-door. But then it came into my Head, How if the Steeple itself should fall? And this thought, it may fall for aught I know, when I stood and looked on, did continually so shake my mind that I durst not stand at the Steeple-door any longer, but was forced to flee for fear the Steeple should fall on my head."

The parallel between Bunyan's case and that of Dr. Cowles's patient, whose experience is so fully described in the remarkable paper before cited, will from this point onwards become interesting to us. It is noteworthy that Dr. Cowles's patient, after some history of childhood fears, beginning at about ten years of age, became, for a time, "well of these morbid experiences," [*] but afterwards, in youth, experienced a fresh form of her previous disorder, and met this relapse at first in the form of "feelings of hesitation in performing simple acts," with a consequent necessity of repeating many such acts to be sure that they were right. "From this point," says Dr. Cowles of his patient, "all the rest follows in its morbid train." The fortunes of Bunyan were to be, up to a certain point, decidedly similar. The childhood period, with its warning terrors, had given place for a time to a healthy youth. But the elementary conscientious fears which now appeared, and which forced

* Cowles, *loc. cit.*, p. 238.

the lately reckless Bunyan to outward acts of unreasonable timidity, were soon to give place, as in Dr. Cowles's patient, to far more insistent and systematized impulses. In both of these cases the topics about which the insistent impulses finally systematized were matters of inner conscientious scruples. In both cases the general outward bearing and conduct long remained as far as possible normal, except where the inner sufferings of the patient must perforce break through and show themselves. In Bunyan's case it is interesting that these first signs of the coming storm were motor reflexes of a timid and partly of a morbidly inhibitory sort, produced irresistibly at the sound of those bells which he had so much loved to hear, and which, as Venables has shown by quotations from his later works, he never afterwards learned to forget.

The conversation of certain poor and godly people about this time revealed to Bunyan that, with all his legality, he had not yet learned what the true spiritual life is ; and herewith began a second stage of his conversion. The consequence was much continuous meditation upon this higher religious life, and "a softness and tenderness of Heart," whereby his mind became " fixed on Eternity," and, for the time, refused " to be taken from Heaven to Earth." Theological controversy with companions added itself to the foregoing to intensify Bunyan's interest in the secret of true faith. He now constantly read the Bible, which, however, to him, in his environment, seemed rather a collection of texts than of connected treatises. Henceforth his inner life was full of a not uncommon, but in his case especially significant, associative process, whereby he was largely at the mercy of any single text of his now well-thumbed Bible that at any moment might chance to occur to him, wholly separated, of course, from its context. He might be depressed. At such a time a threatening or discouraging text would come to mind ; this or that Scripture would " creep into his soul," and wound him, or chill him all through. He could in but very small degree resist the effect of chance association by recalling the original relations or the meaning of this text as determined by its actual setting at the place where it occurs. No, this " word " had come to him alone; alone he must interpret it and apply it to his case. Did its serious import overwhelm him ? Then there was no way but to hunt at random, either in his Bible, or in the recesses of his chance associations, for some other " word " to set over against the first. Then would follow very possibly long processes of this mere balancing of texts. One " word " must be quoted against another, one series of texts must be neutralized by texts whose immediate emotional effects were more comforting. Bunyan also developed, in connection with such tasks, a peculiarly skilful sort of inner dialectic whereby he estimated the force of each text. He reasoned very subtly with these his own shadows. The decision of nearly every such crisis was determined in the end, however, less by the conscious dialectic itself than by the chances of association. At last, perhaps after days, in the later stages of his malady after months, of conflict, some decisive word would come to mind, would more or less irresistibly " dart " into his soul, would even half seem to be spoken within him (a few times with the force of a pseudo-hallucination, and only once or twice with almost complete hallucinatory vigor). The " word " that association thus made victorious might by its very clearness, or by the strength of its emotional setting, banish all the former " words " from mind ; and for the time doubts would leave him. Or again " two Scriptures " would " meet " in his heart, and one of them would triumph. This process is frequently exemplified in the Grace Abounding, and was of course largely determined, apart from the abnormal capriciousness of his associative processes, by Bunyan's religious opinions and companionships. But this method of thinking was of course an inconvenient complication in view of his now imminent disorder.

At the stage of his pilgrimage here reached, he began to read Paul's epistles with eagerness. They did not decrease his dialectical tendencies. One day, when alone on the road, he found himself wondering gloomily, as he had been doing for some time, whether he really had saving faith or no. Whereupon the "Tempter," who of course, in our author's account, has to bear the responsibility for many of Bunyan's insistent impulses, and for a large part of his associative processes, suggested, as he had several times done before, that there was no way for Bunyan to prove that he had faith save by trying to work some miracle; "which Miracle at that time was this, I must say to the Puddles that were in the horse-pads, *Be dry*, and to the dry places, *Be you the Puddles.* And truly, one time I was going to say so indeed; but just as I was about to speak, this thought came into my mind, *But go under yonder Hedge and pray first that God would make you able.* But when I had concluded to pray, this came hot upon me, That if I prayed, and came again and tried to do it, and yet did nothing notwithstanding, then be sure I had no Faith, but was a Castaway and lost. Nay, thought I, if it be so, I will never try yet, but will stay a little longer."

In this account it is of course the hesitancy and the brooding, questioning attitude that is symptomatic, and not the logic of the quaint reasoning process, which, in view of Bunyan's presuppositions, is normal enough in form. To such broodings the dreamer added about this time one very elaborate symbolic inner vision of his unhappy state as related to the state of the godly people whose faith he envied. The vision, which, as reported, is a fine instance of the automatic visualizing process already characterized, need detain us here no further. It is noteworthy that Bunyan reports it without any surprise, as an incident of a type very familiar in his inner life. The striving with chance Scripture passages continued, and now often drove him to his "wit's end." The comforting passages were occasionally hit upon, but only to give way soon to doubts. His questions as to what faith is, and whether he was of the elect, had already reached the limits of the normal. He was "greatly assaulted and perplexed, and was often," he says, "when I have been walking, ready to sink where I went with faintness in my mind." This is one of the few hints that we get of Bunyan's physical state at this time. The "Tempter" was meanwhile quite capable of suggesting, as regards Bunyan's relation to his fellows in the faith, that these [viz., the known "godly people" aforesaid] being converted already, "they were all that God would save in those parts; and that I came too late, for these had got the Blessing before I came." This thought was insistent enough to cause Bunyan great distress, and even anger at himself for having lost so much time in the past. After really desperate and lonely struggles with such wavering hopes, gloomy fears as to his salvation, and insistent questions and doubts on the whole subject, he at length forsook his solitude, and appealed for help to the "godly people" themselves, who took him to their pastor, Mr. Gifford.

But herewith Gifford only made Bunyan's case for the time worse by assuring him that he was a very grievous sinner, and by drawing his attention away from the universal problems about faith and election back to the particular facts concerning the vanity of his wicked heart. The result was a new stage, wherein all the elements present in the two previous stages of his experience were morbidly combined, and the associative processes so inimical to his peace were rendered more automatic and systematic than ever. The first stage, it will be remembered, had been one of systematically insistent scrupulosity as to the details of his conduct, with elementary inhibitions and fears. The

5

second stage had been one of large and more "tender" emotional states, and of generalized broodings and doubts as to faith and election, accompanied with occasional feelings of general physical weakness and faintness. But now this elaborate process of morbid training came to combine both generalized and specialized elements. The first effect was that instead of the "longing after God" which had characterized the immediately previous state of mind, Bunyan now found in himself a perfect chaos of "Lusts and Corruptions," "wicked thoughts and desires which I did not regard before." He must "hanker after every foolish vanity." His heart "began to be careless both of my Soul and Heaven; it would now continually hang back, both to and in every duty; and was as a Clog to the Leg of a Bird to hinder her from flying. Nay, thought I, now I grow worse and worse; now am I further from Conversion than ever I was before. Wherefore I began to sink greatly in my Soul, and began to entertain such discouragement in my Heart as laid me low as Hell. If now I should have burned at the stake, I could not believe that Christ had love for me: alas, I could neither hear him, nor see him, nor feel him, nor savour any of his things. I was driven as with a Tempest; my Heart would be unclean; the Canaanites would dwell in the land." To this fairly classic description of his general state Bunyan now adds for the first time a mention of the presence of insistent "unbelief," whereof we shall soon hear more. Meanwhile, however, as he adds in a most characteristic fashion: "As to the act of sinning, I was never more tender than now. I durst not take a pin or a stick, though but so big as a straw, for my conscience now was sore, and would smart at every touch; I could not now tell how to speak my words, for fear I should misplace them. Oh, how gingerly did I then go in all I did or said! I found myself as on a miry Bog that shook if I did but stir; and was as there left both of God and Christ and the Spirit, and all good things."

When a man has once got so far into the "Slough of Despond" as this, there is indeed no way but to go on. Such insistent trains of morbid association cannot be mended until they first have grown worse. The process of systematization continued in this case, much as in that of Dr. Cowles's patient.* There were for Bunyan, to be sure, the occasional remissions, due to the temporary success of this or that Scripture passage. So, in one instance, the effective suggestion came from without, through a sermon on the text, *Behold, thou art fair, my Love; behold, thou art fair* —a sermon whose pedantically multipled headings Bunyan years later remembered with perfect clearness. As he was going home after the sermon the two words, *My Love*, came into his thoughts, and "I said thus in my heart, *What shall I get by thinking on these two words ?*" Whereupon "the words began thus to kindle in my spirit, *Thou art my Love, thou art my Love*, twenty times together, and still as they ran thus in my mind they waxed stronger and warmer, and began to make me look up. But being as yet between hope and fear, I replied in my heart, *But is it true ?* At which that Sentence fell in upon me, *He wist not that it was true which was done by the angel.* Then I began to give place to the Word, which with power did over and over make this joyful sound within my soul, *Thou art my Love, thou art my Love; and nothing shall separate me from my Love;* and with that Romans eight, thirty-nine, came into my mind. Now was my heart full of comfort and hope . . . yea, I was now so taken with the love and mercy of God that I could not tell how to contain till I got Home." But this mood of course proved to be unstable, and Bunyan soon "lost much of the life and savour of it."

"About a Week or a Fortnight after this," continues Bunyan, " I was much followed by this Scripture, *Simon, Simon,*

---

* Cowles, *loc. cit.*, pp. 240–245.

Satan hath desired to have you. And sometimes it would sound so loud within me, yea, and as it were call so strongly after me, that once above all the rest, I turned my head over my shoulder, thinking verily that some Man had, behind me, called to me ; being at a great distance, methought he called so loud." This pseudo-hallucination of hearing, secondary, be it noted, to the now frequent and insistent automatic motor process of internal speech, whereby Bunyan obviously found such texts forced upon his attention, concluded this special episode, and this particular text, as he expressly tells us, came no more. Hallucinations of hearing form no part of this case in any but this secondary, transient, and "borderland" form—a fact, of course, which has to be clearly borne in mind in estimating the phenomena. Later reflection, of a sort perfectly normal upon Bunyan's presuppositions, convinced him afterwards that this visitation was a heavenly warning that a "cloud and a storm was coming down" upon him ; but at the time he "understood it not." The minuteness of the account hereabouts is evidence, both of the depth of the experiences, and of the remarkable intactness of Bunyan's memory amidst all this condition of irritable nervous instability of mood on the one hand, and of morbidly persistent brooding on the other.

IV.

But now for the culmination of the disorder—a culmination which appeared in three successive and intensely interesting periods or stages, each one of which Bunyan narrates to us with extraordinary skill and vigor.

"About the space of a month after," he continues, "a very great storm came down upon me, which handled me twenty times worse than all I had met with before." Of this "storm" the primary element, as we should now say, was a melancholic mood, of a depth and origin to him unaccountable. Former moods had been largely secondary, as would appear, to his doubts, although primary states of depression had also played their part. But this time the insistent impulses appeared as obviously quite secondary to the mood. The latter " came stealing upon me, now by one piece, then by another ; first all my comfort was taken from me, then darkness seized upon me, after which " (the order is noteworthy) " whole floods of blasphemies, both against God, Christ, and the Scriptures, were poured upon my spirit, to my great confusion and astonishment. These blasphemous thoughts were such as also stirred up questions in me, against the very Being of God, and of his only beloved Son ; as, whether there were, in truth, a God, or Christ, or no ? And whether the holy Scriptures were not rather a fable, and cunning story, than the holy and pure Word of God ? The tempter would also much assault me with this : *How can you tell but that the Turks had as good Scriptures to prove their Mahomet the Saviour as we have to prove our Jesus is ? And could I think that so many ten thousands in so many Countries and Kingdoms, should be without the knowledge of the right way to Heaven (if indeed there were a heaven), and that we only who live in a corner of the Earth should alone be blessed therewith. Every one doth think his own religion rightest, both Jews and Moors and Pagans ! And how if all our Faith, and Christ, and Scriptures should be but a Think-so too ?* "

Bunyan of course sought to argue with these doubts, but this expert in the dialectics of the inner life now very naturally found all the weapons in the enemy's hands. He would try using the " sentences of blessed Paul " against the " tempter." But alas ! it was Paul who had taught both Bunyan and the " tempter " how to argue with subtlety, and now the reply at once came, in interrogative form : How if Paul too were a cunning deceiver, who had taken "pains and travail to undo and destroy his fellows " ? Bunyan's only remaining comfort was at this point the usual one of the patients afflicted with such harassing enemies. He was aware, namely, that he hated his own doubts, and was so, in a way, better than they. But, as he expressively words it: "This consideration I then only had when God gave me leave to swallow my Spittle; otherwise the noise and strength and force of these temptations would drown and overflow and, as it were, bury all such thoughts." Meanwhile insistent motor impulses of a still more specific sort occurred. Bunyan frequently felt himself tempted "to curse and swear, or speak some grievous thing against God." He compares his state to that of a child whom a gipsy is stealing and carrying away, "under her apron," "from friend and country." "Kick sometimes I did, and also shriek and cry; but yet I was bound in the wings of the temptation, and the wind would carry me away." Nor were the fears of hopeless insanity, so common in such patients, absent from Bunyan's mind, so far as his knowledge permitted him to formulate them. "I thought also of Saul, and of the evil spirit that did possess him; and did greatly fear that my condition was the same with that of his." The sin against the Holy Ghost was of course suggested to Bunyan's mind amongst other possible crimes, and it seemed at once, of course, as if he "could not, must not, neither should be quiet" until he had committed that. "Now, no sin would serve but that; if it were to be committed by speaking of such a word, then I have been as if my Mouth would have spoken that word, whether I would or no; and in so strong a measure was this temptation upon me, that often I have been ready to clasp my hand under my Chin, to hold my Mouth from opening; and to that end also I have had thoughts at other times, to leap downward into some muck-hill hole or other to keep my mouth from speaking."

But to follow further this chaos of motor processes is,

for our purposes, hardly necessary. A system there indeed was amidst the chaos, but this system is now manifest enough. Suffice it that the whole race had now to be run. At prayer Bunyan was tempted to blaspheme, or the "tempter" moved him with the thought, *Fall down and worship me.* At the sacraments of the church, which, although not yet a member of the church, he attended as spectator, in hope of comfort, he was also "distressed with blasphemies." There were still no true hallucinations, but "sometimes I have thoughts I should see the devil, nay, thought I have felt him, behind me, pluck my Clothes." As to mood, Bunyan was now usually "hard of heart." "If I would have given thousands of pounds for a Tear, I could not shed one ; no, nor sometimes scarce desire to shed one." Others "could mourn and lament their sin." But he was, as he saw, alone among men, in this hardness of heart, as in the rest of his troubles. The unclean thoughts and blasphemies aforesaid were likely, as is obvious, to appear as reflexes, of an inhibitory type and meaning interestingly analogous to his earlier conscientious scruples themselves. For these blasphemies were excited by and opposed to any pious activity, precisely as the old conscientious fears had been excited by and inhibitory of any activity which his natural heart had most loved. Hearing or reading the Word would be sure, for instance, to bring to pass the blasphemous temptations. The "tempter" was a sort of inverted conscience, busily insisting upon whatever was opposed to the pious intention. Meanwhile Bunyan of course complains of that general confusion of head of which all such sufferers are likely to speak. When he was reading, "sometimes my mind would be so strangely snatched away and possessed with other things, that I have neither known, nor regarded, nor remembered so much as that sentence that but now I have read." This "distraction " was often at prayer-time associated with insistent inner visual images, as of a " Bull, a Besom, or the like," to which Bunyan was tempted to pray.

Bunyan attributes to this condition an endurance of about a year. Detailed and obviously trustworthy as his psychological memory is, his chronology seems to suffer, very naturally, with a tendency to lengthen in memory the successive stages of his affliction. One can hardly find room, in the known period occupied by the entire experience, for such lengthy separate stages as the writer assumes. The present, or first culminating period of the malady, finally passed off by a gradual decline of the insistent symptoms—a decline assisted, as would appear, by a controversial interest which Bunyan was just then led to take in the "errors of the Quakers," to whose condemnation he devotes a paragraph of his text, hereabouts, in his Autobiography. The objective turn which such controversial thoughts gave his mind was used, as he himself feels, by the Lord, to "confirm" him.

One would suppose that the foregoing story, written with the most moving pathos by Bunyan, ought of itself to be a sufficiently obvious confession, even to readers of comparatively little psychological knowledge. The long-trained habits of verbal and emotional association which are exemplified in these repeated experiences with the remembered passages of Scripture, the systematized attitudes of conscientious fear and inhibition which date back to the beginning of our author's conversion, the obvious essential identity between all these mental habits, and those which Bunyan's "tempter," his inverted conscience—equally fear-compelling, equally inhibitory of his present ardent desires —represented, whenever this "tempter" disturbed him at prayer, even as his conscience had in former days learned to disturb him at bell-ringing—all these phenomena give us a most instructive object-lesson concerning the familiar processes by which the human brain, whether in health or in disorder, gets moulded. The emotional instability that lies at the basis of this particular morbid process—an instability without which, of course, just these habits could never have become such formidable enemies—is perfectly clear before us. Of the precise physical basis of this instability we can indeed only form conjectures; but we know that this was an extremely sensitive brain, and that the childhood dreams and terrors had been of a type such as to furnish obvious warnings that this mind needed especial care. We know too that such care was in so far lacking, as this still very young man had now to suffer the anxieties of providing for his family at a moment when his troubles about his soul were intense, and when his poverty was great. Meanwhile, one aspect of the symptoms, which we have already noticed, is as obvious as it has been, in the past, neglected by Bunyan's readers. This man, a born genius as to his whole range of language-functions, had been from the start a ready speaker, had developed in boyhood an abounding wealth of skilfully bad language, and had then, in terror-stricken repentance, suddenly devoted himself for many months to a merciless inhibition of every doubtful word. We observe now that insistent motor speech-functions were the most marked and distressing of his mental enemies, and that both the tempter, and that comforter whose strangely suggested Scripture passages occasionally consoled Bunyan's heart, tended to speak, "as it were," within the suffering soul. When one considers, still further, the careful way in which, by his own description, Bunyan excludes from his case all hallucinatory elements except the few pseudo-hallucinations, how can one doubt the type of patient with whom one has to deal? Memory, as one sees, is remarkably intact. Any tendency to pathological delusion is obviously lacking; for that Bunyan is beset by the "tempter," is for him a mere statement of the obvious facts in the light of his accepted faith, and is, from his point of view, a strictly normal and inevitable hypothesis, which he never in any morbid fashion misuses. For the rest, he retains throughout as clearly critical an attitude towards his case as the situation in anywise permits ; otherwise we should never have come to get this beautiful confession.

And yet, as said, the biographers have repeatedly missed nearly all these psychological aspects of the case, and that, too, whatever their theory of the poet's experiences. Some, as pointed out, have endeavored to conceive all this as merely the deep religious experience of an untutored genius. Religious experience it indeed was ; nor does its deep human interest suffer from our recognition of its pathological character. Genius there also, indeed, is, in every word of the written story. But the specific sequence of the symptoms thus recorded, and the striking parallel with such modern cases as that of Dr. Cowles's patient (who was surely no genius, and whose morbid conscience busied itself with far more earthly matters than the religious issues central in Bunyan's mind)—these things forbid us to doubt that the phenomena are characteristic of a pretty typical morbid process, which has certainly gone on in very many less exalted brains than was that of Bunyan. Other biographers have spoken, as Macaulay did, of "fearful disorder," but have had no sense of the clear difference between an hallucinatory delirium, which could only develop either in a very deeply intoxicated or exhausted, or else in a hopelessly wrecked brain, and a disorder such as this of Bunyan's, which could get thus dramatically systematized only in a sensitive but nevertheless extremely tough and highly organized brain, whose general functions were still largely intact. So sympathetic an observer as Froude, on the other hand, almost wholly ignoring the pathological aspect of the case, can actually suppose that Bunyan's "doubts and misgivings" were "suggested by a desire for truth" ;

because, forsooth, from the point of view of a nineteenth-century thinker : " No honest soul can look out upon the world, and see it as it really is, without the question rising in him whether there be any God that governs it all." Froude imagines, therefore, that Bunyan later went no further in doubt largely because " critical investigation had not yet analyzed the historical construction of the sacred books." But surely thus to argue is wholly to miss what it is that makes a given sort of questioning, or of other impulse, normal or morbid, for a given man, and under given circumstances. And here is perhaps the place to define more precisely this very matter in our own way.

Morbidly insistent impulses, of whatever sort, are, oddly enough, never morbid merely because they insist. For all our most normal impulses are, or may become, insistent. One has a constantly insistent impulse to breathe, a frequently insistent impulse to eat; and one's life depends upon just such insistences. Insistent desires keep us in love with our work, take us daily about our duties, guide our steps back to our homes, seat us in our chairs to rest, are with us, in their due order, from morning to night, whether we bathe, dress, walk, speak, write, or go to bed. To run counter to such normally insistent impulses pains, and may in extreme cases very greatly distress, or even in the end quite demoralize us. Insistence of will-functions is, then, so far, a sign of health, and means only the kindly might of sound habit. An " imperative impulse " of the morbid sort is therefore, in the first place, one that, under the circumstances, opposes instead of helping our normal process of " adjustment to our environment." But herewith we have still only defined, so far, that element of the morbid impulse which the latter shares in common with all defective mental processes. The peculiar *differentia*, however, of all such forms of morbidly insistent thoughts, fears, temptations, etc., as are the ones now in question, is that their

tendency to bring one out of "harmony with his environment" is subjectively expressed, for the sufferer himself, in
the form of a sense that the fear, thought, or other impulse in
question is opposed to his fitting relation to his environment
as he himself conceives that relation. The hallucination
or the delusion gives one a pathologically falsified environment, and then one's adjustment objectively fails, because
one knows not rightly the truth to which one ought to be
adjusted. Confusedness, or mere incoherence of ideas and
impulses, or other such general alteration of consciousness,
equally means failure, but here also without any completer
subjective sense of what one's failure objectively involves.
But the present sort of sufferer from morbidly insistent impulses, whether or no he conceives his environment rightly,
still knows how he conceives it, and has his general plans of
thought and will ; but he himself, meanwhile, finds, within
himself, "in his members," "another law warring against
the law" which he has accepted as his own. Without pretty
definite plans, then, there can be no such morbidly insistent
impulses as are these of Bunyan's tale. Failure or strong
tendency to failure, in the adjustment, as conceived and
planned by the sufferer himself—such failure being due to
this inner conflict—this it is that makes us here speak of
morbidly insistent impulses.

But not even thus do we define all that it is necessary
to bear in mind in judging such cases. Impulses, feelings,
thoughts, more or less inimical to our deliberate plans, are
constantly, if but faintly, suggested to us, by our normal
overwealth of perceptions and of associations. Without
such overwealth of offered perceptions and associations, we
should not have sufficient material for mental selection ; yet
such overwealth is necessarily full of solicitations, tempting
us, with greater or less clearness, to abandon or to interrupt
our chosen plans of action. Nor is there any fixed limit to
the range of those "imaginations as one would," that, as

Hobbes already pointed out, may at any moment be initiated in a man's inner life by chance experience and association. Therefore, mere opposition between our chance impulses and our plans is a perfectly normal experience.

Normal impulses then are insistent. And normal trains of impulse, or plans of conduct, are constantly besieged by the faint but more or less inimical distractions of normal experience. When, then, is any single impulse, as such, abnormal ? When it insists ? No, for breathing is an insistent impulse. When it opposes the current trains of coherent thought or volition ? No, for every momentary inner or outer distraction tends to do that ; and there is hardly any known impulse or thought or feeling of which a normal man may not at almost any moment be reminded, through the chances of perception and of association. What then is the subjective test of the abnormal in impulse ? One can only find it in this : Association chances to suggest any impulse inimical to one's actually chosen plans for "adjustment to the environment." So far there is no essential defect. This happens to anybody. But normally the coherence of one's series of healthily insistent or of voluntary impulses is so great, or the strength of the intruder soon becomes, under the influence of the opposed ruling interests, so faint, that this intruder is erelong sent below the level of consciousness, or harmlessly "segmented," and that with an ease and a speed proportioned to the incongruity and to the felt inconvenience of this enemy itself. But, in the abnormal cases, things go otherwise. Perhaps the intruding impulse is not a chance one, but is itself part of a previously established system of inhibitory habits. Or perhaps it is supported by numerous now partly or wholly unconscious motives, say by masses of internal bodily sensations (as in case of pathological fears, or of certain physical temptations of abnormal vigor). In all such cases it may prove too strong to be controlled. Or again, the general condition of the sufferer is one of irritable weakness. The sustained coherence of normal functions is then already impaired by nervous exhaustion ; the main trains of association hang weakly together ; their general power of resistance, so to speak, is lowered. The intruding impulse, on the contrary, is then the mental aspect of a suggested nervous excitement that, beginning at one point, quickly spreads to others, and for the time takes possession of the functions of this unstable brain. And now, in any of these cases, we have a failure to resist the intruder, a failure which the sufferer himself bitterly feels. Objectively, the failing adjustment appears as hesitation, or as useless repetition of acts, or as unaccountable impulsive " queerness " of conduct, or even as helpless inactivity, with various quasi-melancholic symptoms—silence, hiding, self-reproach, lamentation. Within, the sufferer, who, to suffer decidedly from this sort of malady, must be a person of highly organized plans and of self-observant intelligence, feels a prodigious struggle going on. All seems to him activity, warfare, self-division, tumult.

In judging of such a case, one must therefore carefully avoid being deceived either by the imperativeness or by the quaintness of the particular impulses involved. All depends upon their relations in a man's mental life. The intense interests of the inventor, of the man of science, of the rapt public speaker, are not necessarily at all analogous to the " obsessions " of the sufferer from insistent impulses, although the former are, like breathing, imperative. Nor are the merrily absurd impulses of a gay party of young people at a picnic abnormal, merely because they are for the time incoherent, and are thus opposed to serious thought and conduct. No, it is the *union* of a tendency toward incoherence in feeling and conduct, with an imperative resistance to the actual and conscious plans, whereby the sufferer deliberately intends to be in some chosen fashion coherent—

it is this union of incongruity with insistence that constitutes the subjective note of the morbidly insistent impulse.

These are .commonplace considerations. I should not introduce them here were not the literature of this whole topic so often affected by confusions of conception. In the light of such obvious considerations, Froude's refusal to see the abnormity of Bunyan's insistent questions or " blasphemies " as to the being of God, and the like, becomes sufficiently insignificant as affecting our present judgment. Any man may by chance, in his mind, come momentarily to question anything. That is so far a matter of passing association, and involves nothing suspicious. A modern or, for that matter, an ancient thinker may moreover persistently question God's existence. If the thinker is a philosopher, or other theoretical inquirer, such doubts may form part of his general plans, and may so be as healthy in character as any other forms of intellectual considerateness. But if a man's whole inner life, in so far as it is coherent, is built upon a system of plans and of faiths which involve as part of themselves the steadfast principle that to doubt God's existence is horrible blasphemy, and if, nevertheless, after a fearful fit of darkness, such a man finds, amidst " whole floods " of other " blasphemies," doubts about God not only suddenly forced upon him, but persistent despite his horror and his struggles, then it is vain for a trained sceptic of another age to pretend an enlightened sympathy, and to say to this agonized nervous patient: " Doubt ? Why, I have doubted God's existence too." The ducklings can safely swim, but that does not make their conduct more congruous with the plans and the feelings of the hen. The professional doubters may normally doubt, But that does not make, doubt less a malady in those who suffer from it, and strive, and cry out, but cannot get free.

This observation, that the symptomatic value of these

insistent impulses lies solely in the *relation* between the
impulses themselves and the organized mental life, the
plans, insight, and chosen habits of the patient, reminds us
also in this case that Bunyan's experiences clearly indicate
the essential psychological equivalence of several of the various sorts of *manias* and *phobias* which some authors, im-
agining that the content rather than the relations of the impulses concerned is important, have so needlessly chosen to
distinguish. Bunyan was tempted to doubt, fear, question,
blaspheme, curse, swear, pray to the devil, or to do whatever
else conscientious inhibition and irritably weak speech-functions had prepared him to find peculiarly fascinating and
horrible. There was no importance in the mere variety of
the wicked ideas that the one " tempter " suggested. The
evil lay in the systematized character of the morbid habits
involved, and in the exhausting multitude of the tempter's
assaults.

V

The malady was now, after the passage of this acute stage,
all the more certainly in possession of the man. The temporary remission was sure to prove deceitful. In Dr. Cowles's
patient, after once the morbid habits had become systematized, to a degree similar to the one now reached in Bunyan's case, there was apparently no way out of the gloomy
labyrinth. Whatever devices were tried led, so long as
the patient was under Dr. Cowles's observation, to renewed
struggles with conscientious scruples and with ingeniously
subtle inner temptations, and the sufferer, whatever her temporary stages of relief, was doomed to walk round and round
the charmed circle of doubt, of temptation, of elaborate self-
invented exorcising devices, of failure, of self-reproach, and
of despair. It was to be Bunyan's good fortune to escape in
the end from his tempter. How he was thus to escape, the
next and most agonizing of his acute stages was to determine. The sufferer from such morbid systems is at best, as

all the evidence shows, in a very serious position. That
very strength of certain of his highest brain-functions
which is one condition of the development of his weakness
as to other functions, makes all the harder the task of teaching him wholly new mental habits. Yet without such
wholly new habits he can never escape. Hence the evil prog-
nosis which most observers now unite in attributing to this
type of disorder, viz., to the chronic malady of insistent impulses with intercurrent acute stages. But there is one
rather desperate chance which most writers on the subject
have, as I think, generally neglected. Suppose there appears,
in the life of the chronically affected patient, a new insistent impulse, such that yielding to this particular impulse
brings the patient into some wholly new relation to his environment. Suppose, thereupon, that a novel and profoundly
different life, even if this be a very painful life, is forced
upon him in consequence of his yielding. The result may
be a condition of things in which, diseased though he still
is, the old cares and temptations are entirely set aside by the
fresh experiences given through the new environment. If
the patient has now strength enough to bear the pangs and
the fresh and strongly contrasted nervous distresses of this
changed life, he may actually have time to reform his mental habits before the old "tempter" is able, for his part, to
organize his own inimical nervous tendencies upon the new
battle-field. The substituted pangs themselves may then
pass before the old are renewed. Then indeed, some day,
the old enemy will come back, but the patient will have become, meanwhile, another man, and the whole system of
his formerly insistent opponents will have been broken up.
He will thus find himself thrown back, in some sense, to the
earlier stages of his own case; he will once more have only
elementary doubts and fears to oppose. But these his experience will have taught him to circumvent; and so, at any
rate with a certain degree of defect, he may have become
6

cured. The elements will survive, but will no longer systematize.

This possible good fortune, to be won, if at all, by passing through the fiercest fire of painful impulse, Dr. Cowles's patient tried in vain to find, when she experimented at pretending to poison herself, or, later, deliberately wounded herself with a pistol, not hoping to commit suicide, but only seeking to expiate her faults, and to get peace from her tempter, through novel pangs. Bunyan, without dreaming of such relief, actually won it through what seemed, at the time, the most hopeless of all the woes that had yet beset him.

"For after the Lord had, in this manner, thus graciously delivered me from this great and sore Temptation . . . the Tempter came upon me again, and that with a more grievous and dreadful Temptation than before. And that was, *To sell and part with this most blessed Christ, to exchange him for the things of this life, for anything.*"

The new temptation had its own typical mental context, different from that of the previous stage. This was now no single member of a "flood of blasphemies." It stood nearly alone, as an equivalent for all the rest of the earlier temptations. Still, however, the impulse to *sell Christ* was merely an imperative motor speech-function. No other word seems ever to have substituted itself for the word *sell*; and the only further act involved in yielding to the temptation was a purely formal inner assent to the "selling." The proposed transaction involved, as a matter of course, no actually conceived exchange whatever. Nevertheless, in a most interesting fashion, the imperative impulse now appeared as a reflex, which tended, in consciousness, to enter into a sort of "agglutinative" combination (to use one of Wundt's well-known adopted phrases), with any object of passing perceptive interest; so that the special form of the experience was that the tempter moved Bunyan to *sell Christ for this* or

for that, whatever the insignificant thing might be that
Bunyan was at the moment attending to, or handling, or
dealing with in any active way. The painfulness, the associated fear, and the violence of the thought, were all of the
most intense sort; and this reflex character made the temptation infect Bunyan's whole life most horribly ; " for it did
always, in almost whatever I thought, intermix itself therewith, in such sort that I could neither eat my food, stoop
for a pin, chop a stick, or cast mine eye to look on this or
that, but still the temptation would come, *Sell Christ for
this*, or *sell Christ for that ; sell him, sell him.*"

The struggle this time very soon led Bunyan to that
grave stage where the sufferer from insistent impulses re-
sorts to apparently senseless motor acts that possess for him
an exorcising significance. " By the very force of my mind,
in laboring to gainsay and resist this wickedness, my very
body also would be put into action or motion by way of
pushing or thrusting with my hands or elbows, still answering as fast as the destroyer said, *Sell him ; I will not, I will
not . . . no, not for thousands, thousands, thousands of
worlds.*" This kind of elaboration rapidly grew to its own
hopelessly extravagant extremes. But in vain. A few
added doubts, of the old inhibitory type, meanwhile appeared in the background, but the tempter had now, so to
speak, learned his game, and had no need to waste his forces
upon general devices of inhibition. This one suggestion was
enough. The loathsome triviality of the motor impulse
itself, in its pettiness, and the vast dignity of the eternal
issues imperilled, as Bunyan felt, by its presence, combined
to give the situation all the dreadful and inhibitory features
that had earlier been spread over so wide a mental range of
evil interests.

" But to be brief, one morning, as I did lie in my bed, I
was, as at other times, most fiercely assaulted with this
temptation, . . . the wicked suggestion still running in my

mind, *Sell him, sell him, sell him, sell him,* as fast as a man
could speak. Against which also, in my mind, as at other
times, I answered, *No, no, not for thousands, thousands,
thousands,* at least twenty times together. But at last, after
much striving, even until I was almost out of breath, I felt
this thought pass through my heart, *Let him go, if he will !*
and I thought also that I felt my heart freely consent thereto. Oh the diligence of Satan! Oh the desperateness of
man's heart!

"Now was the battle won, and down fell I, as a Bird that
is shot from the top of a tree, with great guilt, and fearful
despair. Thus getting out of my Bed, I went moping into
the field ; but God knows, with as heavy a heart as mortal
man, I think, could bear ; where, for the space of two hours,
I was like a man bereft of life, and as now past all recovery,
and bound over to eternal punishment."

VI.

The nervous crisis thus passed served to introduce a condition of extremely lengthy, quasi-melancholic, but to Bunyan's consciousness wholly secondary, depression. The
hopeless sin was committed. Like Esau he had sold his
birthright. There was now "no place for repentance."
This, the third stage of the culmination of the malady, was
marked by an almost entire quiescence of the insistently
sinful impulses; for what had the victorious tempter now
left to do ? There were no more minor hesitancies, no
loathsome motor irritations. One overwhelming idea and
grief inhibited all these inhibitory symptoms. The insistent
associative processes with the Scripture passages became,
however, for a good while, all the more marked, automatic,
and commanding. Thus the whole mental situation was
profoundly altered. The secondary melancholic depression
expressed itself occasionally in praecordial anxiety. "I have
felt also such a clogging and heat at my stomach, by reason

of this my terror, that I was, especially at some times, as if my breast bone would have split asunder." But Bunyan even now never long lost his dialectic skill; and hopeless as seemed his case, he from the first set about trying to think of a way of escape from destruction, being throughout "loath to perish"—a fact which, viewed in its results, indicates the relative intactness of his highest mental functions amidst all his gloom.

Except for the automatic processes with the Scripture passages, Bunyan's condition of secondary melancholic depression had, therefore, despite its depth and its fantastic background, many of the more benign characters of normal grief. It had, at the worst, its occasional remissions. It left his reasoning powers formally unaffected. And it had the painful but really invaluable character that, just because his fate seemed decided, he had a long and almost total rest from the irritating motor processes, whose dependence upon his past habits of conscientious anxiety is thus all the more confirmed. For this restless anxiety, the pretty steady assurance of damnation was now substituted. This, as the event proved, Bunyan's heroic disposition was strong enough to endure, despite the "splitting" sensations in the breast, despite the long days of grief and of lonely lamentation; despite his inability to get any comfort or help from his few advisers. The case was still grave enough, but this light melancholia proved to be a decidedly kinder disorder than the foregoing one, and it led the way over to recovery.

In the long tale which follows, in Bunyan's Autobiography, and which is largely devoted to the description of the inner conflicts amongst the Scripture passages (of whose automatic evolutions poor Bunyan's consciousness was now long the merely passive theatre), there are but few things further to be noted for our purpose. But these few are extremely instructive.

The gradual emergence from despair is obviously due, on the whole, to the *vis medicatrix naturæ*. Bunyan's general physical health gradually improved. His conscientious habits of life, freed now from the tempter's teasing interferences, had a chance to become healthily fixed and unconscious. He grieved too deeply to long for distractions, and never thought of returning to his youthful sins as a relief from despair. The doubts and other motor inconveniences were of course still in the background of his mental life, but it is interesting to note how, whenever they appear, they are now simply overshadowed and devitalized by the fixed presence of the ruling melancholic ideas. The tempter is thus at length known as a relatively foreign and mocking other self, whose power over Bunyan's will grows less even while his triumph is supposed to be final. He " becomes humorous," as Froude observes. Bunyan, so the tempter suggests in his old metaphysical way and with the old doubting subtlety—Bunyan had better not pray any more, since God must be weary of the whole business; or if he must pray, let it be to some other person of the Trinity instead of to the directly insulted Mediator. Could not a new plan of salvation be devised by special arrangement, the Father this time kindly acting as mediator with the otherwise implacable Son, to meet Bunyan's exceptional case ? But such suggestions, which in an earlier stage would have been " fearful blasphemies," now have to stand in contrast to the fixed and central grief which constitutes Bunyan's own personal consciousness. Bunyan knows by the very contrast that these suggested words of the tempter are *not* his own. This is the mere fooling of the exultant devil. It is meaningless. For Bunyan is consciously on the side of the grief itself, and the humorous tempter is the sole owner of the blasphemies, which therefore serve all the more to " confirm " the sufferer in his painful faith. A better device than this for the " segmentation " of insistent questionings could not have been imagined by any physician learned in the cure of souls. The victorious tempter had unwittingly dug his own grave. He could never again get possession of this man's central self, nor use this brain as a foundation for systematized evil habits.

Another instructive aspect of the slow process of recovery lies in the fact that Bunyan was, towards the end, able, at some moments, and despite his always busy dialectic processes, to win that attitude of complete resignation, of abandonment of all feverish conscious strugglings and pleadings with fate—that attitude which, as experience shows, is so often the beginning of a final recovery from all forms of deeper mental distress. Such an attitude is consistent, as it was in Bunyan, with a good deal of cool consideration, and with much activity of thought; but it was still effectively assumed. There is, for such sufferers as Bunyan, and for many others, a mood of gentler despair that is often essentially healing, because, as compared to their old feverishness, it is peaceful. It is the sort of despair that Edgar Poe has put on record in the admirably psychological lines For Annie. It is the mood that says, to the tempestuous striving self of former days, " *Ich hab' meine Sache auf Nichts gesetzt.*" One is lost; only eternal mercy can save; one finally is content to leave all to fate or to God, and to " lie quietly," like the conscious corpse of Poe's poem, glad a little that the " fever called living is ended at length." Bunyan is remote enough in type from Poe's lover; and he was never content long to lie quiet. But still, at moments, this essentially curative element also is present in this stage of his experience. The automatic play of the remembered Scripture passages became with him more and more complex, imposing, unpredictable—an inner fate that he often helplessly watched as one watches the breaking of great waves on the beach. Plainly God must be directing the process. Bunyan could only pray that God's will might be

done, and hope that so many kind glimpses of light would
not have been shown to an utter outcast. "God and Christ,"
he says, "were continually before my face," and, painful as
the experience was, since he was facing his judge, this kept
down, as he himself recognizes, all the old temptations to
"atheism." At last "I saw . . . that it was not my good
frame of heart that made my Righteousness better, nor my
bad frame that made my Righteousness worse; for my
righteousness was Jesus Christ himself, *the same yesterday, to-day, and forever.*" And "now," he says, in nar-
rating this last experience, "did my chains fall off my
Legs indeed." Such is the healing virtue of true resignation.

The episodes of this whole long final stage were of course
numerous and of Protean character. There was throughout, despite the prevalence of the general despair, considerable instability of mood. Intervals of peace, resulting from
this or that "sweet glance" of a "Promise," were sometimes
followed by the wildest fits of gloom. Two or three times the
borderland pseudo-hallucinations of speech returned. Once,
in particular, at a moment of this sort, the accompanying
experience of calm "made a strange seizure upon my spirit;
it brought light with it, and commanded a silence in my
heart of all those tumultuous thoughts that before did use,
like masterless hell-hounds, to roar and bellow and make a
hideous noise within me." And this sudden transformation
of mood, produced by a comforting voice that was "as if
heard," was so great that, many years later, though writing
in a very cautious and self-critical spirit, Bunyan could not
refrain, in a later edition of the Grace Abounding, from
inserting this incident, and adding his private opinion that
this might indeed have been "an Angel" that "had come
upon me." Yet no element of actual delusion was, at the
time, involved in the experience. As for the Scripture passages, their automatic effects were such that Bunyan ere

long found himself awaiting with interest what would happen when two, already known and often studied "words" should, by chance, "meet in my heart"—an event which might prove to him of the most critical importance, although, beforehand, he could do positively nothing to hasten or to effect this event by any voluntary consideration of the passages. Only when the suggested passages were numerous, and the "meeting" had already often occurred, could he devote himself, with his accustomed dialectic skill, to considering with care the outcome and its meaning—a thing which, just before his recovery, he learned to do, in some cases, very coolly and with great deliberation.

The passing of this stage of despair was attended, at the end, with many of the usual exaltations and confusions of convalescence. "I had two or three times, at about my deliverance from this temptation, such strange apprehensions of the grace of God, that I could hardly bear up under it; it was so out of measure amazing, when I thought it could reach me, that I do think, if that sense of it had abode long upon me, it would have made me incapable of business."

VII.

The cure had come to pass, but it was, and remained, a cure with a pretty well-defined defect. The tempter could never again obtain control. The diseased habits were reduced to their elements, and were unable to systematize themselves afresh. The elements, however, proved, as one would expect in such a case, too deeply founded in this wonderful constitution ever to be eliminated. At the end of the Grace Abounding Bunyan, with the simplest humility, records the temptations to which his soul is now permanently subjected. His moods of spiritual interest and emotion are to a very considerable extent unstable, do what he may. There are times when he is "filled with darkness,"

however much, at other times, he may have been exalted.
His heart becomes, at the dark times, "dead and dry," and
he can then find no "comfort." He is also still occasionally
tempted "to doubt the being of God and the Truth of his
Gospel"; and this is always the "worst" of moods.
Furthermore, in his preaching, the tempter often besets him
"with thoughts of blasphemy," which he is "strongly
tempted to speak" "before the congregation"; or again, a
strange confusion of head comes upon him as he preaches,
and straitens" him, so that he feels "as if I had not known
or remembered what I have been about, or as if my head
had been in a bag all the time of the Exercise." More subtle assaults of the tempter also come while he preaches—
condemnations of this or that which he knows it to be his
duty to utter, or on the other hand movings "to pride and
liftings up of heart." For a while after his malady, when
he had joined the church, he was tempted to blaspheme
during the sacraments. In any of his illnesses, peculiarly
black and cowardly thoughts always come. At the beginning of his imprisonment he long felt himself to be a hopeless coward, unable because unworthy to suffer for the faith,
and the tempter mocked this weakness with all the old
subtlety.

But now—here is the important thing—all these permanent enemies are still, and remain for the rest of Bunyan's
life, in no wise uncontrollable. His deeper consciousness is
beset, but never overwhelmed, by them. His attitude
towards them becomes objective, resigned. They teach him
to "watch and be sober." They are useful to him, since
"they keep me from trusting my heart." Of one of his
later hours of darkness he says: "I would not have been
without this Trial for much. I am comforted every time I
think of it, and I hope I shall bless God forever for the
teaching I have had by it. Many more of the dealings of
God towards me I might relate, but these *out of the spoils*

won in Battle have I dedicated to maintain the house of God." The words are typical of all the later inner experience of Bunyan; and it is to this spirit in the man that we owe his immortal works.

Of his mental regimen after his recovery a word may yet be said. A wise instinct guided the much-tried wanderer in the darker world to forsake henceforth his solitude, to join himself "unto the people of God," to try to be objectively serviceable, and to keep in touch with the needs of his brethren. His gift of speech hereupon soon discovered itself. He was erelong set to preach. His power won multitudes of listeners during all his years passed out of prison. In prison he wrote busily, and preached to his fellow-prisoners at every opportunity. The motor speech-functions, whose inhibition had led to such disastrously rebellious insistent habits, were never again suffered to remain without absorbing and productive exercise. The decidedly healthy self-contempt engendered by the experience of his own weakness only served to make him more objective in his whole attitude towards life. Henceforth he knows every man to be of himself naught. He has therefore, as Froude points out, no favorites, and portrays, in his literary work, Talkative, and Ignorance, and Mr. Badman, with as much cool devotion to the task and with as much artistic faithfulness, as Christian. He spares no one, himself least of all. Yet he sympathizes with every manner of human weakness, for his own inner life has furnished him with a brief abstract and epitome of all human frailty. His mastery is the mastery of the genius who has really entered the Valley of the Shadow and has passed through. Hence the seeming of the man in the eyes of those who knew him in later life, and who could not easily have suspected, in this modest yet commanding presence, the piteous weaknesses of his younger years, had he himself not so instructively told the wonderful story.

Our result can be briefly stated. This is unquestionably a fairly typical case of a now often described mental disorder. The peculiarities of this special case lie largely in the powers of the genius who here suffered from the malady. A man of sensitive and probably somewhat burdened nervous constitution, whose family history, however, so far as it is known to us, gives no positive evidence of serious hereditary weakness, is beset in childhood with frequent nocturnal and even diurnal terrors of a well-known sort. In youth, after an early marriage, under the strain of a life of poverty and of many religious anxieties, he develops elementary insistent dreads of a conscientious sort, and later a collection of habits of questioning and of doubt which erelong reach and obviously pass the limits of the normal. His general physical condition meanwhile failing, in a fashion that, in the light of our very imperfect information concerning this aspect of the case, still appears to be of some neurasthenic type, there now appears a highly systematized mass of insistent motor speech-functions of the most painful sort, accompanied with still more of the same fears, doubts, and questions. After enduring for a pretty extended period, after one remission, and also after a decided change in the contents of the insistent elements, the malady then more rapidly approaches a dramatic crisis, which leaves the sufferer for a long period in a condition of secondary melancholic depression, of a somewhat benign type—a depression from which, owing to a deep change of his mental habits, and to an improvement of his physical condition, he finally emerges cured, although with defect, of his greatest enemy—the systematized insistent impulses. This entire morbid experience has lasted some four years. Henceforth, nnder a skilful self-imposed mental regimen, this man, although always a prey to elementary insistent temptations and to fits of deep depression of mood, has no return of his more systematized disorders, and endures heavy burdens of work and of fortune with excellent success.

Such is the psychological aspect of a story whose human and spiritual interest is and remains of the very highest.

III.

*TENNYSON AND PESSIMISM.**

THE bitter criticism that greeted the appearance of Lord
Tennyson's second Locksley Hall shows how much people
still loved the first Locksley Hall, and how little they had
learned from it. An almost universal opinion declared the
new poem to be a purely abnormal product, whereas the first
poem, according to the same opinion, was something quite
natural and healthy. The new Locksley Hall was thus denounced as a sort of treason. This cruel father, people said,
sacrifices the child of his own youth. This worn-out old
hero shows himself at last before all the world as a coward,
and whines where once he sang the battle-hymn. This Tory
lord now bids crouch whom the rest bade aspire. Such was
the general sense of popular criticism, at least in this country.
And, at first sight, what could be more natural than this
judgment ? The first Locksley Hall gave us a view of life
so honest, so youthful, so modern, so comprehensible, that it
would seem as if nobody capable of feeling what young men
feel, could fail to adopt that view, or, having adopted it, could
abandon it without regret. If now the creator of this old
ideal appears as its denouncer and destroyer, can we who
loved the old poem do anything but condemn the final
mood of its maker.

* Locksley Hall Sixty Years After, etc. By Alfred, Lord Tennyson.
New York : Macmillan & Co.

But this popular view was no less plausible than unjust. In fact the second Locksley Hall is, despite a certain falling off of technical skill, still substantially the fulfillment of the first. Whatever unhealthiness exists in the latest poem, is in germ in the original one, and, on the whole, the new poem, notwithstanding a number of frantic opinions and of unpleasant lines, is healthier, more manly, more devout, and even more cheerful, in a deeper sense of the word cheerful, than was the first poem. Neither poem is truly sound. Both suffer from the same disease. Both illustrate Tennyson's characteristic weakness. But of the two the old man's poem, if artistically inferior, is ethically higher, and for this reason is far more satisfying. Such is the thesis that this paper wants to defend.

What has made people blind to this is the fact that the disease from which both of these poems suffer is a very prevalent disease. It is a cause of numerous modern superstitions, and casts a gloom over many lives. We need to become conscious of its nature, and to get rid of it from our own minds. For my part, then, I am thankful to our poet for the second Locksley Hall, because, taken with the first, it illustrates so well and so instructively a great man's conflict with this, the favorite disease of his age. I should be glad if people saw this truth more readily, and I venture upon the few hasty suggestions which follow for the sake of helping others, possibly, to direct their attention to the matter.

A devout man is one who believes that there is something in the world which demands both his worship and his loyalty, and who, accordingly, tries to worship and be loyal. Now, if any man seeks to be devout, his great difficulty is that he is all the while in the midst of petty and disheartening things, which at once attract, corrupt, pain and horrify him. In his religious faith, or in his poetry, or in his dreams, he therefore tries somehow to neutralize, or to explain away, or at the worst occasionally to forget, this baseness of the details of life.   Only when he can somehow either transcend or forsake these coarse facts, has he the chance to feel the desired devotion.   " If, therefore, there is anything divine in the world," he says to himself, " I shall not find it while I am joined to these cloying and hateful experiences."   And so he asks of his religious teachers, or of his poets, or of the others who have spiritual wares to offer him, that they shall somehow purge his soul, from time to time, of the corruption of finite things, and show him that divine good, whatever he chooses to call it, which is to be the true object of his loyalty.

Now, since this is the natural desire of a good man, it is also but natural that everybody at some time tries to take the shortest road to this goal of spiritual freedom.   To get above the petty and coarse things of life, we must forget them, so we say.   This seems the only fashion of escape.   In consequence of this resolve, we often ask of our poets not so much that they shall transcend, as that they shall disguise or deny, or ignore, the coarseness of the real world.   " Hide it," we say to them, " declare it unreal, dream it away, talk of it as illusion.   Deliver us from evil by simply destroying the very idea of it, so long as we are in your company."   When we make this demand of our poets, we ask them to be romantic, and the poets who habitually appeal to this demand are called the romantic poets.   As is well known, however, Lord Tennyson himself is a romantic poet.   Always one of the most devout of men, he gives as his ideal of the devout mood something that can be realized only through a more or less complete separation from the world of concrete life.   He offers us the things of the spirit in sacred places, not elsewhere.   His realm of divine truth is and always was for him a dream-land, to be reached through mystical exaltation, or by the ecstatic fancies of hopeful youth.   He has believed in God, but in a God that hideth himself, and that still showeth himself, on rare and romantic occasions, to the devout. This is the God of the Holy Grail, or of the wondrous mystical experience during the night scene on the lawn, in the In Memoriam. This God, to tell the truth, seems afraid of his own world. He doubtless knows our frame, and remembers that we are dust, but he regards us meanwhile with a distant, although mildly pitiful negligence. On occasion he lets us catch glimpses of himself, but there is neither rule nor rationality about the coming of these glimpses. "Look at me if you can," the divine truth says to us. Otherwise we seem to form no part of its business. We are not the sort of people that it habitually meets in a social way.

All this is only a matter-of-fact statement of the romantic spirit, familiar to us, of course, in many poets besides Lord Tennyson. But it is needful to remind ourselves what this spirit means, in order that we may see just now how it expresses itself in the first Locksley Hall. In that poem, to be sure, there is nothing of what one usually calls mysticism. There is, in fact, no theology at all. Hence, indeed, the essentially modern sound of the verses. Lord Tennyson's age is doubtless out of harmony, and from the first has been out of harmony, with the more esoteric and theological element in his romanticism. Yet this age has no sort of objection to divinely significant truth, if only you can express it in terms of well-known astronomical, physical, or biological theories, and can make it sound unmiraculous. That, in a fashion, was what the first Locksley Hall did, by means of a few skilful and even prophetic phrases. What the age views with great dislike, namely, the expression of the higher truth in traditional or in mystical forms, was what the first Locksley Hall ingeniously avoided. Hence people who make little or nothing of In Memoriam, who find all the Idyls of the King at their best too fanciful, and who think the Holy Grail quite unintelligible, may still admire

7

endlessly the dreams about the far-off future in Locksley Hall.

Yet Locksley Hall is percisely as romantic and as full of the remote ideals as is the Holy Grail. You may state the thing in mediæval terms if you like, or in terms of fancies about flying-machines and international Federations. Yet the result is precisely the same. The world that you move in is, in both cases, the old romantic world, the land of magic fire, of talismans, and of a beautiful darkness. You are on a quest for the ideal. It is a sort of creature that won't be caught in a commonplace way. You must go on knightly wanderings, and lose yourself in deserts and oceans. The mighty wind arises, roaring seaward, and you go. Your business is somewhat indescribable. You are sure only that it is vastly important. Its most prominent feature is that it takes you away from earthly relations. You are shamed through all your being to have loved so slight a thing as an actual flesh-and-blood woman, who, of course, must have been quite incapable of understanding such a nature as yours. Nevertheless, after all your misfortunes, the crescent promise of your spirit has not set, and you propose to do something on a grand scale. The outcome of the business will be some sort of ineffable glory for future humanity. The distance beacons, and not in vain. You cry " forward," quite ignorant, of course, of just what the word means, but sure that if we only get far enough away from where we are, we shall not fail to find perfection. The good is something absolutely and fatally destined to be reached by us, although it is also of a certainty something so very remote that we have not the least idea when we shall reach it. Such, then, is your Holy Grail, your increasing purpose that runs through the ages, your divine truth. Your description of its features may vary, but it always has the same " unmistakable marks," by which you may know it wheresoever you go.

This summary may perhaps seem mere scoffing. The matter has, of course, another side. This devotion to a vague and romantic ideal, which is chiefly defined by the fact that it is a good way off, has its strong features. The purity of intention is, in Lord Tennyson's poems, undoubted. Their educating value, in their place and time, is of the highest. How much we owe to this teacher of the ideal in a sordid age, who may know ? But if, for the sake of awaking our enthusiasm, these vague dreams of abstract perfection are invaluable, we must never forget two things about them : first, that they are never the only expressions, never the highest expressions, of the love of ideals; and, second, that the invariable outcome of such dreams, unless they give place to some more solid sort of idealism, is sooner or later hateful and pessimistic despair. This romantic idealism of so many among Tennyson's poems, is, therefore, not only vague, but essentially transient. In case of the mood of Locksley Hall, also, the idealism must give place to a deeper and less romantic devotion, or else it must end in out and out pessimism. The second Locksley Hall especially shows us in what sense the first Locksley Hall was already, in germ, a pessimistic poem.

For in the first Locksley Hall, if we will be honest with it, there is plainly great faith that God is the God of the future ; but in no true sense does he appear as the God of the present. The present is a world of wicked squires, who drink wine and love dogs, of false and fickle cousins—who probably lie awake o' nights weeping because they feel themselves unworthy of our high regard—and in general of social lies and sickly forms. There are a few good people in it, in the foremost ranks of time, namely ; but their concern is not with its absurdities, but with the service of the ideal future humanity. The noble youth of the poem is simply a pessimist as to the world that now is. It is out of joint, and he is not born to set that world right, but rather

to forget it. His optimism concerns the world that is not,
but some day shall be. Of that, all sorts of amusing things
are true. God's attention is plainly devoted to the realms
of dreams, and the divine plan has no place for the squire
and the cousin. This of course is optimism with a vengeance, but is it not also in a much deeper sense pessimism ?
God is not in this place, and Jacob, on a famous occasion,
made a blunder. God is somewhere else, sleeping, as it
were, or on a journey, and we must set out to find him.
Nay then, is not this optimism of progress, this assurance
that the divine truth is still playing truant, a very dark
thought, after all ? "One increasing purpose," indeed ! But
so far it has culminated in the squire and the social lies
aforesaid. What is wanted is still a very great increase of
this "purpose." For thus far we have to curse very frankly, in the poem, pretty much all, save our noble selves, that
the "purpose" has produced. Where then is the "promise
of his coming ?" Or rather, what is it all but a bare and
wearisomely reiterated promise, whose fulfillment is only in
dream-land, and is apparently there to stay for as long as
we can definitely foresee. But then the "distance beacons."
Yet it is only distance, only the far-off. There is no meaning in life save what that far-off gives to it. *Das Dort ist
niemals Hier*. At heart then, despite all our fervor, we are
only pessimists. The good is somewhere, just as "oats and
beans and barley grows where you nor I nor nobody knows."
And that is the whole tale of our airy and meaningless
hopes. We have only to wake up to this fact to turn all
our enthusiasm into disaster and gloom.

Now in so far as the second Locksley Hall is truly pessimistic at all, its pessimism is simply the explicit statement
of the sense of this very thought. Unless God is here, says
in substance the poet of the second Locksley Hall, how do
you know that he is anywhere else ? Unless the present has
divine meaning, how worthless the dreams of a far-off starry

future, dreams comparable only to the fancies about the perfect life that may dwell in the other planets :

Hesper—Venus—were we native to that splendour or in Mars,
We should see the Globe we groan in, fairest of their evening stars.

Could we dream of wars and carnage, craft and madness, lust and spite,
Roaring London, raving Paris, in that point of peaceful light ?

Might we not in glancing heavenward on a star so silver-fair
Yearn, and clasp the hands and murmur, " Would to God that we were
    there ? "

.   .   .   .

" What are men that He should heed us ? " cried the king of sacred song ;
Insects of an hour, that hourly work their brother insects wrong,

While the silent Heavens roll, and Suns along their fiery way,
All their planets whirling round them, flash a million miles a day.

Such are the thoughts that finally determine the poet to give up the optimism of progress. The process of the world, such as it is, is far too vast to be expressed in merely temporal terms. Regarded in time merely, there is doubt about all this plan. There seems at all events to be rhythm as well as growth :

> Evolution ever climbing after some ideal good,
> And Reversion ever dragging Evolution in the mud.

And so much that we take to be progress, after all, turns out not to be such ! Still again, where we are in doubt about the reality of anything that we have called progress, we become appalled at once by the magnitude of the powers of the world. How, looking at them externally, can we be sure of their meaning ?

Forward, backward, backward, forward, in the immeasurable sea,
Sway'd by vaster ebbs and flows than can be known to you or me.

To be sure, even now we can repeat our youthful dreams of the future peace and perfection of humanity. Perhaps there will come an " end after madness " for our poor earth :

> Every tiger madness muzzled, every serpent passion kill'd,
> Every grim ravine a garden, every blazing desert till'd,
>
> Robed in universal harvest up to either pole she smiles,
> Universal ocean softly washing all her warless Isles.

But then, not only are these things hard, even as dreams
(" Who can fancy warless men ? "), but just behind all that
is the picture of the physical death of our planet, a death
sure to come at last. Is not the moon dead ? "The moon-
light is the sunlight, and the sun himself will pass." For
the old dreams we therefore have left only the gloomiest of
mysteries, and the saddest of assurances.

But, after all, does not the true secret of this pessimism
lie in our original abandonment of the real world about us
for that world of dreams ? When we sought the ideal far
off, and refused to recognize it in human life as it is, were
we not already just what we have found ourselves to be,
pessimists ? Can we not then escape our outcome by abandoning our romantic mood ? To a certain extent, Tennyson
undertakes to do this in the new Locksley Hall, and this is
what makes me say that there is, with all the weakness and
the gloom of this latest poem, a far healthier view of life, in
many of its lines, than we find in the old Locksley Hall.

First then, in general, the poet distinctly recognizes at
last that, if this is God's world, what others have called the
" perfection in imperfection" of just these struggles, sins,
tears, strivings and loves about us to-day, must be the expression of God's will. The sins are none the less sins that
they and the struggle with them are alike necessary to the
genuine realization of the good. We need cry out no less
against evil whilst we still hold evil to be, not the transient
absence of the god of Evolution from his world, but the
living strife in the midst of which the true God maintains
himself *in* his world. This view of evil is the one that
among recent poets, Browning has especially been commis-

sioned to illustrate afresh for us. This is what he has said
in all his best poems. But this view is the one that Tennyson's romanticism has always tried to escape. Tennyson
has lamented the evils of life, but has never been ready to
take them for what they are, the evils of God's own world.
They have seemed to him the accidents of God's remoteness.
In this latest poem he somewhat haltingly recognizes, amidst
all his complaints, the inevitable fact. The good simply is
not and cannot be realized, save in the midst of the conflict
with evil. Yet that truth makes the good no less good, and
the world no less divine. Through all his despair the poet
now at last turns towards this light as his only guide :

> Follow you the Star that lights a desert pathway, yours or mine.
> Forward, till you see the highest Human Nature is divine.
>
> Follow Light, and do the Right—for man can half-control his doom—
> Till you find the deathless Angel seated in the vacant tomb.

It is with this new sort of faith in mind that the poet
says of our earth, not, as of old, that it is a joy to see her
spinning down the ringing grooves of change, but that

> Ere she reach her earthly best, a God must mingle with the game.

He feels too that there are " those about us whom we
neither see nor name." He is sure that, amid all the mysteries of the heavens, mysteries upon which the word Evolution throws no sort of light, there must still be a living
presence :

> Only That which made us, meant us to be mightier by and by,
> Set the sphere of all the boundless Heavens within the human eye,
>
> Sent the shadow of Himself, the boundless, thro' the human soul,
> Boundless inward, in the atom, boundless outward in the Whole.

This faith is still vague, it is still clouded, it still loves
romantic forms of speech. But after all it is more genuine
than that blind old trust in whatever might happen to fill

the remote future. For if this mysterious world is even now the world of a divine plan, boundless both in the whole and in the atom, if we wait not for some far-off divine event, but believe in the actually present God, then our lives become, for all their horror and their problems, at any rate genuine lives. It is a game, at worst, this life of ours, and not a procession. We play it, and do not simply watch it to see what is some day to follow:

> You, my Leonard, use and not abuse your day,
> Move among your people, know them, follow him who led the way,

> Strove for sixty widow'd years to help his homelier brother men,
> Served the poor, and built the cottage, raised the school and drained the fen.

The man who does his commonplace business in the living present is, after all, the true man. He fights the good fight, and the good is nothing if it is not the good fight.

The particular true man, however, whom Leonard, the " grandson " of the new poem, is to follow, is none other, be it noticed, than the old squire himself, that dog-loving creature, who used to hunt in dreams, and behave otherwise disagreeably. There is a beautiful completeness about the late apology which the poet now makes to that much abused person. Every reader will be amused by the apology. But possibly some reader may not note its full significance. Returning, as the poet does from the world of vain dreams to the world of human beings, he finds not only horrible and gloomy things, such as fill him with fear, but true and genuine things, such as express God's own heart. Among these things are the very relationships that the romantic youth had affected to despise. Amy, to be sure, is gone, long since. But the old squire has lived even until yesterday. The poet has come at last to be present at his funeral. And when one sums up the squire's hearty, simple, benevolent, unromantic life, one sees what it meant:

Worthier soul was he than I am, sound and honest, rustic Squire,
Kindly landlord, boon companion—youthful jealousy is a liar.

After all, it is the straightforward and manly life that
is praiseworthy. Once it seemed to us mere Philistinism,
and perhaps in its narrowness it may often have been nothing better. But narrowness is not cured by negations.
"Forsake this present life because it is narrow," our romantic youth had said. Now we see that it is in this present
life, not out of it that we are to find God. Take this commonplace life, and without denying it, without forsaking it,
make it no longer narrow. Make it large and full, but
keep it concrete: that is the lesson that the old squire has
taught us, and we thank him for it as he lies dead. We
have no better advice for Leonard than that he shall follow this example.

Thus then, Tennyson's latest pessimism is not without
its brighter comrades, courage, and faith in the real world.
In so far as our poet has reached this view he has distinctly
progressed from disease toward health. The old man thinks
gray thoughts, for he is gray; but not all his thoughts are
of death. Experience has brought him the end of romantic
dreams, and his only hope is now in the actual.

One hears nowadays, very often, of youthful pessimism,
prevalent, for instance, among certain clever college students. When I hear of these things, I do not always regret
them. On the contrary, I think that the best man is the
one who can see the truth of pessimism, can absorb and
transcend that truth, and can be nevertheless an optimist,
not by virtue of his failure to recognize the evil of life but
by virtue of his readiness to take his part in the struggle
against this evil. Therefore, I am often glad when I hear
of this spread of pessimistic ideas among studious but undeveloped youth. For I say to myself, if these men are brave
men, their sense of the evil that hinders our human life,
will some day arouse them to fight this evil in dead earnest,

while, if they are not brave men, optimism can be of no service to cowards. But in any case I like to suggest to such brave and pessimistic youth where the solution of their problem must lie. It surely cannot lie in any romantic dream of a pure and innocent world, far off somewhere in the future, in Heaven, or in Isles of the Blessed. These things are not for us. We are born for the world of manly business, and if we are worthy of our destiny, we may possibly have some good part in the Wars of the Lord. For nothing better have we any right to hope, and to an honest man that is enough. We may be glad that our poet won at last the possession of this truth.

IV.

THE KNOWLEDGE OF GOOD AND EVIL.*

In a remarkable paper on Moral Deficiencies as determining Intellectual Functions, published in the July number of this Journal, the learned author has made a very interesting contribution to that famous discussion which was begun, according to a very respectable tradition, in the Garden of Eden, and which, in much more recent times, was continued in the incomparable conversation between Mephistopheles and the student in Faust. Every thoughtful consideration of so interesting and momentous a question is welcome, and no reader can doubt the thoughtfulness, and in many ways the instructiveness, of the admirably candid and fearless essay referred to. In attempting, as I shall here do, to explain some of the relations between moral and intellectual development from a point of view not wholly identical with that of the author of this former paper, I shall do best to give my argument as little as possible the directly controversial form. Something of controversy will indeed creep into these paragraphs; but the matter at issue is in fact too real and tragic to warrant very much of the weighing of the accuracy or adequacy of this or of that individual phrase which one may chance to find in the speech of one's conscientious fellow-student. Our

---

* International Journal of Ethics, October, 1893. The paper was suggested by one written by Professor Georg Simmel, of Berlin.

words easily differ, and may even be open to grave misunderstandings—never more so than when we write on the
intricate relations which obtain between moral defect and
intellectual skill. It is easy therefore to misinterpret or to
misuse another's expressions upon such subjects; and this
fact, while it certainly seriously increases the responsibility
of any one who feels called upon to give public utterance to
his views as to such delicate problems, makes doubtless
only the more unprofitable too detailed a controversy over
words that have once been uttered. It is, after all, the
cause involved that is here of moment. For the problem :
To what extent does an experience of evil add to our intellectual ability ? is indeed so complex as to make only too
possible expressions of opinion that, by reason of the difficulty of the subject, may prove to be erroneous, and that, by
reason of the practical moment of the issue in question, may
in consequence easily cause the judicious to grieve.

Meanwhile, of the reality of the issue itself there can be
no doubt. The words rendered, *Eritis sicut Deus, scientes
bonum et malum*, were felt by the author of the original
tale to embody a paradoxical truth that, for us who come
after him, has only grown more wealthy in its paradoxes as
time has gone on. As for the part later played, in the discussion, by Mephistopheles, in the passage just referred to,
the significance of these as of other utterances of Faust's
tempter lies just in the fact that they contain, in all their
cruel irony, an aspect of the real truth. Moral goodness, as
an attainment, is doubtless something very different from
innocence. And attained goodness is only won through a
conflict with the forces of evil, which involves a pretty deep
knowledge of evil. But knowledge of evil, in us men (and
for excellent " psycho-physical " reasons, too) frequently
leads to sin, and very commonly does so, in any given individual, before it actually leads the individual himself to the
possible goodness that lies for him beyond and above this

knowledge of evil. Therefore, on the way that leads the triumphant towards the goal of attained goodness, there will be found many who pause by the way, and who are content, after their fashion, with this or that sort of knowledge of evil, and with the sin in which, in their cases, this knowledge has actually involved them. Among these numerous wayfarers, moreover, there will be found many in whom such knowledge is a very marked feature of their whole mental life. Some of them, accordingly, will be very clever and ingenious persons, and will owe much of their wit to their lack of innocence. As against the innocent—the dwellers, as it were, in Eden—these knowing sinners can always assert that there is something more advanced—more Godlike, in fact, as the serpent said—in their wisdom, than in the ignorance of those who cannot conceive of sin. And thus insight and moral defect will come to have that frequent actual association, which the writer of the paper here referred to has noticed as a fact in the life of the world, and which is, in truth, the source of so serious a tragedy in human life. For it is precisely this association which often helps to make evil so keenly attractive in the eyes of the young and curious. But if one examines more closely, one finds that the paradox of the serpent is but one special case of an universal paradox of all human consciousness. And it is only necessary to state this paradox in its extremest form to deprive it of half its susceptibility to misunderstanding. There will, of course, indeed, always remain a great number of perplexing special problems in this as in all regions of our life; but at least we shall no longer be misled in our principles of judgment, when once we have grasped the deepest source of the difficulty. The common mistake, in dealing with all such matters, is the half-truth, and it was just in the half-truth that the wisdom of the original serpent consisted. Even so, however, to point out in succession now this, now that case where an intellectual advance results from some particular moral deficiency, may be to any extent confusing and disheartening. To discover, however, a principle so universal that it would determine *a priori* the existence of many such paradoxical cases in any moral world, even the best, so soon as that world were conceived as more than one of transparently empty innocence —this is an undertaking worthy of the serious moralist; and, properly set forth, such an undertaking can be in no wise either confusing to the little ones, or disheartening to the earnestly-minded. And, after all, why should science, in its cool regard for truth, need to be disheartening when the truth happens to be inspiring, or choose to be confusing in order to prove itself to be dispassionate.

As a fact I find, since writing the body of what follows, that the author of the essay here in question actually recognizes, in its universality, precisely that principle which I am about to expound afresh, and has elsewhere,* in the already published first volume of his treatise on ethics, discussed in a general and significant way the close relation which exists between the ethical worth of the individual and the presence of evil tendencies and temptations in his consciousness. Little or nothing of what I here write will therefore seem new to him, and therefore it is indeed better that I avoid the controversial tone. But in the essay now in question, on the Moral Deficiencies, our author has written as if he had forgotten or chosen to neglect his own former discussion. This his former discussion itself, moreover, has just come into my own hands, and the following essay, written before I had seen the first volume of the Einleitung in die Moralwissenschaft, must therefore be regarded as, on the whole, far less a reply than an independent contribution to our topic. Where what I shall here say agrees,

---

* See Einleitung in die Moralwissenschaft, by Georg Simmel. Berlin, 1892, vol. i., 3tes Kapitel, on Sittliches Verdienst und Schuld.

then, with our author's former chapter, in his published Einleitung—the chapter on Verdienst und Schuld—I shall only be supplementing his more recent essay by the thoughts presented in his previous publication.   Where my own views run altogether counter to his, the contrast may still be of service.

I.

It is an old observation, which recent research only makes more impressive and concrete, that all organic processes involve a certain balance of opposing forces, and that, in particular, there is in all of them such an union of conflicting tendencies as is, for instance, expressed by saying that the phenomena of physical life involve at every instant, as a part of themselves, all the essential phenomena of the death of tissues.   As I read, at the moment, in the current journals, I come upon two very recent expressions of this now fairly commonplace fact.   In an article on The Nerve-Cell,* by a well-known English expert, I find, in an argument upon the functions of nerve-fibers, the words, "Since the chemical processes which accompany death of living tissue appear to be very similar to the chemical processes which accompany activity, as is seen, for example, in the case of muscle, it is very possible," etc.; but the rest of the argument concerns us not here.   Meanwhile, a paper in the Revue Philosophique, on the movements of lower and higher organisms,† contains, in the author's summary of some recent discussions of the chemical processes at the basis of such movements, the statement, "Nothing more resembles the phenomena of the irritation (of living tissues) than those of death; and it was a stroke of genius in Claude Bernard to insist as

* The Nerve-Cell Considered as the Basis of Neurology, by Professor Schafer. Brain, 1893, Parts LXI and LXII, p. 156.

† Origine et Nature du Mouvement Organique, by J. Soury. Revue Philosophique for July, 1893; see, in particular, p. 55.

much as he did on the truth that every function of life is a function of organic death; that in every movement of man and of the animals 'the active substance of the muscle is destroyed and burned,' just as the brain, in thinking, is consumed; and in a word, that life is death (*La vie c'est la mort*)."

Now, here is mentioned an union of opposing tendencies in one of the best-known and most-frequently studied of organic processes. I need not for the moment insist upon the true analogy, which some at first sight would think a strained one, between these objective physical phenomena and certain others which are observable in the subjective world, among the activities of consciousness. Of that genuine analogy I shall indeed speak in a moment. But just now I shall confine myself to the mere interpretation of phrases. And here, for the first, what it concerns us to note is that there does appear, in the account of the vital processes, a necessity of stating their nature in essentially paradoxical terms, and that yet nobody is likely, in this region, to fall a prey to certain apparently easy misunderstandings of the meaning of the phrases used. *La vie c'est la mort:* it is not hard, in the light of the concrete facts of the metabolism of tissues, as the biologists explain them to us, to understand the significant half-truth, the apt paradox, of such an expression. But suppose that some one began to draw conclusions as to the implication of these words if taken in too abstract a sense. Suppose that one passed from the processes to the products. Suppose that he said, "If the processes of life are essentially processes of death, surely it follows, then, that all live things are, as such, dead things." This consequence would no longer be a happy paradox, a half-truth. It would be nonsense. The process is an union of balanced but opposing tendencies. But the product can not be expressed in merely negative or in indifferent terms. Living involves, yes, as it were, at every step, consists, in dying; but life is utterly different from death.

Well, without insisting just yet on the reality of the analogy of such, without dwelling on anything but the parallelism of the phrases, suppose that we do find, in our conscious life, processes whose nature has to be expressed in a paradoxical language similar to the one thus occasionally used in biology. Shall we let this necessity deceive us? Shall we be so neglectful of the complications of truth as to seem to forget that you may have to affirm of a process what would be nonsense if affirmed of the product, or if so affirmed as to confuse product and process? To become morally wise, for instance (if moral wisdom involves an understanding of moral issues), involves becoming acquainted with impurity. Shall we accordingly say, "All the morally wise, as such, are impure?" Or, taking another view of the case, shall we conceive the "moral man" just as a product, in whom, by definition, there is to be no evil, and shall we then say, "The moral man lacks the physical experience which gives the immoral one so thorough a comprehension of the immorality of others?"* Surely such views are confusions. It is as if we either said, on the one hand, "The live tissue must lack all the essential characters by which either dead or dying tissues resembles one another;" or, on the contrary, "All the living tissues, as such, are dead." No, if the matter is merely one of comprehending phrases, we need not even take the physiological processes as our basis for illustrating this sort of confusion. If we are determined to confuse a process with either a stage or an outcome of a process, regarded as something fixed and stationary, we may as well turn Eleatics at once. Surely (for so in substance argued Zeno), the flying arrow,

---

* The latter, though not the former, of these supposed assertions is an actual quotation from the article that has suggested the present one.

8

whenever it moves, *is* somewhere. But *somewhere* means a place—yes, *one* place. And so, as of old, " the flying arrow rests " — rest precisely as all the live things are dead, and precisely as the morally wise man remains essentially impure. For the process of wisely conceiving the moral truth involves as a moment the " psycho-physical " impurity of thinking evil; and the process of the arrow's flight involves of necessity that the arrow should be somewhere in order that it may fly. As a fact, however, the arrow that rests in its place does *not* move, the tissue that *merely* disintegrates is dead, and it is the thought that *dwells* in impurity, that is impure—not the thought that comprehends impurity only to overcome it.*

But I indeed am not content thus merely to dwell upon the analogies of phrase involved in the similarity between our current accounts of biological and of moral processes. I insist upon the actual and enlightening analogy of the two sorts of processes themselves. In so far as the life of a conscious being runs parallel to the biological processes of his organism, it is not surprising that just such a balancing of opposing tendencies, just such a unity of conflicting activities, just such a Heraclitean καλλίστη ἁρμονία ἐκ τῶν διαφερόντων, as is everywhere found on the physiological side, should be represented in our consciousness in more ways than one. For the just mentioned relation of the death and the activity of tissues is but a single case of the presence of this union of opposing tendencies on the physiological side; and more complex instances of such union, instances that reach the grade of the co-operation of antagonist muscles in

---

* Here again it is well to say that these words were written before I had seen the Einleitung in die Moralwissenschaft, where, vol. i, p. 268, the contrast between " *ruhende Qualität* " and "*Prozess*" is admirably applied to the very case now before us. It is strange that the essay on Moral Deficiencies seems so much to have neglected this aspect.

a voluntary movement, are already pretty obviously represented in consciousness. We are well aware that we give
complex voluntary movements precision by "holding ourselves back." We know that true freedom of action is
inseparable from elements of self-restraint and of self-control. We consciously rejoice in ruling ourselves. We are
aware, in general, that our will, in every organized form,
involves a consciousness of opposing tendencies—a consciousness which very obviously has not only this its conscious aspect, but its whole psycho-physical embodiment
and expression. And from this point of view we get
already a general notion of the true analogy that connects,
in the one world of life, the most complex organic functions
—those to which our consciousness corresponds, with those
simpler physical processes which characterize all life, and
which make the union of contrary tendencies so familiar
an affair throughout the organic realm. It is therefore
more, then, than an analogy of phrases, it is a real resemblance of type, which makes the lesson gained from a general survey of such organic activities useful when we turn
to a study of the facts of consciousness.

But this resulting lesson, so far, is, that if I am talking
of something conceived as the product or outcome of an
organic process—such a product as "a live organism," or "a
good man," or "virtue," or "intellect"—I must not be surprised to find, in the process of which this product is not
merely the result but the embodiment (the ἐνέργεια, in Aristotle's sense), factors which, taken by themselves, are distinctly opposed in their character to the positive but highly
abstract definition that the product, if conceived merely as
something finished and at rest, would necessarily possess.
Just as in the living and active tissue I find, as an essential
factor of its activity, that going on which, *if it were alone*,
would mean death, just as in the voluntary movement I
find that stimulation of the antagonist muscles going on

which, *if it were alone*, would mean an utter defeat of the intended movement, just as every important nervous stimulation seems to involve, as part of itself, the excitation of processes that tend to inhibit it, so, too, I must expect to find in all forms of the higher life, and, in particular, of the moral life, a similar complexity of structure. And I do find, as a part of moral excellence, be it of whatever grade you will, that there are tendencies present which, *if they were alone*, would be the very opposite and the destruction of every such excellence. And this must be the case, not because of the weakness of man, but because of the organic dignity and consequent complexity of virtue; and not because the moral world is a mere maze of perplexing confusions, but because the very principle of every organic life is the combination in harmony of opposing tendencies.*

II.

And now, in the next place, for some illustrations (drawn directly from the moral world itself) of the way in which this union of opposing tendencies works in that region. Then we shall be able to apply our result to some of the special problems suggested by our author.

It is of the essence of moral goodness that positively good deeds should be the result of what we call choice— that is, that morality should be a matter not of fate, but of consciousness. There is no virtue in digesting wholesome food when I am in sound health and have once eaten it. There may be virtue in choosing, against momentary appetite, a wholesome food instead of a tempting but pernicious dainty. But if the moral processes are thus processes of

---

* Here again I have to go over ground which the aforesaid 3tes Kapitel of the first volume of the Einleitung in die Moralwissenschaft has on the whole admirably treated, while the essay on the Moral Deficiencies has strangely neglected the same considerations.

conscious choice, it follows that every such choice involves a knowing of something *against* which one chooses, as well as something in favor of which one decides. But that against which one chooses is necessarily a motive, an interest, a solicitation, a temptation. For the moral choice is an inner one ; the rejected alternative is not an outer enemy, but an internal " spring of action " (to use Dr. Martineau's phrase). If so, then of necessity every distinctly moral choice involves the previous presence of a certain tendency to choose the wrong. Yes, moral choice is essentially a condemnation of the rejected motive, as well as an approval of the accepted motive. Otherwise it could be no moral choice. A being possessed of but one motive could have no conscience. But if this be so, then the consciousness of every moment of moral choice involves, also, a consciousness—a confession, if you will—of the presence in the chooser of that which he himself regards as evil. He not only coldly knows, he includes, he possesses, he is beset with some evil motive ; and, nevertheless, he conquers it. This is involved in the very formal definition of a moral act. You might as well try to define the king without his subjects, or the master without his servant, or the captor without his captive or his prize, as to define a moral deed without the presence in the agent of some evil motive. The case, then, is here quite parallel to the case of the relation of life and death in the functions of the active tissues. Once define a given man as moral in respect of any one given deliberate act of choice, and then, indeed, you can no longer without contradiction conceive him as failing to possess at least *one* significant psychical experience of evil—namely, the experience of precisely that evil motive which he has then and there deliberately rejected as evil. Had he not first known that evil motive, and known it as verily his own, he certainly could not have deliberately chosen against it. Or am I moral because I choose not to act on the motives that I can only abstractly conceive, as possible and remote temptations, which attract others and not me ? If so, how vast my morality ! Like the moralizing schoolmaster in Hegel's Philosophy of History, who is represented as warning his class against the ambitious passions of the great men of history, I can place my virtues above those of Alexander, for, unlike that glory-seeking man of blood, I have no ambitious desire to conquer Asia, or to overthrow Darius, but I leave all nations to fare as God pleases.* This sort of virtue is indeed cheap, and "moral" men in this sense are as plenty as are the weaklings; while if one points out that we possess *such* virtues not in so far as we comprehend life, and are skilful, but in so far as we are limited, and ignorant of life, and unskilful, I have no objection to offer to such an argument. Only the virtues of Hegel's schoolmaster are simply not virtues *in actu*, and one cannot even be sure that they are virtues *in potentia* until the virtuous schoolmaster has proved by his deeds his capacity for self-conquest. Put the schoolmaster in Alexander's place, and what will he do with Darius and with Asia ? Who can tell ? Nay, he himself cannot tell, and that is just why he is here ignorant *both* of the temptations of Alexander, and of the virtues that Alexander might have possessed, but perhaps did not possess. Here, then, ignorance conditions not only the lack of temptation, but the entire absence of the corresponding virtues as well.

Hegel skilfully said, "*Die Tugend ist nicht ohne Kampf; sie ist vielmehr der höchste, vollendete kampf.*" †

---

* Hegel, Werke, IX, p. 40: Woraus sogleich folgt dass er, der Schulmeister, ein vortrefflicherer Mensch sey, als jene (Caesar u. Alexander) weil er solche Leidenschaften nicht besässe, und den Beweis dadurch gebe, dass er Asien nicht erobere, den Darius, Porus, nicht besiege, sondern freilich wohl lebe, aber auch leben lasse.

† Logik, Werke, IV, p. 63. I venture to refer to my own discussion of this general topic, and to my statement of Hegel's view of it, in my Spirit

" Virtue is not without strife, but is rather the highest, the fulfilled strife." But forgetting this perfectly obvious consideration, people often so ignore the element of conflict in the process, while they think only of the assumed perfection of the product, that when some one suggests, in the interest of the " intellectual functions," how an insight into life must involve a knowledge of evil, people at once assume that the washed-out soul of the colorless and inane person whom they have imagined as the model good man cannot possess such knowledge, and thereupon they lament the sad conflict which seems to result between the interests of virtue and those of insight into life. As a fact, however, the whole case stands thus : The good man as such is neither an innocent nor an inane person, but a knowing, a warm-blooded, a passionate servant of the good. Meanwhile, neither virtue nor knowledge exists *in abstracto* among us men. There exists always some concrete virtue, which shows itself in good choices in favor of this or of this good, as against that or some other evil end, or motive. And as to knowing, it too is no abstraction, but there exists always some concrete knowledge, which is knowledge of this or of that thing. We therefore, to be sure, cannot compare the virtuous man in the abstract with the knowing man in the abstract, to see whether the two concepts can be made to agree. Doubtless many stupid men, meanwhile, have some virtues, and many of the base are clever. Nobody, moreover, has all virtues, or all knowledge. The only possible comparison is therefore between two men as to a particular virtue, either in exercise or *in potentia*, or between the same men as to the knowledge of a particular thing. Well, this being so, let it be a question of the actual and conscious exercise, in a deliberate and not in a

---

of Modern Philosophy, p. 210, *sq.*, and in my Religious Aspect of Philosophy, pp. 452–459.

merely accidental way, of a given virtue, as concretely applied to a given case. Let one man choose the positive exercise of that virtue; let another, with equal deliberation, wilfully reject it. Which now of these two is just then the more knowing as to the motives involved in this virtue? I say that, so far as we have yet defined the case, there is no difference in intellectual capacity defined as between the two. Both know the good and the ill involved. For neither could consciously choose unless he in some measure knew both the good and the ill. The good man knows the ill, and is aware of the temptation to do it; otherwise his " virtuous " act would be a matter of blind health, like his digestion, or of mere lack of interest, like his present avoidance of any wicked ambition to conquer Asia. He knows the rejected ill, he is tempted, and he deliberately resists and overcomes the temptation (whether with or without free will I decide not here). The other also knows, but chooses the ill. Which is so far the more knowing? The virtuous man can surely say, " Show me thy knowledge without thy virtue, and I will show thee my knowledge *by* my virtue. For by knowing the ill and the good it is that I choose the good with open eyes." Of the later knowledge which for the sinner alone, not for the good man, results from the consequences of this sin, I shall speak hereafter.

Doubtless one may indeed still insist that, unless by the actual assertion of a freedom of indeterminate choice, the foregoing precise equality of knowledge between these two men cannot in the end be maintained. Well, be it so. I am, as I have said, not here arguing the free-will issue. Admit, if you please, that there must be a difference of motive between the two, and therefore a difference of knowledge : the question will then once more arise, Which of them is, at the moment of choice, the *more* knowing? For the same reasons as before, both of them alike must at

least in some genuine measure know both of the motives
between which they choose. Else there is mere blind
prevalence of interest without any clear deliberation.
Shall one say, as to the different degrees of knowledge
now subsisting, It is the chooser of the good who knows
not the full allurements of the other's temptation? Or
shall one say, It is the sinner who is blind to those manifold excellencies whose presence to consciousness determines the good man's choice? Here, if anything, the
chances are largely in favor of the greater knowledge of
the virtuous chooser, since in general strong temptations
are comparatively elemental, while the reasons in favor of
goodness are in nature usually complex and abstract. A
mere boy can have a full sense of many temptations to
vice; it takes reflection to see fully all the reasons why
vice is intolerable. But herewith, as soon as one admits
differences of knowledge, as between these two, one enters
afresh the realm of the indeterminate. My object was only
to show that in order to have the same choice presented, in
its essential features, to two agents, one virtuous, one vicious
in his decision, it is necessary to have essentially the same
motives, and so the same elements of knowledge present in
both cases. What further differences of knowledge there
may be is indeed a matter of accident; but the chances are
at least even that the good chooser is more knowing than
the sinner.

But if this is so whenever an individual case of comparison is taken up, how far, then, extends the possible growth,
in insight into life, of those agents who grow in active virtue; and how does their possible collective insight concerning mere temptations compare with that of the sinners?
If every active virtue involves a knowledge of evil in order
to be a conquest over evil—the presence of temptation in
order that the active virtue may be a victory over temptation—then what insight into life is there that will not some-

where form part of the insight, and so of the virtue, of some
virtuous agent ?   No, it would seem that there is no insight
into life that is alien from every possible virtue, and that
no sinner can say to *all* the good, "I comprehend temptations that no one of all of you can possibly understand."
For had the sinner not only possessed his temptation, but
won the victory over it, he would now be, with reference
to that temptation alone, surely no less than he is, in insight
or in being, and he would then have stood among the
virtuous, where even now there may well stand some one
who has been tempted in all points as he was, but who is,
in this matter, without sin.   I still postpone, to be sure, a
discussion of the knowledge that the sinner gets from the
consequences of his sin—from the experiences that follow
upon it.

   This view of the nature of virtue is, however, indeed apparently open to one or two more or less plausible objections, which it may be well still to mention.

   " If this view of virtue is right," some imaginary objector
may say, "then it must follow that a good man is good
merely in proportion to the number and the gravity of his
resisted temptations.   But if so, then a man who should be
constantly tempted to murder his mother, to steal church
property, to be a cannibal, and to kidnap and eat children,
and who nobly resisted all these temptations, would be a
more virtuous man than one who was never thus tempted,
but who lived without friction the devoted life of a philanthropist, and of a public servant, always loyal and chari-
table of heart.   As this result is absurd, it follows that
virtue indeed implies, as the author of the essay here in
question asserts, a certain ignorance of evil motives."

   This objection is obvious, but trivial.   No one would be
deceived by the parallel assertion in case of the organic
processes before referred to.   Life involves disintegration
of tissue, and so constant death, always counteracted, indeed,

by the processes of tissue-building. The more life, and the more activity of tissue—the more disintegration, and the more building up. And so, for instance, in a warm-blooded animal, a more rapid dying process goes on than in a cold-blooded animal. It does not follow that, in a given organism, the life would grow in general vigor if disintegrating processes at random were set up, and were then just counteracted, in the struggles of a pathological condition, by the upbuilding processes that preserved the life. The death-process is not alien from my physical life, but is a part of it. The more active the life that I get, the more dying will be going on in my tissues. But the simple converse of this proposition very surely does not follow. I do not necessarily produce more life by introducing more death into my tissues. What is clear is, that if some disintegrating disease is present in my tissues, *then* I get life, if at all, by conquering this pathological disintegration. But without just that form of disintegration, I might, indeed, have a richer life.

Just so it is too with the process of virtue. Any actively virtuous man can say, at the moments of deliberate exercise of virtue, " My virtue involves as one of its elements temptation to evil. Hence in doing good I know evil." Ignorance of a given evil may be *per accidens* a condition of a given virtue, but every active virtue involves some knowledge of evil. On the other hand no sinner can say, " My knowledge of temptation depends upon my viciousness, and if I had been good at the moment of choice in respect of the deeds wherein now I am evil, I should *ipso facto* have diminished my intelligence, in acquiring my virtues, since I should then have failed to know these temptations." For here the answer is simply : You could have known these temptations just as truly if you had resisted them. You would then have no less insight as to temptation, but much more virtue as to life. But these things being granted, it

may well be that some virtues are better worth knowing
than other virtues, just as some life is more vigorous than
other life ; so that virtues whose knowledge involves the
knowing and resisting of pathological temptations may
be far less interesting, both to the afflicted sufferer from
the pathological enemy, and to the lover of conscious or
of moral life in general, than are other active virtues,
based upon the conquest over more normal temptations
Meanwhile, there can be no doubt whatever of the moral
excellence of the man who, being burdened with a distinctly
pathological temptation, nobly resists it, just as there can be
no doubt that he loses no intellectual skill or insight, but
rather cultivates both, by resisting his temptation. But
since, unfortunately, the burdened man as much lacks
knowledge of the normal life as the normal man fails to
comprehend the depths of abnormality, the real problem
here is, Which of these two sorts of knowledge of life is
most worth having ? And this question is in no respect
any longer a question of the relative value for the intellect
of virtue and of vice, but it is a question of the relative
value for the intellect of two sorts of knowledge, whereof
one is normal, the other unhealthy, but whereof both alike
may involve either virtue if a temptation is known and
conquered, or vice, if the temptation is known and preferred.

For the rest, the kindly and public-spirited philanthropist
of our example is indeed as virtuous as his burdened, but still
triumphant brother, only in case the philanthropist really
struggles as seriously as the latter with his own much more
elevated, but none the less genuine moral problems and
temptations. And the moral order actually demands of him
that he shall do so. He has more talents ; from him, then,
more moral life is required. He may think that he finds in
himself only kindliness ; but if he looks sharply as he goes,
he will erelong find in himself sloth, or pride, or self-com-

placency, not to speak of a horde of more elemental if still normal passions. If he contends with these and with their outcome, he will get as rich an experience of the evils of his own world as his weaker brother gets of the evils of his. In general, then, it is here not our virtue that is responsible for our ignorance, but rather our inevitable ignorance of life that limits the scope of our virtues. The healthy man cannot have the virtues of the sick man, nor the pathologically burdened soul the sort of goodness that distinguishes the genius in holy living ; not, however, because virtue means ignorance of life, but because the naturally limited insight into life which each man possesses limits his possible virtues. But within his limits, the more any given man knows of life the more chance he has to be virtuous, if he chooses to be so.

Another objection, and a common one, to the foregoing view of virtue has reference to the influence of training upon the exercise of active virtues. The virtuous man of Aristotle's original definition is such not merely by reason of his acts, but by reason of the attained character that, in the long run, he earns by his acts. The habitual and successful resistance of any given type of temptations involves, of necessity, the gradual elimination of at least those special temptations. The cultivation of active virtues leads towards a virtuous perfection of disposition in which just these active virtues no longer have to be cultivated. In so far it is indeed true that the aim of the good man is to acquire an ignorance of certain evils which he now knows only too well. If he actively exercises virtue only in the presence of an actual knowledge of evil motives present in himself, he aims, nevertheless, at the ultimate attainment of a state in which these evil motives will no longer have meaning for him. In this fashion, then, it would seem that the attainment of holiness is, in some sense, the attainment of ignorance ; and so once more the argument of our author would receive a certain confirmation, and the price of possessing certain "intellectual functions" would be the retaining of certain "moral deficiencies."

Once more, however, the general biological analogies will aid us in comprehending the true sense of the facts here brought before us. The question is now the familiar one as to the relation of habit and consciousness.* I am not conscious of the detailed execution of what is so completely an habitual function of my organism that I accomplish this function swiftly and without hesitancy. I am conscious in general only of my relatively hesitant functions in so far as they are hesitant. This, again, is a psychological commonplace. On the other hand, the more by practice I exercise my consciousness of a given process, and so perfect any now hesitant function, the more I tend to bring its execution below the level of my consciousness. In this sense, to be sure, we find another paradox—and one of a most familiar and characteristic sort—in the life of the highest organisms. Consciousness, namely, is working, as it were, on all levels, in the direction of its own extinction, in so far as it is a consciousness of just this unfamiliar object; very much as the living tissues are constantly busy in compassing their own death, precisely in so far as they are tissues with just this energy becoming free in their processes. I am conscious of a given function, and so of the objects to which this function is related, because the function is relatively novel, is imperfectly learned, is not thoroughly habitual. But it is precisely this unfamiliarity of the function and of its object that is unsatisfactory to me. I try to perfect my mastery over this function and to render its objects perfectly familiar. I train the function until it is smooth-running, facile, free from hesitancy, and so until

* In this aspect this question is interestingly discussed in the Einleitung in die Moralwissenschaft, vol. i, p. 227 et seq.

it is no longer an object of consciousness. I now ignore
both the function and its familiar objects. This I am everywhere tending to do, precisely in so far as I engage in any
special business of consciousness.   I am conscious of the
syntax of a foreign tongue while I am learning that
tongue ; but the object of my conscious toil is to learn the
language so well that I shall forget its syntax and speak its
sentences with absolutely unreflective fluency.

But now, on the other hand, although consciousness thus,
as it were, aims to compass, on every stage, and in each of
its special functions, its own extinction, still, all of us who
love insight talk of consciousness as being an end in itself,
and are conscious that we want not less, but more of it.
Our general aim as conscious beings is opposed, in this
paradoxical way, to each and every one of the special aims
of our own consciousness, in so far as the latter is a process whereby the unfamiliar is rendered familiar, and is so
gradually brought below the level of consciousness, while
our general aim as conscious beings is not to get less, but
more, concrete insight, and so more consciousness.

Here again, *La vie c'est la mort.*   " Die to live " is a
philosophical motto that Professor Edward Caird loves to
repeat in his writings. It may be important to vary the
phrase, as, with the aid of M. Soury, I have here tried to do.
But Professor Caird is unquestionably right as to the substance of the thing. Consciousness, like living tissue, loves
to feed on its own process of endless self-extinction. And
the way in which it thus feeds is obvious enough. When I
have no longer to be conscious of the syntax of the new language, I shall have acquired a new organic power—namely,
the power to be conscious of the relatively new and unfamiliar things that I shall want to say in that language. The
more numerous the familiar and so unconscious habits that I
have come to possess, the more capacity I have acquired to
adjust myself to complex novel situations, and so to have, in

general, more consciousness. As for the paradox of the whole situation, it is also a case of the general paradox of the will, as noted by Schopenhauer. The will wants to live. But life means specific desires, and each specific desire longing, as it does, for the possession of its object, really longs for the quenching of its restless fires in the dark Lethe of a fulfillment that means its extinction as this desire. The will, then, in longing for life, longs for that which in every concrete manifestation, as this specific desire, it longs to see extinguished. Schopenhauer's paradox is but the expression, in conscious terms, of the essence of all those organic processes to which our consciousness runs parallel, and of which it is a very inadequate expression. As for Schopenhauer's pessimistic comment on this essential restlessness of the inner world, the discussion of that belongs elsewhere. Restlessness does not, as a fact, mean misery, and a wise joy in the genuine paradoxes of life is of the essence of the highest reason.

There is, then, nothing peculiar about the problem involved in the case of the growth of the virtuous man towards a perfection wherein he ceases to be conscious, both of his former defects, and of the active virtues whereby he overcame these defects. Above all, the problem is in no wise one of an opposition between "moral deficiencies" and "intellectual functions." Such as it is, the paradox applies equally, and for the same reasons, to the intellectual and to the moral functions. The one sort has here no advantage over the other. The intellectual skill involved in any stage of our human consciousness, in aiming at its own perfection in the form of the acquisition of finished, habitual, intelligent functions, aims at what, as a fact, when attained, will involve its own extinction as this particular conscious activity. Just so, any growing and active virtue aims at its own extinction, as this particular virtue, by means of the establishment of virtuous habits that will

render the exercise of this conscious virtue no longer necessary or even possible. But virtue thus no more aims at its
own extinction in general than intellectual skill aims at its
own general abolition, or than Schopenhauer's will, in
longing for fulfillment, ceases in general the desire to live.
This must pass—this desire—this stage of growing intellect
or goodness ; but there is more that is desirable, there is
more virtue, just as there is more wit, beyond. This
is the universal rule of conscious life. *Die Leidenschaft
flieht, die Liebe muss bleiben.* When I have so well learned
this virtue as no longer consciously to possess it, but to be
possessed by it as by a mere instinct, well, then, indeed my
active moral goodness will indeed cease as to this matter ;
but, on the other hand, I shall consciously be able to possess far more, and more complex, active virtues, than ever,
for I shall have more powers, and so be able to undertake
harder tasks, to go on new quests, and to fight stronger
moral enemies. When I shall have mastered my present
intellectual puzzles, and accordingly shall have forgotten
their details in the possession of unhesitating and unconscious functions, I shall then be able to possess not less but
more consciousness ; for I shall have more unconscious functions upon which to build new insights.

The parallelism of virtue and of intellect in respect of
the "deficiencies" thus involved in progress is here perfect.
Whatever happens to the one happens to the other.
Learning is based upon forgetting, conscious power upon
unconscious habit, the new life upon the extinction of the
immediate presence of the old. "Moral deficiency," if regarded as a lower state in a progressive growth, involves
"intellectual functions" only in the same sense as that in
which intellectual deficiency itself involves such present
intellectual functions.

It is, then, one sign of intellectual power, just as it is one
sign of moral power, to have forgotten, as well as to have

9

remembered, many things. Such "deficiencies" are necessary moments of our human perfection. To a vain young man, full of the learning freshly acquired at school, the old and erudite scholar may often justly say, " Yes, you indeed have many things in mind that I now ignore ; but see, I have myself forgotten far more than you ever knew." Even so, a persistent sinner, vaunting his present knowledge of temptation as against the state of the virtuous man who has outgrown and learned to ignore the movings that are still clearly present to the consciousness of the sinner, may say, " I know life ; for I know these temptations, and you are no longer aware of them." But a by-stander, considering the life of the virtuous man, and seeing in him the hero of many past conflicts, may retort, " Ay, but he has forgotten, because he has transcended, more temptations than you ever knew." Which " deficiency " is the preferable one ?

To sum up, then : The knowledge and presence of evil form, in very manifold and complex ways, a moment in the consciousness and in the life of goodness. And this must be so. It is no confusing chance puzzle of the moral world ; it is a necessary result of the very essence of all life, which is everywhere an union of opposing elements. The knowledge of this fact is not disheartening, but inspiring ; since all the seriousness of the moral world depends upon it. As to the relation of " deficiencies " and " functions," so far as we have yet seen, the close parallelism of the intellectual and moral processes, as well as their intimate interdependence, taken together with the general nature of life just insisted upon, renders this relation extremely, and yet very intelligibly, intimate on both sides. First, in both the intellectual and the moral life, every " function," of necessity, depends, in the lives of us human individuals, upon a corresponding " deficiency." We think in order to grow wiser, and therefore all our thinking is due to relative ignorance. We choose the right in order to avoid the tempting wrong; and therefore all moral functions depend upon present moral imperfections. Meanwhile, as to the cross-relation of moral deficiency and intellectual function, the rule holds that, since active goodness involves knowledge of temptation, the morally deficient have herein no essential intellectual advantage over the doers of good. As to the ignorance or intellectual deficiency of the being higher in the scale of life as against the being lower in the scale and burdened with temptations unknown to the higher being, it here follows (1) that the "deficiency" of knowledge in question is shared by both beings, in so far as neither fully understands the other; (2) that in neither case does this deficiency of knowledge as to the other being, or possession of knowledge as to one's own moral office and temptations, determine by itself either any moral excellence or any moral defect, since either of the two beings is doing active moral work not in so far as he is by nature high or low in the scale, but in so far as he rightly deals with his own temptations. We call the higher being more virtuous, when he does well, not because, being ignorant of baser temptations, he fails to resist them, but because his virtues, when once they exist, seem to us as a part of a normal and more finished life, better worth knowing than his fellows'. As to moral progress, that does indeed involve a transcending, and so a forgetting, of earlier and simpler virtues; but here moral progress is simply parallel to all intellectual progress.

In general, then, intellectual functions seem to involve moral deficiencies in precisely the same sense as that in which moral functions themselves involve moral deficiencies, and as that in which intellectual functions also involve intellectual deficiencies, every function in our life involving the presence of its own antagonist, and being successful in so far as its antagonist comes to form an organic moment in its own process, instead of being it its turn the triumphant and absorbing factor. But, on the other hand, it does not follow that you can produce a given function, intellectual or moral, by simply introducing the corresponding antagonist or deficiency into a given organic process. All active virtue implies temptation ; but it does not thence follow that by increasing temptation you increase virtue, or that you remain virtuous by nursing your temptation in order to resist it. Change and progress play the same part here that they do elsewhere in the great drama of life. And if living is constant dying, it does not follow that the more death there is the more life there will be.

III.

So much for the main principles involved in our present issue. But now let the question be no longer of principles, but of cases. Moral deficiency shall be essentially involved in certain intellectual functions, or shall determine the latter. When ?—First, for so it may appear, whenever the comprehension of certain forms of evil itself involves such a participation in the evil as amounts to sin. But when does this take place ?   " The task of understanding," so one answers, " certain elementary passions of the human soul is very difficult from the height of official station, as well as in the normal and correct life led by many scholars " ; and so " undeniably this is a point in which a theoretical knowledge gains depth from an experience of comparative immorality, either present or past." *

In judging of such assertions one's first reply is, *Distinguo.* The " elementary passions " of the human soul are indeed the most common source of sin ; but they are not themselves sins in so far as they are elementary passions, but in so far as, in a given context of life, they are persistently preferred, despite the fact that they prove to be in-

---

* These quotations are, as before, from our author's cited article.

capable of organization, or destructive of existent rational good order.   They are evil, in other words, in so far as they are anarchical, fighting against an already established organism, and not in so far as they are "elementary."   It is *in a context* that they become temptations; and the sinfulness of an "elementary passion" always depends on its relations to the other interests of life.   It is as related to such a context that a virtuous man finds what would be an innocent accident of his organization a solicitation to evil. Experience of passion, of the "elementary" in life, is therefore as such never a sin.   The fault of a man is not that he has elementary passions, but that he cannot make out what to do with them, or do it when he has made it out.

In saying this I speak simply the voice of the wholesome consciousness, of the Greek as of the modern man, as against any merely superstitious asceticism which condemns some natural impulses as essentially diabolical.   The wise man does not regret the elementary impulses of his temperament as such, whatever these impulses may be. What he does regret is that they are so ill reduced to order, so poorly trained to an objectively significant service. Even the "pathological temptations" before referred to are pathological not by reason of the elementary impulses involved, but by reason of the union of such impulses into complex groups of motives hostile to the general peace of society, and to the whole rational system of a man's inner life.

It is not needful to waste here many words over this matter, which has been endlessly discussed.   Hatred is a fairly "elementary" passion.   Shall one call it essentially a bad "spring of action" because it is necessarily "malicious"?   On the contrary, if we find superstitious men in the world who let cobras multiply, because of a superstitious kindliness, we shall wish that these men had more hatred of snakes, as well as less superstition.   All depends upon where and when and what you hate—in other words, upon

the context of your passion. If hatred in battle makes
given soldiers fight better against the enemies of their
country, then surely, if patriotism is a virtue, this virtue
may demand, for these men, the cultivation of precisely
such hatred. For the rest, just those passions of humanity
which, under certain conditions, appear as the grossest, the
fiercest, the basest, are notoriously the passions upon whose
organized cultivation, and upon whose subtle influence,
when once they are cultivated, the whole social structure
and its most sacred relations depend.

It would be the saddest of cant, then, to say that a good
man, as such, can have no experiences of the truly " elementary passions "—even the most elementary and vigorous. The fact that many moralists are and have been
bloodless creatures, who have written about life without
themselves possessing any temperament to speak of, is a
lamentable historical accident, due in no wise to the nature
of philosophy, but rather to those economic conditions of
the thinker's profession, which have driven many persons to
turn would-be philosophers, because they have failed in
other walks of life to prove themselves capable men. With
the author who has inspired this paper I regret this accidental ill-fortune of philosophy. The philosophical thinker,
the moralist above all, should first be a man of experience
in a wide range of elementary human life. And the great
heroes of ethical speculation (yes, even a man of the gentle-
ness of a Kant) are never without indications in their works
that they have really and deeply experienced at least some
part of our human nature. But now this does not mean that
the thinker needs to be a sinner above other men in order
to be wise. Elements are one thing. The organization of
life is another. It is not necessary to experience many
forms of chaos in order to understand good order.

But is not sin, too, an experience ? And can the good
man possess that experience ? We have said, in our dis-

cussion of principles, that temptation to evil is an essential element in every exercise of active virtue. But a conquered temptation, although an evil, which is conquered by the good man just because it is an evil, is still no sin. Sin proper, however, is, in us mortals, another experience, and is *ipso facto* no part of the experience of the good man as such, just as an active disease is no part of the life of a healthy organism. Here indeed is the body of death from which the good man, as such, longs to be delivered altogether. His resisted temptation is part of his life—the death in life of which before we spoke. But his sin is no element of his good life.

And yet, since sin forms so large a part of human life, and is, for us men, vastly more than temptation, and since the endless consequences of sin—remorse, all the arts of concealment, all the ingenuity of effort to repair—the rejoicing, too, of the froward in their frowardness—the fierce sense of freedom of which our own Hawthorne tells in the Marble Faun as an experience that follows upon a crime—the long and perplexingly fascinating agony of the consciousness of a life of sin—the revelry and the fruitless later repentance of the Faust of the original story—the contrition of David— the conversion of the dying thief on the cross—the raptures of a saved Mary Magdalene :—since all these, and countless other human experiences flow not from resisted temptation, but from actual sin, were we then not one-sided in our discussion of principles, where we limited ourselves to the study of temptation, and said that the sinner knows no more of the motives of sin (which are the temptations) than does the good man, equally tempted, who resists and conquers the temptation ? That, as an one-sided view of life, may be true. But temptation is but a small part of the sinner's experience. It is consequence that he knows, and herein consists his intellectual opportunity. Here, indeed, is a " moral deficiency " very positively conditioning an

" intellectual function." In hell and in purgatory they do thus know what must needs be wholly unknown to the angels, and but ill-conceived by the saints, excepting as the saints remember the long life in sin from which some of them escaped. This being true, can one (to use still the convenient allegorical fictions)—can one, as a moralist, comprehend the world of human life, unless he has lived in hell and in purgatory, as well as among the good ? What sort of a moralist is, then, one who has had little or no experience of sin ?

The first answer is so obvious that I wonder that any one should miss it. Such moral deficiencies do indeed determine certain intellectual functions, but precisely as they also determine certain moral functions. And the way in which they determine the latter is very enlightening as to the significance of the whole controversy.

Sins, I say, are possible conditions, not only of a deep intellectual knowledge of certain very common and momentous human experiences, but also of certain extraordinarily heroic moral deeds. Nobody has harder moral work to do than many a sinner who has repented. Nobody, therefore, can show us, on occasion, a more brilliant example of active virtue than he may learn to do. The outcast on account of a crime sometimes has a peculiarly good opportunity to become at one great stroke a saint. The thing has occasionally taken place ; for the shock of the consequences of crime has sometimes been enough to shatter the habits of a sinful career in one moment of conversion. Apart from sudden conversion, which is rare, the most serious moral tasks of many men are furnished to them by the office of building up through their newly-acquired virtues what their former waywardness has destroyed.* And in

* A brilliant literary example of moral recovery and of the heroic rebuilding of a shattered life one finds depicted in Sienkiwicz's remarkable

this way, indeed, the wrath of man is sometimes taught to praise the good.

But surely the fact that certain peculiarly great opportunities for virtue in the way of reform and of making atonement are furnished to the sinner by his own past crimes—opportunities which those of the virtuous who should never have swerved from the right could not get— this fact, I say, does not at all tend to confuse us as to the nature of sin and of virtue. Sin, when past, furnishes especial opportunities for future virtue. But one who desires virtue will not think that he shows thus his desire for virtue by first sinning that grace may abound. When we once have sinned, our exceptional opportunities to atone may encourage us to begin afresh with zest the moral task. But whoever sins under pretense of seeking hereby for this exceptional opportunity to get a new and higher virtue by means of his intended repentance, such a man does not deceive us by his pretenses. He is a liar and the truth is not in him. He sins because he wants to sin, not because he wants any new moral function to be determined by his previous moral deficiency, and until he learns not to lie he will remain deficient and without further function.

I say that this very familiar determination of future moral opportunities and excellencies by past misdeeds shows, first of all, that here, as earlier in our discussion, the dependence of function upon deficiency holds within the moral sphere itself precisely as much as in the comparison of moral with intellectual function and deficiency, so that the case is one of an universal problem of life, and not merely one of certain specific oppositions between moral and intellectual interests. I say, also, that the reason for this dependence of the opportunity for new goodness upon

romance, The Deluge, recently translated from the Polish by Mr. Curtin. Kmita, the hero of this romance, is a magnificent instance for the moralist.

past sin is obvious enough, and the outcome in so far not at all misleading.

But now, further, just as the moral function depends on the previous moral deficiency, precisely, and only, in so far as one does not remain in the deficiency, but transcends it, so (as I think that experience will show) it is not our mere dwelling in sin that ever enlarges our deeper insight into life so much as it is our looking back upon our sin, and representing it in precisely the light which makes it appear as sin, and so as rationally condemned, that enables us to read the intellectual lesson of the sinful experience itself. Regarding the matter, then, for the moment, solely as an " intellectual function," it is Macbeth after the murder, or in his latest monologues, who sees the truth of his case as it is. It is Dostojevsky's hero in Crime and Punishment, just before he gives himself up to the police, whose eyes are truly open. This is the lesson of countless works of art in which the moral tragedy is portrayed. However coolly planned beforehand, the crime is still relatively blind. The still cooler and far deeper intellectual insight of later moments lifts the ransomed criminal above himself. He reads now the lesson of his case ; but he reads only to condemn. His intellectual function is itself, if his eyes get opened, the beginning of a moral function.

Moreover, this not only often is, but always must needs be the case. If the right is, as it is, not the object of superstitious dogma, but of science and of reason, and is known to be the right as soon as one clearly sees the situation, then a true intellectual insight into sin means a condemnation of it, and one has not the true " intellectual function " until one has really begun to transcend the " moral deficiency." After all, the freest act of sinful choice doubtless involves a certain deliberate ignorance of the reasons in favor of the good, which itself involves intellectual defect. If so, however, the relation of the " moral deficiency " to the " intel-

lectual function " is precisely like the just noticed relation
of any moral deficiency to the often very noble moral functions that may be founded upon it.   The latter relation is
inspiring when we have sinned, because it shows us the
way out.   But the expectation of getting this " far off interest " of crime, of plucking this flower that blooms in hell,
attracts of itself nobody into crime ; and whoever says that
he commits crime with any such noble purpose in view is,
I repeat, a liar.   But just so, whoever pretended to choose
sin for the sake of that possible sin-transcending insight,
would be but pretending.

For the reasons now explained, it is also clear that wilful
sinners, who have not learned to repent, are on the whole,
as respects the cultivation of intellectual functions, far less
instructive to themselves than they are to the intellect of
any observant student of human nature who, not being
slave to their sin, has leisure to study their varied experience, and temperament enough to interpret life with respectable skill when he sees it.   The sinners whose eyes are
finally opened have transcended their "deficiency."   The
relatively blind, who are still slaves to their sin, are in many
ways an open book to the wiser among their fellows.   And
it is indeed true that it is the right and the duty of every
moralist to learn, with due prudence, but without foolish
timidity, whatever he really needs to know of the disorders
of the moral world, from an observation—not cynical but
humane—of the records of sinful experience in his fellows.
Thus indeed their deficiency may very directly and usefully
condition his function.   And he will learn of life while learning also how to help the sinners themselves towards virtue.

But now shall we descend from these matters to mere
trivialities ?   Shall we illustrate the relations of function
and deficiency elsewhere ?   Shall we seriously inquire
whether a successful liar is not naturally a more skilful
person than a mere blunt speaker of the truth ?   Shall we

reason that a liar, like the skilful hero in the fairy tale, or
like Odysseus with the Cyclops, must hold at least two ideas
at once in his head, while his giant or other dupe thinks of
but one at a time ? Well, if these things must be argued, it
is indeed an old notion, precisely as old as those fairy tales
whose heroes are liars, that lying is a peculiarly clever business, and is so precisely for the reason that obviously guided
the authors of the fairy tales—namely, because it is so
much more skilful to think two ideas at a time than one
idea. But surely the civilized man, for whom truth, whether
legal, commercial, political, or moral, has now grown to be
so complex an affair, has transcended such trivialities. In
all the more serious practical affairs of our modern lives, we
wholly exhaust our stock of ingenuity in trying even to
think the truth as it is, and fail at that. We may lie all we
choose, and may even succeed as liars, but we shall get no
more cleverness thereby than would be at all events needed
to think or to say even the blunt truth in its nakedest simplicity. We no longer live in a world where there is question of stupid giants with one idea, and clever heroes with
two at a time. The honest man's wits are all needed in
order to meet even the demands of honesty. For the rest,
if a liar needs cleverness to think his supposed two ideas, as
in the fairy tale, what would an honest man need who must
learn to defeat the liar ? Surely he would have to think of
the truth, and also of the liar's false idea, and finally of the
proper plan for meeting the liar's falsehood and for bringing it to naught without lying himself : in sum, then, at
least three ideas to the liar's two. But herewith such trifling
computations may as well cease. Not thus are moral deficiencies, as such, at all peculiar in being sources of some
sorts of intellectual ability. There is no possible degree of
cleverness or of ingenuity that is not sadly needed in our
complex world for every good cause whose undertakings
are serious.

But surely there still remain—do there not ?—vast regions of knowledge which it is unholy for any given individual to tread upon. And to enter these fields would therefore involve "intellectual function," and still also true "moral deficiency"; or would it not ? Yes, indeed, it is as easy as you please, and as trivial, to mention, in case of any of us, any number of such forbidden regions. My neighbor has left his house unguarded, his desk unlocked. It would greatly amuse my curiosity to read his diary, his love-letters, his other confidential documents. And yet I may not do so. Why ? Because the intellect is somehow mysteriously opposed in its interests to the conscience ? No : but for the simple reason that this would be theft. This knowledge is not mine. These secrets are his property, like his purse, save in being more sacred. Here the mystery of the relation between ignorance and virtue is merely that of the existence of any private rights whatever. As his money is good for what it can buy, but is not mine to spend, so his knowledge is here a good thing to have, but it is not for me to purloin. But now, under the category thus illustrated, countless types of actually forbidden knowledge fall, of knowledge, however, that is forbidden not because the intellect ought as such to be limited in its scope, but because a man must keep to his own, and in a world where men live together possession has to be private, and therefore exclusive. My neighbor's house, his land, his affairs—anything that is his—I must not steal or covet. If this limitation involves not only respect for material property, but for countless, and often nameless privacies of his inner and outer life, then it is not the rights of the intellect that are at stake, but the rights of the person.

On the other hand, as to the rights of the intellect itself, knowledge, *as such*, we must maintain, is always an innocent, and frequently a holy possession. Its moral limitations, its perils, its implied sinfulness, these always belong to it *per accidens*, and with respect to specific conditions and individuals. There is no knowledge whatever to which somebody may not conceivably have a right. That not everybody may, without sin, possess a given sort, or degree, or fact of knowledge, depends always upon specific and perfectly comprehensible conditions relating to this sort, or degree, or fact. I may not seek to know another's secret by stealth ; I may not seek to know the results of a sin by myself deliberately sinning ; I may not seek to add to my present burdens a temptation that I have not now, and that, when I get it, may prove corrupting to me. But, on the other hand, the man whose secret this is may be blessed in knowing it. The man who has sinned may gain inspiration for reform from coolly considering the very heart and the essence of his sin, that he may find in its fruits the seeds of coming virtue. The man who has the temptation, by facing it, and so by knowing its secret, may win control over it, and may thereby use his opportunity for holiness. When in progress I abandon one knowledge for another, I do so because the other is more of a knowledge. And thus it is never my business as a moral being to shun knowledge as knowledge, but always it is my task to get wisdom as wisdom, and then to use it in the cause of the right.

NATURAL LAW, ETHICS, AND EVOLUTION.*

THE discussion seems to me to have reached a stage where it is just as well to supplement controversies over the precise meaning or the bearings of Professor Huxley's address, by a few independent efforts, however imperfect these may be, to deal with the questions. (1) Whether the " ethical process " is a " part of the cosmical process " ; and (2) whether it stands in a relation of opposition or of harmony to the tendencies of this cosmical process ; and (3) finally, in case the relation of the " ethical process " to the " cosmical process " is one of opposition, what the source of this opposition is. The following paper is a sketch of such an effort.

The student of nature is trying to reduce observed facts to universal laws. In so far as he can do this, he succeeds in what certain recent students of the Logic of Science (e. g., Mach) have called the description of the facts. The fundamental principle of empirical science is, that you can only tell what a given fact is, in so far as you can describe its nature in universal terms—i. e., in terms which identify this nature with the nature of other facts. Were all the facts of our experience single, discontinuous, unrepeated even in memory, and as different from one another as tones

---

* An essay contributed to a series of papers upon the well-known address of Professor Huxley. The discussion, in which several other writers took part, was published in the International Journal of Ethics. The present contribution appeared in July, 1895.

are now different from odors, or as brightness is different
from swiftness, then we might all of us experience the
world ; but we could none of us describe in the least what
it contained. This world might even be allowed to have *one*
sort of uniformity in it—viz., it might be as richly delightful a world as you please, from moment to moment ; but it
would be not only an uncomprehended, but an unreported
world—a world of whose facts no record could be made. On
the other hand, a world where experience can be recorded,
reported, described, has two characters : First, there are in
it facts whose similarities can be noted—i. e., there are
"wholes" or "groups" of phenomenal elements, which are
alike in some respects ; and, secondly, the noted similarities
are such as permit you, in terms of these similarities themselves, to define certain complex groups of phenomena, as
" having the same structure," or as " being built up according to the same rule," or as " exemplifying the same law,"
so that at least some of the details of each fact noted are
"explained " by this law. To " explain " a given phenomenal detail, noted in your experience, say d, by the " natural
law " which is said to " require " its presence, or to " make it
necessary," is simply to point out that the phenomenon d is
part of a larger whole, a " fact " in the substantive sense—
viz., $abcd$, and that this " whole fact," $abcd$, has a structure,
or " make-up," a describable " build," a " typical constitution," which other whole facts of experience, viz., ABCD, or
$pqrs$, also exemplify, while this constitution is such as to involve the presence of d in case a, b, and c are present, and in
case the whole is to preserve the aforesaid typical structure.
You then say that, since the whole fact $abcd$ resembles
ABCD, or $pqrs$, not in its details as such (i. e., in its contents), but in their structural relations—i. e., in the general
type or build of each of these whole facts—therefore the
same rule or law which defines D by its relations to the
other phenomena, A, B, C, of its own group, and which

defines *s* by its relations to the other phenomena, *p*, *q*, and *r*, of the group *pqrs*, can be realized or exemplified when you pass to an *abc* group, only if there is present a fourth phenomenon, *d*, which is such as to have the same structural relation to *abc* in the whole fact whereof *abc* and *d* are parts, as was present in case of the facts ABCD and *pqrs*.

My statement is abstract. But the principle is simple. It means that you cannot describe whole facts—i. e., that you cannot report, record, verify, or comprehend their structures, without conceiving the phenomenal details of these facts as subject to laws—i. e., to rules of structure, which are exemplified by other whole facts of experience as well as by the fact that may be, at any time, under discussion. The " uniformity of nature " is thus the *conditio sine qua non* of the describability of her facts. And on the other hand, to report whole facts is, to some extent, to explain their details. It is, therefore, not one thing to describe facts, and another thing to explain the elements that enter into their constitution. But, *in so far as you describe the wholes, you explain the parts of these wholes.* There is, indeed, no *a priori* principle that every experience which may occur to anybody is describable at all. Anybody's experience might be, to any extent, apparently or really unique. In so far as it was unique, science could only ignore it, as being a " private " or " personal " experience. But if an experienced fact is to be described, it must be, in some respect, capable of indentification with other facts. And different facts can be describably identical only as regards their structure. But if two facts have the same structure, then their details, the elements of which they are made up, stand in relations to one another which exemplify this structure. Any one element, then, will appear in each fact, as explained by and conformable to the law which links it to the other elements of the whole fact of which it is a part. The presence in the world of various whole facts that exemplify the same structure, is

10

then a condition of the describability of each of these whole facts. But the describability of any whole fact involves what appears as the explanation of the parts or elements of this fact by the law or structure of the whole to which they belong. In brief, the structure actually common to many facts also appears as the law which explains or necessitates the constituent elements of each fact.

Nature then, *in order to be describable*, has to be viewed or conceived as such that the details of every natural phenomenon shall be " subject to," " determined by," or " necessitated by," the laws which describe the structure of the phenomenal wholes of which each detail is a part. If any given natural phenomenon, itself a mere fragment (e. g., the petal of a particular flower, the tooth of a carnivorous animal, the total phase of an individual lunar eclipse), is to be conceived as a part of a certain whole, then this part must be *conceived as if* " explained," or " necessitated," by the law which describes, in universal terms, the whole " thing " or " process " of which the fragment is a part. And this is what is meant by the " necessity " of natural events. Natural necessity is an incident of the conceived describability of natural phenomena when grouped in whole facts.

That natural phenomena shall be *conceived as* necessary, or as subject to rigid law, and that the " cosmic process " shall be viewed as one where " mere necessity reigns," is therefore not a belief capable of any but a relatively subjective and human interpretation. Experience comes and goes in its own way. No mortal has ever " experienced " the absolute necessity of any cosmic process whatever. Chance, as Mr. Charles S. Peirce has well observed, streams in through every channel of our senses. Trust then to mere experience, as it comes to any one of us, and such experience can never prove that there are " cosmic laws."

But natural science depends not upon merely accepting, but also upon reporting, and upon recording, the phenom-

ena, upon comparing notes, upon trusting nobody's private
experience as such, upon a process, then, of publicly verifiable description of facts. This process—not now the cosmic
process, but the process of description—involves noting uniformities, and depends for its success upon our ability to note
the latter. The describable uniformities are structural uniformities—i. e., those expressible in terms of universal "rules
of structure" or "laws." The law of structure of a given whole,
be this whole a "thing" or a "process," a coexistent whole, or a
whole of successive elements, appears, in our slowly formed,
socially communicated, and gradually verified scientific
conceptions, as determining the necessity of every element
of any fact by virtue of the whole to which the element belongs. The only further assumption upon which the doctrine of the *objective* universality of rigid cosmic laws, as
distinct from the foregoing subjective and human need for
such laws, depends, is the assumption which I have elsewhere examined at some length *—viz., the assumption that,
in our human experience, *only* the relatively describable
data stand for the external or physical world *as such*—the
endless indescribabilities of our experience, the "chance" of
Mr. Peirce's account, being viewed, by scientific thinking, as
standing for the merely "individual" or "internal" element
of our experience, or for the limitations of the individual
point of view. For science, as I have just pointed out, is an
essentially social affair. The described "cosmical" fact is
a fact which others are conceived to be capable of verifying
besides the observer who now describes. And as only the
describable aspect of our experience is communicable to
others for them to verify, and as only the verifiable is, scientifically speaking, to be viewed as "cosmical" at all, it follows that, while private experience is full of what seems to

---

* Cf. the Philosophical Review for September, 1894, and The Spirit of
Modern Philosophy, lecture xii, on The World of Description.

be chance, we all have come to regard the cosmical process as one subject to the most rigid law. But one must carefully bear in mind this genesis and meaning of the whole concept, both of necessary natural law and of the cosmical processes themselves, in any comparison of the "cosmical process " with the "ethical process." Hence our present need for this rather technical summary.

On the other hand, the conception of moral laws, by which given acts are to be judged, and of "ethical processes," such as what is called "Progress"—processes which involve a gradual approach towards a conformity of given facts to given ethical ideals—this whole conception of the moral world as such, involves an entirely different point of view in presence of human experience. To conceive the "cosmical process " as such, you have to conceive it as in every detail subject to laws—viz., to precisely the cosmical laws. But you can well view the facts in the light of a moral ideal, while believing that the now existent physical facts run in some ways directly counter to the ideal. Yes, so to view the facts is inevitable whenever you have ideals. For you derive your ideals, ultimately, from an aspect of your experience which has not to do with describing experienced facts, but with desiring ideal objects that are absent when you desire them. It is true that what you rationally desire, you can, in general, both describe, and hope, with the aid of a possible good fortune, some time either to verify yourself, or to view as verifiable by somebody else, in whose interest you desire this object. But you do not desire the object *in so far as* it is describable. And furthermore, just in so far as you desire any object, its presence is not yet verifiable. One desires the absent. The cosmical fact—i. e., the physical fact, viewed as subject to natural law, is, then, an object in so far as it is *both* describable *and* verifiable. The object of our ideal is desirable *not* in so far as it is describable, and, again, *precisely in so far as it is not* yet verifiable. Herein, then, lies a double contrast between the natural fact as such, and the object of desire, as such. The contrast comes out well in case of future facts. The future eclipse, as natural phenomenon, is but an incident in the vast describable whole fact called the process of the solar system. As such, the eclipse can be predicted as something necessary, because this process, as a whole, is conceived as one describable in terms of known and universal law. The eclipse is also verifiable, at the time of its occurrence, by all rightly situated observers. But so far the eclipse is no object of desire. Desire is as vain as would be prayer. The eclipse is to be verified only at the computed time, but then it *must* be verifiable. Science does not aim at the eclipse, nor does she pray for the eclipse. She predicts, verifies, reports, records—all in due season. But the eclipse is not only natural fact, but interesting experience in the lives of the men who come to see it. *In so far*, one can desire to live to see the eclipse, can made an ideal of being present when it occurs, etc. But in desiring the experience, one does not compute the eclipse, nor does one verify the computation. One desires the eclipse in so far as one still expects but cannot yet verify its coming. And to desire to see the eclipse is simply not to compute its coming, but just to make this sight as such an ideal, and not to view the eclipse itself as a cosmical fact.

In consequence, our present contrast might be stated thus : Phenomena are desired (or dreaded) precisely in so far as they appear to be *interestingly novel*. Novelty, then, is a *conditio sine qua non* of all ideal value when regarded from a temporal point of view. But phenomena are explicable precisely in so far as they are conceived as *not* novel, but as mere cases under law. And again : The desired, or the dreaded, must be, as such, *now* unverifiable. But the explained is known to be such precisely in so far as universal explanations are actually verified. When I recognize

something as a case of a " cosmical process," my recognition,
as such, involves therefore no desire. One may say, indeed,
that the actual can be approved, as conforming to an ideal
standard. But, for us mortals, this approval, whenever
desires are concerned (and a purely contemplative, æsthetic
approval concerns us not here), is the approval of the fact
in so far as it *has been* desired. In brief, then, the explained or necessary phenomenon of the " cosmical process "
is such in so far as it embodies the universal law in a specific case. But the object of desire is such in so far as the law
or rule which this desire involves has not yet been embodied
in the precise sense in which it here needs to be embodied.

Here is the root of the endless conflict between the ethical view of the world and the explanatory or " scientific "
view. For a rational ethical doctrine is simply some uni-
versalized system of desires. What the right system may
be concerns us not here. Enough, if one has an ideal, he
bases it on some type of desire. If nothing were desirable,
there would be no ideals. A man with an ethical doctrine
has simply taught himself what he now thinks to be wisely
desirable. But he still desires. Thus desiring, he looks out
upon experience. There occur phenomena. These his science " apperceives," recognizes, describes as cases of law,
explains, calls necessary. But the very nature of this explanatory or descriptive sort of consciousness is that it says,
" these phenomena are not novel." The consciousness of
the possessor of ideals, however, essentially asserts, at every
breath one draws, " Yet the novel, in so far as it justly appears novel, is precisely what I want." The explaining
consciousness insists : " The law is eternally realized. What
has been will be. There seems to be alteration. There is
none." The ethical consciousness retorts : " The law is not
yet realized. In this ' not yet ' is my life. I have no abiding city. I seek one out of sight." Meanwhile, of course, it
is perfectly possible to point out common territory, where

these two views seem to meet without direct conflict.
" You must use my insight," says the explaining consciousness, "if you want to realize your ideals. In vain do you
desire as ideal what my laws forbid as forever unverifiable." The ethical consciousness must accept this inevitable comment. But it still responds : "Whatever laws of
yours I recognize, they become to me not my ideals, but
the mere material for realizing my ideals. If I could not
interfere with the phenomenal expression that your laws
are to get, my work would be utterly vain. You point me
the means. But I set the goal. I do not quarrel with your
laws. But I use them."

Hereupon, of course, the explaining consciousness makes
one retort which does, indeed, appear to be crushing. "Realize your ideals if you will and can," it says ; " yet what is
your realization but a mere incident of my cosmical process ? Your realization, when it comes, will be a natural
phenomenon, a part of a whole fact, like the rest. I shall
explain this phenomenon, and show, whenever it happens,
that it is nothing new." To this, of course, the ethical consciousness may make either one of two responses. It may
say : " Granted. As a fact, I admit that you are right. My
realization of my ideals will itself be only a nature-process,
involving no true novelty. I admit that my view is, in the
last analysis, illusory. 'Nature is made better by no mean,
but nature makes that mean,' just as Mr. Herbert Spencer
quotes. Nothing really new ever happens. Hence no
ideals, viewed *as* ideals, ever do realize themselves, any
more than eclipses come because we hope for them. But
still our human experience has its limitations. Some events
seem novel. Some desires seem, as such, productive of
what nature did not before contain. As a fact, the ' star-
mist' contained everything—good, evil, possible, necessary.
But, ' *Der Mensch, der beweglich Fühlende, der leichte
Raub des mächtigen Augenblicks*,' *feels* the thing other-

wise. I view the world as it seems to active beings; and so I *must* view the world. Hence you have the truth; but I, as practical common sense, must live in my necessary illusions; and it is in *this* sense that I remain forever in opposition to you—viz., just as an inevitable, if illusory, point of view."

This is what the ethical consciousness *may* say; and it is saying this which, to follow out to their just consequences the views of many writers, ought to constitute what such writers should consistently regard as the true " philosophy of evolution." The real world, thus viewed, is one of rigid cosmical law. In such a world, nothing essentially new ever happens. If we, as scientific observers, could come to comprehend this truth, we should no more talk of a genuine realization of ideals before unrealized in the universe, than we should regard the swing of a pendulum as a dramatic action. The pendulum bob, in its regular vibration, rises and falls, moves right and moves left, moves swiftly and moves slowly; yet all the time engages in but one describable cosmical process, which involves nothing novel at any point. So with the cosmical process, in its wholeness. New passions and desires, as well as their significant potency in transforming the world, are and must be illusions, *if* describable natural law, as such, is universal. From this conclusion there can be, *upon this hypothesis*, no possible escape. For to explain is to see the apparently novel, in all its essential details, as an instance of the old, whose former type is, down to the least genuinely true element, merely exemplified once more in this seemingly novel situation. Either, then, desires, passions, ideals, are not subject to the laws of the describable and necessary cosmical processes, or else they, if mere incidents of a describable process, are nothing new, and bring to pass nothing new, in all the universe. What has been will be. There is, then, nothing truly ethical. There is only the cosmical. This, I say, is the only possible

" philosophy of evolution," *if* natural law is an account of the absolutely real world. Evolution, as a process, is in that case the mere appearance of novelties to unwary or to necessarily ignorant observers. It does not and cannot involve anything truly historical. But meanwhile, of course, the philosophical evolutionist of this type could make practical concessions, to his public, to himself, and to the ethical consciousness, so long as he did not forget that these concessions were such—mere accommodations to human ignorance and to the practical point of view. He could say, " A portion of the cosmical process—namely, our own voluntary activity, appears as if it were ethical—i. e., as if true novelty, genuine progress, effective ideals, historically significant passage to something never before realized, were there present. This illusion is human, inevitbale, and even useful. When we write on ethics we have to treat this illusion as if it were true ; and to do so is as harmless as to speak of the sunrise, remembering all the while the cosmical truth."

Such ethically disposed, but consistent, partisans of natural necessity ought, however, still to admit that the ethical process, when thus abstractly sundered from the cosmical process, of which it is all the while held to be a part, does indeed appear in very sharp contrast to the rest of the cosmical process. In the ethical world, illusory as it is here said to be, it still *seems* true that the pendulums do not merely swing, that the old does not merely recur, that the creation moves towards some far-off event, divine or diabolical. One now has to talk (although such speech is, by hypothesis, but illusory) of progress, which means novel good entering a world that has thus far lacked its presence. One has to treat nature as if she could be made better. One looks to the future with hopes which, for many evolutionists, become rather sentimental. And to do this is to abstract from the supposed fact that the " star-mist " contained it all, and that nothing essentially novel occurs, or will ever occur. But the abstraction is in sharp contrast to the assumed truth. The ethical world is, when conceived, in vehement, even if in illusory, opposition to the natural process; and Professor Huxley's discussion will have done great good, in so far as it leads to the recognition of this inevitable fact. How one states the details of the opposition is of small consequence. The opposition itself is deep and universal.

But the ethical consciousness, instead of thus surrendering, might decline thus to abandon its assertions. It might say, "But, after all, my view is right. I not merely, in the seeming of my ideals, contrast my illusions with a supposed truth, but I rightly, and in the name of truth, oppose my view of the real world to any physical view. After all, does experience prove the real universality of the 'cosmical process'? Certainly, experience, as such, does not. That nothing new occurs is a proposition directly opposed to the seeming of every individual experience. Why may not this seeming be well founded? Why may there not be true novelties, effective ideals, genuine progress, transformations, evolution which is not a mere seeming of growth, spiritual processes which were not present in the star-mist in any form?"

To these queries would, of course, come the reply: "Supernaturalism, this—base supernaturalism." "But, no," one might retort; "not what that word usually suggests to some people, but merely what Kantian idealism long ago made familiar, and distinguished from all *Schwärmerei*—this alone is what we mean."

As a fact, the assertion of the universality of rigid cosmical process, and of what I have elsewhere called the reality of the "World of Description," is unquestionably a human, and, as I myself should affirm, a distinctly social theory for the interpretation of one aspect of our experience. Take human experience from that special point of view, and *then*, indeed, you have to conceive the world of experience *as if it were known to be* one of cosmical processes, which are the same yesterday, to-day, and forever. In that world, the only philosophy of evolution is that all evolution is to be called appearance. The only ethical process observable is one which, upon this hypothesis, is to be conceived as unreal. There is no question of warring against the cosmical process. But there is question of an undying opposition between the inevitable ethical consciousness and the hypothetically true cosmical consciousness; for the one forever looks to the future for the novel, the coming, *das Werdende*, conceived as the possibly progressive; the other asserts that all *Werden* only manifests the changeless truth of the cosmical process itself.

But now, the other view of human experience, the one which regards the universe as what I have elsewhere called "The World of Appreciation," is, as a fact, equally true to experience, and equally inevitable. For nature we know, as a fact, only through our social consciousness,* and the social consciousness is ethical before it is physical, appreciates more deeply than it describes, recognizes nature for reasons which are, in the last analysis, themselves ideal, and is conscious of novelty, of progress, of significance, in general of the human, in ways which, in the last analysis, make the whole cosmical process a mere appearance of one aspect of the moral world. Yet this doctrine is not "supernaturalism," because the true opponent of the natural is not the "supernatural," but the human. The "cosmos," in the sense of empirical science, is a conceptual product of the human mind. Man is indeed but a fragment of the absolutely real

---

* I may be allowed to refer again to the before-mentioned paper in the Philosophical Review, and to the later essays in this volume upon Self-consciousness, Social Consciousness, and Nature.

universe. But that genuine universe of which he is a fragment is not the world of Description, but the world of Appreciation—a world at which the phenomena of nature indeed richly hint, but which they do not reveal.

It is true that, when viewed in the light of such a doctrine, the facts of evolution get an interpretation, not here
to be expounded, which does away with much of the opposition between the ethical and what had seemed the cosmical, in the sense in which we have so far used that word in
this paper. Meanwhile, I should still hold that, as points
of view, the view for which the ethical process exists at all
is very sharply opposed to the view which, in the sense of
physical science, deals with cosmical processes as such.
Call the whole matter one of phenomena and of human
opinion, and then indeed this opposition need lead to no
misunderstandings. It will then be *merely* one of points of
view, no assertions of ultimate truth being made on either
side. But if it be a question of a philosophy of reality, then
one must choose between the two points of view, or else
reject both. There is no chance of reconciling the metaphysically real and ultimate universality of the so-called
cosmical, i. e., physical process, or processes according to describably rigid laws, with any even remotely ethical interpretation of the same reality.

The questions asked at the outset are then to be decided
thus : (1) Conceive the "cosmical process " as one of describably rigid law, as all explanation in natural science
does, must do, and ought to do, and *then* the " ethical process " can form no part of the "cosmical process." (2) In
essence the " ethical process," in so far as you conceive its
presence at all, is utterly opposed to all "cosmical processes " when they are thus physically conceived. (3) The
nature of the opposition lies not in any world of "things in
themselves " at all, but in the peculiarity of the ethical
point of view which, in dealing, as both this view and its

rival concretely do, with mere human appearances, estimates ideally, and desires essential novelty, progress, and
the thus far unattained as such ; while the descriptive or
explanatory point of view conceives its purely phenomenal
world as if it were known to contain no novelties whatever, and nothing ideal.

VI.

THE
IMPLICATIONS OF SELF-CONSCIOUSNESS.

THE present paper is an effort to set forth in brief some
of the evidence for an idealistic interpretation of the nature
of reality. My argument is in its essential features identical with the one presented in a chapter on The Possibility
of Error in my book called The Religious Aspect of Philosophy, published in 1885. Another statement of the same
considerations is to be found, in a summary form, on pages
368–380 of my study entitled The Spirit of Modern Philosophy. In the latter book I have also given an extended
account of the historical relations of this line of argument
—especially of its relations to Kant's Deduction of the
Categories, and to the philosophical development from
Kant to Hegel. That these relations are intimate, needs
here no further express declaration. The discussion in my
chapter on The Possibility of Error was criticised in some
detail by two French writers—by M. Paulhan, in the Revue
Philosophique for September, 1885 ; and by M. Renouvier,
in La Critique Philosophique, for 1888, pp. 85–120. To both
these critics I owe a hearty acknowledgment, and I have
tried to profit by their objections, though I cannot here
consider them. In a later and extended form my view
of the doctrine here in question has so been expounded
in a work entitled The Conception of God, published in
1897.

I.

What is it to be conscious ? What does self-consciousness imply ? Such are the questions with which philosophical idealism begins. It is by examining these questions
that a philosophical idealist hopes to get a clearer notion of
the world in which he finds himself, and of his relation to this
world. A successful estimate of such a doctrine can never
be made unless one comprehends how it has been reached.
It is the road that here determines the result. In vain does
one, as philosopher, try to pass the gates of this heaven of
theory, and to get the beatific insight for which the idealist
hopes, unless one has first followed the straight and narrow
path of thorough-going self-critical reflection. Whoever
has approached his idealism by this road will no longer
imagine, like a good many of the superficial critics of idealism, that the God of idealism "may be safely treated as
' une quantité négligeable' " (to quote the words of one such
critic). The careful student of the path will have learned,
as he went, the worth of the goal. His own insight may be
still very incomplete, but he will know that the truth with
which he deals is not " négligeable " merely because, like
the earth in Browning's poem, it "keeps up its terrible
composure," and declines to have a market value, or
to show itself in the precise guises which tradition had
led us to expect it to wear. For the idealist whose mind
is as I think it ought to be, the Infinite is unquestionably a Person, and this Person is as unquestionably the
world-possessor. The finite does not vanish in him ; but
he appears to us, although very imperfectly, through and
by means of the finite. Yet what it is and means
to be a Person, and to be also infinite, and to be the world-
possessor, only a successful philosophical analysis can
hope to make, in general terms, clear. It is useless to
approach such problems with only our accidental and

traditional prejudices, concerning what personality may mean.

It sometimes seems to me that to many minds the word "person" has come primarily to mean one who can and perhaps will on occasion strike back at you if you first hit him; and doubtless the notion in question does in fact reveal a certain aspect of the ultimate truth. The world is indeed a moral order, and the moral law is a hard master, and hard masters do strike down rebels; and to many, who would reject very scornfully the crude language that I have just used, the idea of God and of his personality is, in fact, based upon an unconscious elaboration of just such simple categories as these. I do not question the relative value of such categories. We have in childhood to get our theology in these terms, and we never ought altogether to forget our childhood, or to ignore the sinewy and healthy truths then impressed upon us by tradition. Only such truths should not pretend to be ultimate. Imagery of this kind does not reveal the inmost meaning of the word "personality." Ideas of this sort ought not to be treated as final tests of all philosophical definitions of God. It is perfectly true that in our immediate inner experience, in our uncriticised finite self-consciousness, fragmentary as it is, we mortals learn at the outset, in a first rude example, what personality means, and it is by reflection upon this rude example that we have to proceed. But we need not wonder to find that the deeper meaning of the word "personality" is only to be got at by a long study of the significance of the rude facts themselves. For, as a very little analysis shows, we are none of us at the outset able to answer sharp questions concerning the true extent, or the nature, or the limitations, or the significance, of this familiar reality which we call our self-consciousness. In other words, we are self-conscious, but very imperfectly so. The question, "Who am I?" is not easily answerable, yet no question is more obviously a fair one. The problem, "What is a person?" is, then, not to be solved by a mere glance within.

In seeking after God, there are many who do indeed begin by asking the question, "Who am I?" but who thence proceed by offering some facile answer, such as the well-known one, "I am a thinking substance," or the still more familiar one, "I am a being possessed of free choice and volition," and on such a basis a theology is quickly built up. This theology will therefore, indeed, take a comparatively naïve shape. I am a person. God, of course, is another. For I have free volition. That constitutes the essence of me, and so of any person you please; and this fact is obvious, and for reflection nearly if not quite ultimate. Now, in the exercise of my free volition, I meet resistance from without. This resistance indicates a world of outer objects. But obviously only a will can resist a will. Hence there is will, and so personality, outside of me. The unity of law in the world of my objects, the cleverness of the manifold contrivances of nature, or, better still, the extent and the wisdom of plan which I see exemplified in the facts of organic life and of evolution—all these things assure me that, in knowing the physical world, I am dealing with the doings of one great Person, whose creation is this natural order. He is free, and so am I. He limits me; and, so far as I am free, I limit him. We are two; and hence the world is a moral order. Any more monistic interpretation would be immoral, for I should not fear God unless he were another person; nor regard him as my Father unless I felt his resistance whenever, in the exercise of my free volition, I push against his reality, After all, it is the muscular sense that, from such a point of view, becomes the chief revealer of the divine personality to us finite beings; and hence those who insist upon these categories love to exalt their "dynamic" character.

11

All such brief sketches of the views of opponents have of course to be inadequate, and therefore in a measure unjust. It is only to show in what direction I myself should look for more light that I make this brief hint of the unreflective nature of all these notions of a good deal of current theology. They are derived from a very simple inspection, so I must insist, of the world of the inner life. They have their relative truth, but they need deeper criticism. " Conscious of free choice," " conscious of outer objects resisting my free choice," " conscious of dynamic principles beneath all reality "—how profoundly problematic are the categories contained in each one of these phrases ! What is it to have free choice ? What is it not only to have, but also to know one's own free choice ? What is it to know outer objects ? What is it to know one's Self ? Yes, what is it to be conscious at all ? What is a Self ? All these are just the questions of philosophy. Whoever says, " But I *do* know all these things, and there is the end of it—no matter about the *how* "—such a person is perfectly welcome to his assurance, but he is not philosophizing. It is precisely the *how* that concerns one in philosophy.

So much, then, for an indication of the reason why the idealist, knowing at the outset something of his own bit of finite self-consciousness, but longing to know more, declines to state *à priori* his notion either of Personality, or of the world, or of free will, or of the nature of knowledge, but aims to get at the true ideas of these things by means of a better analysis of the implications of self-consciousness themselves.

II.

Our questions, then, are no doubt fundamental, and worthy of scrutiny. They promise rich fruit. Yet, in approaching them, we must, in the present paper, limit our undertaking pretty carefully. Amidst the wealth of these problems we must choose what most directly concerns us in getting a general notion of the nature of the idealistic doctrine. Let our choice be as follows.

Idealism of the post-Kantian type is distinguished by two especially noteworthy features. It first 'involves a criticism of the inner nature of finite self-consciousness. I, the finite thinker, it says, must be in far more organic and deep and wide relations to my own true selfhood than my ordinary consciousness easily makes clear to me. In essence, then, I am much more of a self than my immediate consciousness, as it exists under human limitations, ever lets me directly know. The true Self is at all events far more than the "empirical" self of ordinary consciousness. This is sure because, upon examination, one finds that the flickering and limited self-consciousness of any moment of my life logically implies far more than it directly contains. I am never fully aware of the content, or of the meaning, of my present self. Unless, then, I am in deeper truth far more of a self than I now know myself to be, I am not even as much of a self as I now suppose myself to be. In other words, it is of the essence of finite consciousness to be, in its logical implications, transcendent of the limited character of its momentary inner contents. This is the first assertion of idealism. Put negatively it runs : Finite self-consciousness never directly shows me how much of a self I am. Therefore finite self-consciousness never directly reveals to me the true nature, or extent, or limitations, or relations of my own personality.

The second feature of our idealistic doctrine appears in its theory of the relation of any finite self to what we call the " external world." The idealistic view here is, that if on the one hand the self of finite consciousness is in any case, by implication, far more than it can directly know itself to be, on the other hand this self, in order to be in true relation to the outer objects which it actually thinks about, must be, by implication, so related to these outer objects that they are in reality, although external to this finite self, still not external to the true and complete Self of which this finite self is an organic part. If the analysis of consciousness has first shown me that my true Self is and must be far more in its essential nature than I can now directly know it to be, the analysis of the definition of "my world of objects" shows that, in order to be *my objects*, in order to be external, as they are, to my finite thoughts about them, "my objects" must be such as my true Self already possesses—objects which it is aware of because they are its immediate objects, and which it knows to be mine because it includes both my meaning and their inner essence.

Uniting these two features we have, as our idealistic metaphysic, this result: The self of finite consciousness is not yet the whole true Self. And the true Self is inclusive of the whole world of objects. Or, in other words, the result is, that there is and can be but one complete Self, and that all finite selves, and their objects, are organically related to this Self, are moments of its completeness, thoughts in its thought, and, as I should add, Wills in its Will, Individual elements in the life of the Absolute Individual.

I begin here at once with the first of these two considerations. It is a familiar assertion ever since Descartes, yes, in fact, ever since St. Augustine, that, whatever else I am doubtful of, I am at least directly sure of my own existence. I am I. What truth, so people say, could be clearer ? I exist, and I exist for my own thought ; for I doubt, I wonder, I inquire —in short, I think. And in my thinking I find myself, not as a possible dream of somebody else, or as a fiction, or as an hypothesis, or as a matter of doubt, but I find myself existent for myself. Such is one familiar way of stating the initial assurance of human thought.

A popular misunderstanding of the nature of idealism in philosophy supposes that, beginning thus with his own individual existence as somehow a thing very much clearer in nature and in definition than the existence of anything besides himself, every idealist as such must proceed, in a solipsistic sort of way, first to reduce all objective reality to his own ideas, and then to find, among these ideas of his, certain ones which dispose him, on purely subjective grounds, to assume the existence of outer objects.   It is historically true, of course, that such methods have been followed by certain students of philosophy.   It is also a fact that such methods have a value as means of philosophical analysis, and as preparations for deeper insight.   As such I myself have made use of them more than once for purposes of preliminary instruction: not that they constitute the essential portion of the teachings of a metaphysical idealism, of the sort which the post-Kantian thought in Germany developed (for they do not), but merely because they are pedagogically useful devices for introducing us to the true issues of metaphysics.

As a fact, however, before one could undertake, in a serious fashion, to be even provisionally and hypothetically a " solipsist " in his metaphysical teaching, it would be needful to define the Self, the *Ipse*, whose solitude in the world of knowledge the " solipsistic " doctrine is supposed to maintain.   The reason why in the end our post-Kantian idealism is not in the least identical with " solipsism," either in spirit or in content or in outcome, is that the definition of the Self, the answer to the question, "Who am I ?" is logically prior to the metaphysical assertion that a being called " I " is better known than is any being called " Not-I."   This assertion itself may be true.   But in vain does a doctrine declare that a being called by any name, x or y, mind or matter, not-self, or Self, obviously and with absolute assurance is known to exist, and is more immediately known to exist than is any other being, unless the doctrine first defines what being is meant under this name.   Self-consciousness can only reveal my own substantial existence with absolute, or even with merely exceptional clearness, in case self-consciousness first reveals to me what I mean by myself who am said thus so certainly to exist.

Idealism, then, has no more right than has any other doctrine to fire its absolute assurances "out of a pistol." That I exist is at the outset only known to me in the sense that this thinking, this consciousness, of mine, is no unreality. What reality it is, I shall not know until I shall have reflected long and with success. First, then, to say, "I clearly know myself, but I know not certainly anything beyond myself," and then by analysis to reduce the outer world to "my Idea," and then to say, "Beyond my ideas I can never certainly go"—all this method of provisional and halting reflection, which assumes "the Ego" as something perfectly transparent, may be useful enough as a propædeutic to philosophy. It is not yet thoroughgoing self-criticism. Nor is it upon such imperfect reflection that the idealistic doctrines of modern philosophy have been built up. Fichte, who is popularly supposed to have done his work in just this way, actually made the Self the central assurance of philosophy only in so far as he also made it the central problem of philosophy. Its very existence is, for him, of the most problematic kind, so that, in the first form of the *Wissenschaftslehre*, the true Self is never realized at all, and exists only as the goal of an *unendliches Streben*, an endless travail for self-consciousness. No sooner has Fichte declared at the outset that it exists—this Self— than he finds the very assertion essentially paradoxical, in such wise that, unrevised, it would become absurd. Moreover, as Fichte insists, the natural consciousness is far from a real self-awareness. "Most men," declares Fichte (Werke, vol. i, p. 175, note) ," could be more easily brought to believe themselves a piece of lava in the moon than to regard themselves as a Self." In such a philosophy the *cogito ergo sum* no longer means that I, the thinker, as *res cogitans*, am from the very beginning an obviously definite entity, while all else is doubtful. The first word of such a doctrine is rather the inquiry, *Who, then, am I?* It is the Self which needs winning, and which requires definition, and which is so far unknown, just because it is the object of our reflection.

Beginning thus our consideration—asking, What is the Self whose existence is to appear to a wise reflection as the fact surely involved in our consciousness?—we find of course at once that the larger empirical Ego of the world of common sense is by no means this Self whose truth is to be thus directly certified by the thinking and doubting with which philosophy is to be initiated. *I exist* cannot mean, at the beginning of our reflection, "I—Caius or Titus—I, this person of the world of common sense, calling myself by this name, living this life, possessed of these years of experience—*I* think, and so I am immediately known to exist." For the Self of the world of common sense is inextricably linked with numberless so-called non-Egos. He exists as neighbor amongst neighbors, as owner of these books or of this house, as father of these children, as related in countless ways to other finite beings. As such a creature, self-consciousness does not at first immediately reveal him. As such a being amongst other beings, reflective philosophy, at the outset, must ignore him. His existence is no more immediately obvious at any one moment, at the outset of our philosophical reflection, than is the "lava in the moon." When Fichte's opponents accused him of teaching that Professor Johann Gottlieb Fichte was the only person or reality in existence, and that his students, and even the Frau Professorin, were only ideas that Johann Gottlieb was pleased to create—such critics forgot that *das Ich* at the outset of the *Wissenschaftslehre* is not named Johann Gottlieb, and at this point of the system could not be, and that the beginning of Fichte's philosophy ignores the German professor named Johann Gottlieb as absolutely and mercilessly as it does the castles on the Rhine, or the natives of Patagonia, and knows as yet of nothing but the necessity that a certain pressing and inexorable problem of consciousness, called *das Ich*, must be fathomed, since every possible assertion is found to involve the position of this as yet unfathomed Self.

The Self which constitutes our present problem is, therefore, like Fichte's *Ich* at the beginning of the *Wissenschaftslehre*, a still unknown quantity. Its existence we know only in the sense that, in dealing with it, we are dealing with no unreality, but with a central problem and principle of knowledge.

How much of a Self, then, is clearly to be known to our most direct reflection ? If we look a little closer, we next feel disposed to answer that if the Ego, as directly known in consciousness, is not as yet the whole empirical Ego of common sense called in case of any one of us by his proper name, and involved in these external social and personal relationships, then the best account one can give of the immediate subject of the *cogito ergo sum* is, that it is *the knowing Self of this moment.* Here, in fact, is a definition that has become comparatively frequent in philosophy. I myself cannot accept this definition without modification. But it is necessary for us to examine it ere we proceed further. I know directly, so it has often been said, nothing but what is *now* in my consciousness. And now in my consciousness are these current ideas, feelings, thoughts, judgments, and, in so far as I choose to reflect, here am I myself, the subject in whom and for whom are these momentary thoughts. This is what I can directly know. To all else I conclude with greater or less probability ; or, again, the rest of reality is an object of my faith, or of my practical postulates. As for myself, I know myself just as the knower of these current thoughts of this moment. Thus, then, is our question to be answered.

Yet once more, is this new answer quite clear ? For *how much* does the present Self, the self of this moment, immediately know ? And does that which the self of this moment knows belong wholly to this moment ? As soon as we try to answer these questions, we enter upon a labyrinth of theoretical problems as familiar, in some sense, as it is intricate. I should not venture to weary the reader with even a passing mention of these subtleties were not the outcome of the necessarily tedious investigation of such importance.

I am to know, then, " this moment," and I am to exist for myself here as " the knower of this moment." Very well, then, shall I, taking this point of view, say that I know immediately the past in time ? No, apparently not. I have a present idea of what I now call past time. That must be all that I " immediately know " of that so-called past. Do I immediately know the future ? No, again ; I have a present idea of what I now call future time. I am limited, then, in " immediate knowledge," to the present in time. This moment is of course, as the present moment, to be cut off from past and future. Very well, then, how large a moment is it, and how long ? Is it quite instantaneous, wholly without duration ? No, for I must surely be supposed immediately to know, in this moment, a passing of time. My psychological present is a " specious present." It looks backward and forward. It lasts a little, and then insensibly glides over into the next moment. Such at least seems to be the definition that this doctrine of the " present moment " must accept as a good account of what the " present " is.

But, alas ! the present, as thus defined, is only the more left undefined. This gliding " specious present," when does it cease to be present ? When does it become past ? Where are the boundaries ? How much is there of it ? For, remember, I am looking for the immediately certain truth.

I wanted to know who I am, as an immediately sure reflection shall find or define me. The answer to my inquiry was, "I am the knower of this moment." So much I am to be quite surely aware of about myself. Well, I have tried to define this assurance, and of course, if it *is* immediate assurance, I must be able to give at once its content, i. e., to define just what is contained in this moment. But unfortunately I at once find myself baffled. And as an actual fact, if I look a little closer, I shall always find that, despite the assumption that I do know only the "present moment," I cannot tell reflectively the precise content of my present moment, but can only answer certain reflective questions about the consciousness which is no longer quite my own, because, before I can reflect upon it, it has already become a past moment. As a fact, then, the assumption just made about my knowing fully the content of the "immediately present moment" turns out to be an error. For I know *not* now in full what it is that is present to me, nor who I myself am to whom this is present. And I find out that I do not thus fully know myself at any present moment, just because, when I try to tell what I know, what I tell about is no longer my present, but is already my past knowledge.

This problem about the definition of the "present moment" is one of the most characteristic of the problems of self-consciousness. Let us give some examples of its curious complications. Let the present moment, for instance, be a moment of a judgment. I judge that the paper before me appears extended. This, as it would seem, I just now know immediately, since I chance to notice it. But extension even now already involves, for my consciousness, all sorts of consequences, which will begin to appear upon reflection. If extended, the paper is divisible. In so far as it appears to me as what I call paper, I already begin to think of it as something that I could fold or tear. Yes, upon reflection, I perceive that, even while I saw and felt it as extended, I all the while " sub-consciously " perceived it to be smooth to my hand as I wrote, and also saw it to be white, and knew it to be partially covered by my handwriting, and knew to some extent what letters I was writing, and had furthermore in my mind the train of my more abstract thoughts. All this mass of " mind-stuff " was in me in a more or less latent form. What portion of it was immediately present to me at any moment during the writing of the foregoing half-dozen sentences ? Yes, *how much of it all is even now immediately present to my consciousness ?* I cannot tell. I know not. " This moment " has ceased to be " this " before I have observed its content, or written down its name. I know all the while that there just now was a present moment; and all the while also I am just coming to know this now flying moment. That is the actual situation. My " immediate knowing " ceases to be immediate in becoming knowledge, and the knowledge that I now have crumbles forever as it passes over into my immediately present state of feeling. I judge what just was my feeling, and feel what may straightway become an object for my judgment.

Enough ; I shall never thus define in any precise way who I am. It is here I who ceaselessly fly from myself. My moments as such have no power to define in any sharp fashion their own content. I can therefore only say they must actually have such fleeting content as a perfectly clear and just Reflection would judge them to have. That alone is what I seem to be sure of. For they have *some* content. What it is, however, I can endlessly inquire ; but I can never fully and at the same time immediately know. Unless I am an organic part of a Self that can reflect with justice and clearness upon the contents of my moments, these moments contain a great deal that exists *in* me, but *for* nobody. So much, then, for the first result of our inquiry.

So much for the effort to define the "Ego" apart from the "external world."

Have I learned anything about myself by this weary and baffling process of reflection ? Yes, one thing I have learned. It is the thing that I just stated. It is a difference which I inevitably find myself making between myself as I really am, and myself as I haltingly take myself to be from moment to moment. I am twofold. I have a true Self which endlessly escapes my observation, and a seeking self which as endlessly pursues its fellow. What I really am, even in any given moment, I never find out in that moment itself. I can, therefore, only define my true Self in terms of an ideally just reflection upon the contents of my moment; a reflection of an exhaustive character, such as in fact I in my momentary capacity never succeed in making. I must exist, to be sure, for myself; and as I really am I must exist for myself only. With that consideration one begins in our present inquiry. It is reflection that is to find me. It is my consciousness that is to discover me, if I am ever to be discovered. But the Self for whom I am what I am is not the self of this moment, but is thus far an ideal Self, never present in any one moment. To repeat, then, by way of summary : The Self is never *merely* the self of this moment, since the self of this moment never fully knows who he even now is. It is of his very essence to appeal beyond the moment to a justly reflective Self who shall discover and so reflectively determine who he is, and so who I am. For I am he.

III.

Another way of stating the foregoing result would, therefore, be to say that, unless I am more than the knowing and the immediately known self of this moment, I am not even as much as the self of this moment. For this moment implies more consciousness than I am now fully aware of. That which is just now in me to be known is far more than

I just now know. That is the paradox, but it is also the inevitable fact, of my inner life; and thus I already begin to
see how large may be the implications of self-consciousness.

But herewith our task is by no means done. We have
studied the problem of the Ego viewed apart from a world
of "external objects." What we have learned is, that the
subject of the *cogito ergo sum* is in the beginning, strange
to say, at once the best and the least known of the possessions of our knowledge. I cannot doubt its existence. But
I am not yet aware how much of a self it is, nor how much
it truly knows, nor whether it is or is not limited to a single
series of moments of consciousness and reflection, nor how
it stands related to any sort of inner or outer truth. Those
who have begun philosophy by saying, "The self at least is
known," have usually forgotten that the self as known is at
the outset neither the empirical Ego of the world of common sense, nor yet merely the so-called "self of the one
present moment." It is not the first, because philosophy
has not yet at the outset come to comprehend the world of
common sense. It is not the second, for the consciousness
of the "present moment" can only be defined in relation to
a reflection that transcends the present moment; whilst, on
the other hand, no human reflection has ever yet fathomed
perfectly the consciousness of even a single one of our moments. The self, then, is not yet known to us except as the
problematic truth exemplified by the still so mysterious fact
of the *cogito* itself. Much less then is the relation of the
Ego to outer objects as yet clear.

To this latter relation we must, however, next turn. Perhaps there we shall get a light which is refused to us so
long as we confine ourselves to a merely subjective analysis
of the inner life of this baffling Ego. The self undertakes
to be not merely conscious of its own states, but of outer
truth. Is its power in this respect indubitable? And if it
is, upon what is founded our assurance that we do know a

world of real objects outside the Ego? Possibly in getting a solution of this problem we shall come nearer to a true definition of the Ego itself.

The only way of answering the question about the external world lies in first asking, in a thoroughly reflective way, what is *meant* by a world of objects beyond the Ego. It is useless to try to find the philosophical evidence for the existence of a world of outer objects, unless you first define what an object beyond your consciousness is to mean for you. Amongst the numerous definitions of the meaning of the words *external object*, I may therefore choose three, which seem to me of most importance for our present purpose, and may consider each in its turn. The third will be my own.

1. "The term *outer object* means for me the known or unknown cause of my experiences, in so far as I do not refer these experiences to my own will"—such is a very common account of the nature of the external truth for the Ego. I need not expound this view at great length, since it is so familiar a notion. According to those who hold to this definition, it is somehow perfectly evident to me that my experiences need a cause, and that I myself am not the cause of all or of most of them. The Ego itself is thus definable as that which is conscious of more experiences than it causes, and which therefore looks beyond itself for the causes of most of these experiences. An "external object" means just such a cause, known or unknown.

It is strange that this, the most familiar definition of the nature and meaning of the word "object," should be the most obviously inadequate. In case of my perception of a house, or of a hot iron when I touch it, or of a wind in my face, I do indeed conceive myself as in relation to an object which is causing experiences in me. But most of the external truth that I usually think about and believe in is not truth now perceived by my senses, nor, *as* I think it, is it *now* in any causal relations to me at all. I at present believe in it because I "trust the validity of memory," or "have confidence in the testimony of mankind," or follow some other such well-known criterion of common-sense opinion. When I read my daily newspaper, light-waves are causing retinal disturbances in my eye; but as for me, I am thinking, not about these causes of my experience, but about the news from Europe, about the Russian famine, about the next Presidential canvass, and about other such "external objects," all of which objects I believe in, not because I reflect that my present experiences need causes, but because I trust tradition, or "current opinion," or the "consensus of mankind," or my own memory, or whatever else I am accustomed to trust. Only in the case where I attend to immediate perception, is the object of my belief at the same time the cause of my belief. Our "belief in the reality of an external world" is concretely definable, then, much more frequently as our belief in the validity of our memories and social traditions, than as our belief that our experiences have present causes. We all of us believe in the future of this external world of ours. There will come the time called ten years hence, or a million years hence. Something will be happening then among the things of the physical universe. That future event is an "external reality"; we all accept it as real, however little we know of it. But is it for us a "cause" of our present experiences? We are sure that such an event will come. Does that future event now "cause impressions" in us?

Yet more, were "my object" once defined as that x which causes my inner experience, my feeling, f, then one would still have to ask, What do I mean by causation? Causation is a relation between facts. I must myself have some inner idea of such a relation before I can attribute to the outer object the character of being a cause. By hypothesis, x, the object, is outside me. Its causal relation to my feeling is therefore also, in part at least, external to me. To believe in my object, x, as the cause of my feeling, f, I must therefore first believe that my notion of causation, derived from some inner experience of mine (e. g., from my own consciousness of my "will" or from my exercise of "power"), does itself correspond to an objective truth beyond me, namely, the outer causation of x, as bringing to pass f. In other words, I make x my object, if all this account is true, only through *first* holding that the inner experience of a relation, called "causation" in me, corresponds to an outer truth, namely, the external causation, whose validity is needed to give me an idea of the very existence of x.

But this means that there is here at least *one* external truth, and so one "object" (viz. :—the external fact of the causation itself), which I believe in, not because it is itself the cause of my idea of the causation, but because I trust that my idea of causation is valid, and corresponds to the truth. And it is only by *first* believing in this objective truth, viz., the causation, that I come to believe in x the cause.

Hence it follows that even in case of immediate sense-perception, my belief in the external object is always primarily not so much a belief that my experiences need causes, as an assurance that certain inner beliefs of mine are as such, valid, i. e., that they correspond with that which is beyond them.

2. "By *object*, then, I mean that which, beyond me, reduplicates, repeats, corresponds to, certain elements or relations of my own ideas." To this definition the foregoing one, as we have now seen, must lead us, when once properly understood, and when freed from the inadequacies thus far noted.

Here is a definition of what I mean by "outer object"— a definition which is far more true to the facts of consciousness than was the foregoing. My belief in such external objects as the space beyond Sirius, or the time before the solar system was formed out of the primitive nebula, or in the existence of Cæsar, or in the presence of monasteries in Thibet, or even in the things that I read about in the newspapers, or learn of daily in conversation—my belief too in your existence, kind reader—all such beliefs are assurances that subjective combinations of ideas have their correspondents beyond my private consciousness. So far then this definition appears adequate. And yet it is really not enough.

For this is not *all* that I mean by an outer object of my thought. It is not enough that beyond my thoughts there should be truths whose inner constitution and relationships resemble those of my thought. For the world of my own external objects is not merely a world which my thought does resemble, but a world which my thought, even as it is in me, intends to resemble. Here I cannot do better for my present purpose than to repeat language that I have used in the Spirit of Modern Philosophy, p. 370. " My object," so I had just been saying, " is surely always *the thing that I am thinking about.* And," as I continued, " this thinking about things is, after all, a very curious relation in which to stand to things. In order to think *about* a thing, it is *not* enough that I should have an idea in me that merely *resembles* that thing. This last is a very important observation. I repeat, it is *not* enough that I should merely have an idea in me that *resembles* the thing whereof I think. I have, for instance, in me the idea of a pain. Another man has a pain just like mine. Say we both have toothache, or have both burned our finger-tips in the same way. Now my idea of pain is just like the pain in him, but I am not on that account necessarily thinking about *his* pain, merely because what I *am* thinking about, namely my own pain, resembles his pain. No, to think about an object you must not merely have an idea that resembles the object, but you

12

must *mean* to have your idea resemble that object. Stated in other form, to think of an object you must consciously *aim at* that object, you must pick out that object, you must already in some measure possess that object enough, namely, to identify it as what you mean."

If this be what is meant by the relation of a self to an outer object, then the relation surely becomes, once more, highly problematic. Unless, namely, the self in question has already its own conscious idea of its object, it cannot formulate its belief in this object. But just in so far as it has its own conscious ideas of the object, the Ego under consideration would seem to possess only inner knowledge. It defines for itself the object of its belief. The definition is internal. The self appears as if cut off from the object. Its ideas shall be " its own." The object, as it seems, is beyond them. The only relation that can exist is so far correspondence. But, alas! this relation is not enough. Another relation is needed. If the self in question is actually thinking of the object, it is already meaning to transcend its own ideas even while it is apparently confined to its ideas. And it is actually meaning, not self-transcendence in general, but just such self-transcendence as does actually bring it into a genuine and objective relation to the particular object with which it means to have its ideas agree. Am I really thinking of the moon ? then I not only have ideas that resemble the objective constitution of the moon, but I am actually trying to get my ideas into such correspondence with an external truth called the moon. In other words, whether I succeed or not in thinking rightly of the moon, still, if I am thinking of the moon at all, my thought does transcend my private experience in a fashion which no mere similarity or correspondence between my ideas and other realities can express. The true relation of thought and object needs another formulation.

Shall we attempt such a formulation ?   In so far as I am

fully conscious of my meaning, in any thinking of mine, I am confined to my private ideas. But in so far as I am to be in any relation to an object, I must really be meaning that object without being, in my private capacity, fully conscious that I am thus really meaning just this object. At the moment of my thought of the object, I am conscious only that I am meaning my ideas to be not merely mine, but actually related to some object beyond. Am I, however, actually thus related to a particular outer object, then my present consciousness of my meaning is so related to that which is truly, although at present unconsciously, my meaning, that, were I to become fully conscious of my meaning, the object would no longer be external to my thought, but would be at once recognized as the object that I all along had meant, and would be included in my now more completely conscious thought. Complex as is this formula, it is needed for the sake of expressing the facts.

In other words, the only way in which I can really mean an object that is now beyond me is by actually standing to that object in the relation in which I often stand to a forgotten or half-forgotten name when I seek it, or to the implied meaning of a simple and at first sight obviously comprehensible statement, when, as in studying formal logic, I have to reflect carefully before I discover this meaning. And thus we are led to the following formulation of our own definition of the phrase "my object."

3. "My object is that which I even now mean by my thoughts, although, in so far as the object is beyond my private conscious thought, I cannot at present be fully conscious of this my relation to it. Yet the relation, although just now to me unconscious, must in such wise exist, that a true reflection upon my own meaning would even now recognize the object as actually meant by me. Such a reflection would, however, be an enlargement of my own present thought, a discovery of my own truer self, a con-

sciousness of what is now latent in my consciousness. On the other hand, as a consciousness of my meaning, if complete, could still contain only thoughts, my object, as my object, must even now be a thought of mine, only a thought of which I am not now, in my private capacity, fully aware. In other words, my world of objects, if it exists, is that which my complete self would recognize as the totality of my thoughts brought to a full consciousness of their own meaning."

To sum up both aspects of the foregoing argument, whether you consider your inner life or your supposed relation to a world of objects external to yourself, you find that, in order to be either the self of "this moment," or the being who thinks about "this world of objects," you must be organically related to a true and complete reflective Person whom your finite consciousness logically implies, fragmentary and ignorant though this consciousness of yours is.

Thus, then, the essential nature of our idealistic view of reality begins to come into sight. I know not directly through my finite experience who I am, or how much of a personality I truly possess. If, however, I am really a self at all, as even my fragmentary finite self-consciousness implies, then my true Self is aware of its own content and of its own meaning. If directly I cannot through finite experience exhaustively know my own nature, I can examine the logical implications of my imperfect selfhood. And this content and this meaning, which, as I find, are logically implied by even my finite selfhood, must include my whole "world of objects," as well as the whole truth of my inner life. If, then, this analysis of the concept of Personality be sound, there is logically possible but one existent Person, namely, the one complete Self.

Yet perchance to the foregoing argument an answer may be suggested that will seem to some readers, at first sight, conclusive. This idealism, it will be said, is, after all, unable to give any notion of the extent, or of the content, or of the magnitude, of this world of the complete Self. What is proved is at best this, that *if* my thought is truly related to objects outside of my finite consciousness, then in so far as this relation exists, that is, in so far as I truly think of these objects, they are in themselves objects possessed by my true or complete Self, whereof this finite consciousness is only an aspect or organic element. But perhaps the assumption that I ever think of objects beyond my finite self is itself an error. How, at all events, can I ever do more than postulate, or hope, or believe, that it is no error ? How can the way to an objective knowledge of the objective relations of my finite thought ever be opened to me ? How can I ever transcend my finitude, to know that I am really thinking of objects beyond, or that I am implicitly meaning them ?

It is at this point that the argument concerning the " Possibility of Error," as I developed it in my chapter so entitled, in the Religious Aspect of Philosophy, becomes immediately important to the present discussion. If, namely, in my finitude, I am actually never meaning any objective truth beyond my finite selfhood, even when I most suppose myself to be meaning such truth, then one must accept the only alternative. I must, then, be really in error when I suppose myself to be referring, in my thoughts, to outer objects. The objective truth about my finite consciousness must then be, that I never really refer to any objective truth at all, but am confined, in a sort of Protagorean fashion, to the world of the subjective inner life as such. I think, let us say, of the universe, of infinite space and time, of God, of an opposing philosophical doctrine concerning these things, of absolute truth, of the complete Self as he is in himself, or of what you will. Well, these are all, it may be supposed, subjective ideas of my finite self. It may be an error to regard them as more. No objects outside my finitude correspond to them. I do not really mean any outer truth by them. I only fancy that I mean outer truth by them. Could I clearly reflect on what I mean by these objects, I should see this illusion, this error, of supposing that I really have in mind outer objects. So our sceptical objector may respond to all the foregoing considerations.

But, once more, if this be true of any of my ideas, if my intent to mean outer truth by them is itself an illusion, then under what conditions, and under what only, is such an error, such an illusion, possible ? I err about any specific object only if, meaning to tell the truth about that object, I am now in such a relation to it that my thought fails to conform to the object meant. I cannot be in error about any object, unless I am meaning that object. If, then, when I think of infinite time, or of infinite space, or of the universe in general, or of the absolute truth, I err in supposing that there is beyond my finite self an object corresponding to any of these notions of mine, then my error can only lie in this : that whereas my finite self *means to mean* outer objects, my true Self, possessing a clear insight into what truth really exists beyond my finite self, completing the imperfect insight of my finitude, discovers that what I take to be an outer object is only an idea of mine, and that in the world of the complete insight there exists nothing corresponding to my intended meaning. But thus, after all, we surely change not the essential situation which my finite self must really occupy. For still, whatever its errors, my finite self is an organic element in the correcting insight of the true Self. My notions of time and of space, of truth and of the universe, may be as imperfect, in all specific respects, as you please. Only, in so far as they are erroneous, the complete Self, having possession of the complete truth, corrects them. And even if I do not *mean to mean* an outer truth at any one moment when I imagine myself to be in relation to such truth, even then, this paradoxical situation can only be the objective, the genuine situation, in which my finite consciousness stands, in case my truly reflective Self detects the meaninglessness of my finite point of view in just this case. For, in the case as thus supposed, I am still defined as objectively in error, just in so far as what I *mean to mean*, namely, some particular kind of outer truth, is, from the point of view of the Self that knows my objectively true relations, not in correspondence with what I really mean.

Or, again, to put the case once more in concrete form : I am trying to think of an outer object. I conceive of that object as existent. But I am supposed to be in error. I care not what the supposed outer object shall be—infinite time or infinite space, or any other form of being. If I am in error, then, even now, unknown to my finite self, the objective situation is this, namely, that the world of truth as I should know it if I came to complete self-consciousness, that is, to complete awareness of what I have a right to mean, would not contain this my finite object, but would contain truth such as obviously excluded that object. In any case, then, we cannot escape from one assertion, namely, the assertion upon which the very "possibility of error" itself is based. This is the assertion that there is, even now, the existent truth, and that this exists as the object of my completely reflective Self.

But, finally, does one still object that the completely reflective Self, the possessor of my complete meaning, and of its genuine objects, the Self aware of the world of truth in its entirety, is still, after all, definable only as a possible, not as an actual, Self, namely, as the possible possessor of what I should know *if* I came to complete self-consciousness, and not as the present actual possessor of a concrete fullness of conscious insight ? Then we must reply that the whole foregoing argument involves at every step the obvious reflection that, if at present a certain situation exists, which logically implies, even as it now stands, a possible experience, which would become mine if ever I came to complete self-consciousness, then the possibility thus involved is *ipso facto* no bare or empty possibility, but is a present and concrete truth, not, indeed, for me in my finite capacity, but for one who knows the truth as it is. Idealism is everywhere based upon the assertion that bare possibilities are as good as unrealities, and that genuine possibilities imply genuine realities at the basis of them. A merely possible pain, which nobody actually either feels or knows, is nothing. Yet more, then, is a merely possible reflection, which nobody makes, an unreality. But the foregoing argument has been throughout devoted to proving that the finite consciousness implies the present truth of an exhaustively complete and reflective self-consciousness which I, indeed, so far as I am merely finite, never attain, but which must be attained, just in so far as the truth is even now true.

IV.

Mere outlines are always unsatisfactory. The foregoing argument has been merely a suggestion. There has been no space to answer numerous other objections which I have all the while borne in mind, or to carry out numerous analyses which the argument has brought more or less clearly into sight. My effort has been to make a beginning, and to lead this or that metaphysically disposed fellow-student to look further, if he finds himself attracted by a train of thought to which the whole of modern philosophy seems to me to lead.

Such, at all events, is the path of philosophical idealism. What, now, is the goal ? What definition of the complete Self does one thus, in the end, get ? I have elsewhere used the tentative definition : " The Self who knows in unity all truth." I have accordingly laid stress upon this character of the divine World-Self as a Thinker, and have labored to distinguish between this his fullness of Being, as idealism is obliged to define it, and those customary notions which define God first of all in "dynamic," rather than in explicitly rational terms, and which, to preserve his almighty power as the director of Nature, and his exalted separateness from our weakness in so far as He is to be our moral Judge, find it necessary, first of all, to make Him other than his world of truth, and only in the second place to endow Him with a wisdom adequate to the magnitude of his "dynamic" business. All such opposed definitions I find, indeed, hopelessly defective. But in insisting upon thought as the first category of the divine Person, I myself am not at all minded to lose sight of the permanent, although, in the order of logical dependence, secondary, significance of the moral categories, or of their eternal place in the world of the completed Self. That they are thus logically secondary does not prevent them from being, in the order of spiritual worth and dignity, supreme. That evil is a real thing, that free-will has a genuine existence in this world of the Self, that we beings who live in time have ourselves a very "dynamic" business to do, that the perfection of the Self does not exclude, but rather demands, the genuineness and the utter baseness of deliberate evil-doing in our finite moral order, and that Idealism not only must face the prob·lems of evil and of moral choice, but as a fact, is in possession of the only possible rational solution for these problems —all these things I have tried elsewhere to show in a fashion which, as I hope, if not satisfactory, is at least sufficiently explicit to make clear to a careful reader that the God of the Idealist is at any rate no merely indifferent onlooker upon this our temporal world of warfare and dust and blood and sin and glory. To my mind, one of the most significant facts in the world is furnished by the thought that all this is, indeed, his fully comprehended world, and that if these dark and solemn things which cloud our finite lives with problems are in and of the universe of the crystal-clear Self, then, whatever the tragedy of our finitude, our problems are in themselves solved; while, as for our own personal destinies, they are, after all, and at the worst, part of his self-chosen destiny. For, as I have elsewhere explained, an absolute Reason does not exclude, but rather implies, an absolute choice; while such a choice does not exclude, but of necessity implies, as it includes, a finite and personal freedom in us. That this our moral and individual freedom belongs, after the fashion first indicated by Kant, not to the temporal order of our daily phenomenal world, in so far as it is merely temporal and phenomenal, but to a higher order, whereof we are a part, and not unconsciously a part —all this does not militate either against the true unity of the Self, or against the genuineness of the moral order. Every being who is rationally conscious of time, is, by that very fact, living in part out of the world of time. For what we know we transcend. To live in time by virtue of one's physical nature, but out of time by virtue of one's very consciousness of time itself, is to share in the eternal freedom, and to be a moral agent.

VII

SOME OBSERVATIONS ON THE ANOMALIES
OF SELF–CONSCIOUSNESS.*

In the present paper I shall venture to lay some stress upon certain familiar factors whose psychological influence upon the growth and the anomalies of self-consciousness, both in normal and in abnormal human beings, seems to me to have been, from the purely theoretical point of view, rather unduly neglected. In particular, I shall try to indicate how these theoretically neglected factors may help to explain certain well known types of variation, and of abnormality, to which the functions of self-consciousness, as they empirically appear, are subject. Meanwhile I shall of course avoid, in this paper, any positive reference to the distinctively metaphysical problems which the word self-consciousness easily suggests. The philosophical aspects of the problem of self-consciousness belong altogether elsewhere. Starting this evening with the mere empirical fact that any normal man has, as part of his mental equipment, conscious states and functions that involve, in one way or another, his experience, his knowledge, his estimate, or, in general terms, his view, of himself, and remembering that, in many defective and disordered people, these, the functions of individual self-consciousness, undergo changes of a manifold and interesting sort, I shall try to illustrate

---

* A paper read before the Medico–Psychological Association of Boston, March 21, 1894.

aspects of the purely psychological theory of our topic. I speak to practical men, who are also men of science. I need make then no apology for introducing here a problem, which, whatever its difficulty, is full both of scientifically attractive, and of practically important elements. For surely the alterations and defects of the functions of self-consciousness are among the most frequent phenomena in the region of mental pathology.

I.

In its inner aspects and relations, what we mean by self-consciousness, in any one man, is an enormously complex function or rather a little world of functions. But this world of functions is centred about certain well known habits and experiences which at once serve, not to explain it, but in a measure to begin for us the definition of our problem. There are, namely, in any mature person, certain established motor habits, which, according as they appear to be intact or not, enable us at once to test, from without, the relative normality of whatever belongs to that which one may call the mere routine of an individual's self-consciousness. There are also certain inner experiences, in terms of which the normal individual himself, from moment to moment, can feel assured of the apparent natural-ness of his own notion or estimate of himself. A mature man whose self-consciousness is normal, if his means of ex-pressing himself are intact, must be able to explain "who he is," i. e., he must be able to tell his name, his business, his general relations in life, and whatever else would be essential to the practical purpose of identifying him. Fur-thermore, his account of himself must be able to show an estimate by no means adequate or infallible, but at least not too widely absurd, of his actual degree of social dignity, of his personal importance and of his physical capacity. He will, to be sure, quite normally estimate his value, his prowess, or even his social rank, not, in general, precisely as his fellows do. But this sort of estimate has its normal, if rather wide, limits of error. If these limits are passed, the man's account of himself proves the presence of a derangement of self-consciousness. Finally, as to this account which the normal man can give of himself, he must show a certain degree of correctness as to what he can tell us of his body and of its present state. Here, of course, the limits of error are very wide, but are still pretty definite. A man is normally a very poor judge of his internal bodily states. But if he says he is made of glass, or that he is aware that he is a mile high, or that he is conscious of having no body at all, we recognize a disorder involving alterations of self-consciousness.

Within his own mind, meanwhile, and from his own point of view, a man normally self-conscious is more or less aware of a great deal about himself of which, it is notoriously hard for him to give any exact account whatever. Yet this internally normal self-consciousness has, at any time, a definitive, if not easily definable content, which, in its relatively inexpressible complexity of constitution, far transcends what one expresses when he tells you his name, his place in life, his *status*, or his notion of his bodily condition. This normal inner self-consciousness involves, in the first place, what we are now accustomed to call, from a psychological point of view, masses of somewhat vaguely localized bodily sensations, which, just in so far as they affect our general consciousness, are not sharply differentiated from one another. The origin of these sensations lies in the skin, in the muscles, and, in part, in the viscera. Moreover, the visual perception of the body, the auditory experiences of the sound of one's own voice, and yet other sensory contents, including the more general sensations of bodily movement, obviously determine, now more, and now less, the content or the coloring of normal self-consciousness. If any of these masses of sensory contents are suddenly altered, our immediate self-consciousness may be much changed thereby. Dizziness, sensations of oppression in the head, a general sense of bodily ill-being, a flushed face, a ringing in the ears—any of these may involve what we primarily take to be a general alteration of our feeling of self, and only secondarily distinguish from the self as a separate and localized group of experiences. In general, the more sharply we localize our sensations, and the more we refer them to external objects, the less do these sensory experiences blend into our total immediate feeling of ourselves. The localized or objectified sensory state appears as something foreign, as coming to us, as besetting us, or as otherwise affecting us, but not as being a part of the self; and only a relatively philosophical reflection regards even our perceptions as part of ourselves. Our more naïve self-consciousness tends to regard the sensory or immediate self as a vague whole, from which one separates one's definite experiences of this place on the skin, of this color or tone, or of this outer object.

Yet our inner notion of the self of self-consciousness is by no means confined to this cruder appreciation of massive sensory contents. In addition, our normal mature awareness of who and what we are means what one may call a collection of feelings of inner control, of self-possession, or, as many would say, of spontaneity. If such feelings begin to be altered or lost, one complains of confusion, of a sense of self-estrangement, of helplessness, of deadness, of mental automatism, or of a divided personality. As a fact, since the associative processes always depend upon conditions of which we are not conscious, our sense that we can and do rule our whole current train of conscious states is, as it is ordinarily felt, a fallacious sense. But if we cannot really predetermine, in consciousness, what idea shall next come to consciousness, but are dependent, even in the clear-

est thinking, upon the happy support of our associative
mechanism, it is still normal to feel as if, on the whole, our
inner process were, in certain respects, relatively spontaneous, i. e., as if it were controlled by our ruling interests and
by our volition. This sense of inner self-possession is, to be
sure, an extremely delicate and unstable affair, and is constantly interfered with, in the most normal life, not only by
a series of uncontrollable sensory novelties, due to the external world, but by baffling variations, either in the play of
our impulses and ideal associations, or in the tone of our
emotions, or in both. Yet, when we are alert, these little
interferences continually arise only to be subordinated. We
have perhaps momentary difficulties in recalling names or
other needed ideas, of an imperfectly learned group, or we
feel equally momentary indecisions as to what it is just now
best to do, or we find our attention wandering, or our emotional tone disagreeably insistent, or our impulses numerous
and wayward. But in all such cases we can still, in the
normal case, " keep hold of ourselves," so that we accept as
our own whatever content triumphs in the play of associative
processes, and find our essential expectations met, from moment to moment, by the inner experiences which form the
centre of the mental field of vision. If this rule no longer
holds of our inner life, then our self-consciousness begins
to vary, and we suffer from confusion or from other forms
of the sense of lost inner control.

Thus the self of ordinary self-consciousness appears at
once as a relatively stable group of unlocalized sensory contents or contents of feeling, and as the apparent controller
of the train of associated ideas, impulses, and acts of attention or of choice. Of course these two aspects of the self
are closely related. It is the associative potency of the
ruling feelings and interests that most secures the fact and
the sense of inner self-control. But meanwhile the self also
seems, or may seem, to its possessor, much larger than any

group of facts or of functions now present. One notoriously regards the present self as only the representative of a self which has been present, in the remembered past of our lives, and which will be present in the expected future to which we look forward. Nor does self-consciousness usually cease with this view. The characters, attributes, functions, or other organic constituents of the self commonly extend, from our own point of view, decidedly beyond anything that can be directly presented in any series of our isolated inner experiences, however extended. When one is vain, one's self-consciousness involves the notion that one's self really exists, in some way or other, for the thoughts and estimates of others, and is at least worthy, if not the possessor, of their praise or of their envy. When one feels guilty, one does not and cannot abstract from the conceived presence of one's self in and for the experience of a real or ideal judge of one's guilt. In all such cases the self of self-consciousness thus appears as something that it would not and could not be were there not others in the world to behold, or to estimate it, to be led or otherwise influenced by it, or to appeal to it. It is now from such points of view that the self of self-consciousness comes, in the end, to get form as a being who takes himself to have a social position, an office, a profession—in brief, a vast group of functions without which the self would appear itself to be, relatively speaking, a mere cipher, while these functions are at once regarded as organically joined to the self, and centered in it, and, nevertheless, are unintelligible unless one goes beyond one's private consciousness, and takes account of the ideas and estimates of other people.

Every normal man thus knows what it means to be a person with a social position, or a dignity, or a place in the world, or a character, a person vain of himself, or ashamed of himself, or socially confident or timid about himself, or otherwise disposed to view himself either as others seem to view him, or as he fancies that they ought to view him, or as he has faith that God views him. And such a view of one's self cannot be satisfied with any group of inner facts, however extensive, as containing within it the whole of one's ego. This view conceives the office, calling, dignity, worth, position, as at once a possession, or a real aspect, of the self, and as a possession or an aspect that would vanish from the world were not the self conceived as existing for others besides itself, in other words, were not the self conceived as having an exterior as well as interior form of existence.

The self of normal self-consciousness, then, is felt at any moment as this relatively stable group of inner states; it is also felt or conceived as the supposed spontaneous controller of the general or of the principal current of successive conscious states; it is remembered or expected as the past or future self, which is taken to be somehow more or less precisely the same as the present self; and finally, it is viewed as having a curious collection of exterior functions that involve its actual value, potency, prowess, reputation, or office, in its external social relations to other actual or ideal selves, e. g., to its neighbors, to humanity at large, or, in case one's faith extends so far, to God.

And, now, just as the immediate self of the mass of inner sensations and feelings can vary, or just as the self of the sense of self-control can be more or less pathologically altered; so too the identical or persistent self of memory can be confused, divided, or lost, in morbid conditions; and so too finally, the self of the social type of self-consciousness is subject to very familiar forms of diseased variation. The social self above all can come to be the object of a morbidly depressed or exalted inner estimate. One's social prowess, position, office and other relations, both to God and to man, can be conceived in the most extravagantly false fashions. And furthermore, as I wish at once to point out, the most

13

noteworthy alterations of self-consciousness, in insanities involving delusions of suspicion, of persecution and of grandeur, appear upon their very surface as pathological variations of the social aspect of self-consciousness. Note at once the possible significance of this fact. However you explain delusions of guilt, of suspicion, of persecution and of grandeur, however much you refer their source to altered sensory or emotional states, they stand before you, when once they are well developed, as variations of the patient's habits of estimating his relations to other selves. They involve, then, *maladies of the social consciousness.* The theoretical significance of this fact surely seems worthy of a closer consideration than it customarily receives.

Since the psychologist, as such, can afford to be quite indifferent to the question whether any real being, to be called an Ego, exists, or not, and since he is therefore still less interested in the philosophical problem as to the forms of being which a real Ego can possess, in case it exists—I am here very little concerned to answer one question which these latest considerations may have already suggested to some of you. I mean the question whether an Ego really can possess that equivocal sort of exterior existence, outside of its own train of conscious experience, which, as we have seen, the social sort of self-consciousness seems to attribute to the self. When I feel humble or exalted, abased or proud, guilty or just, or when I say, " I am in this social office or position," I seem to myself as one whose actual nature and functions include more facts than can ever be crowded into my own consciousness. For unless I believe in my real relations to my neighbors or to God, and conceive those relations as somehow a part of myself, I should have no material out of which to weave my notion of my rank, or my duties, and of my external importance. But whether this idea of myself is defensible or not, from a philosophical point of view, is far from us here. It is enough for us that a man common-

ly has just such a view as to his own nature, and that pathological variations of such a view are familiar and important
phenomena.

II.

In the foregoing sketch, I have been simply reporting
familiar psychological phenomena. That our human self-
consciousness involves all these various elements, is, one
may say, agreed. The problem is, how have all these elements come thus to hang together ? And so we next have
to attack the central problem just mentioned, i. e., we have
to ask, in a purely psychological sense : How does this elaborate mental product called self-consciousness get formed
out of these numerous elements and why, when once formed,
is it so variable, and, finally, why, when it varies, does it
vary in the directions so frequently reported ?

It is here that our theoretical knowledge is at present
so poor. The collection of observed facts is, to be sure, at
present, considerable. Readers of Ribot's book on the Diseases of Personality know of the general types of varying
self-consciousness to which attention has been most attracted. Loss of the sense of personality ; or again, the
delusion that one is dead, or is lost, or is an automaton ; or
the feeling or idea that there is a foreign or other self
within one ; or the attribution of one's own thoughts, or
acts, to another and wholly external person or persons ; or
the alternation or the apparently actual multiplication of
one's own personality ; or the refusal to regard one's present
self as identical with one's past self : such are some of the
variations to which self-consciousness is subject, in addition
to the before-mentioned alterations of the obviously social
type of self-consciousness. But when we ask why any of
these alterations takes place, we have so far only one unquestionable, but theoretically inadequate answer, viz. : In
all such cases there are alterations of the common sensibility,
or of the memory, or of both. Now one sees, without doubt,

that self-consciousness involves the common sensibility, in the sense before indicated. One sees then that if this core of normally stable, vaguely localized sensory conditions and feelings gets altered, one's notion of one's self may also naturally change. And, not to leave the limits of ordinary experience, one knows and understands what it means to say, when these central masses of feeling do more or less change : " I feel queer ; I feel altered ; I am no longer quite myself ; I am not my old self." By a little stretch of imagination one can also understand such a delusion as " I am made of glass," quite as well as one can understand any other delusion. For here our dreams help us to see our way, and we have only to suppose that a certain association of ideas, whereby a partial anæsthesia gets interpreted, becomes fixed, and exclusive, in order to see how the delusions as to bodily condition or constitution, present in a measure in all hypochondriacs, can assume such extreme forms. Just so too the mere assertion " I am lost," or " I am dead," is, on the face of it, just an insistent verbal statement, or at best an inner judgment whose exclusive presence in consciousness is due merely to morbid habit, and whose meaning or logical consequences we often need not suppose the patient to develop in any delusionally definite form at all. These phenomena involve, where they are alone, or are segregated from the rest of the patient's life, rather pathological simplifications of the contents of consciousness, morbid associations of sensations with simple groups of words or of ideas, than any other processes. So far, then, we see some light.

But now the case is otherwise when one says " There are two of me," and proceeds actively to develop the consequences of this inner variety of self. Here, to be sure, the phenomena of dreams, and of the commoner forms of transient delirium, as in fevers, bring this sort of doubleness within the remembered experience of very many persons ; and familiar moral and poetical statements about the two selves or more that dwell in one's breast, assimilate such experiences to those of normal people.   But one's conscious-ness, in such cases, throws little direct light upon how the phenomena arise.   Sometimes, to be sure, in delirium their basis is plainly hallucinatory, as when a fever patient sees himself, in bodily presence, standing at a distance, or lying in the bed.   But even then one wishes for more light as to the question whether and how such a tendency to patholog-ical duplication has any natural foundation in the under-stood habits of normal life.   This problem seems even the more insistent when one observes that the sense of the in-wardly doubled personality often arises without any obvious basis in hallucinations of the special senses.   But in such cases, our present theories often fall back again upon the variations of the common sensibility.   Yet here one fails to see how any easily conceivable alteration in the contents of the central core of the sensory self is by itself sufficient to explain a tendency to apperceive that self as double.   One does not doubt the existence, in such cases, of an altered common sensibility ; what one fails to follow is the link be-tween such alteration, and the new habits, of judgment, or of apperception, which tend to get formed upon this basis.

But I do not wish to burden you with a mere enumera-tion of problems, and I will not here further dwell upon the inadequacies of the current theories of the factors of self-consciousness, whether these theories lay stress upon the common sensibility, or upon the memory, as the principal factor in their explanations of the variations of the ego.   It is only necessary to show that, while both the common sen-sibility and the memory are certainly largely concerned in the constitution of the self, the problem of self-consciousness is not thus to be fully solved.   One must look to other fac-tors as well.   One has in fact only to remember that some large alterations of the common sensibility seem to involve

very little change of self-consciousness at all, in order to see
how complex the problem is.

And now, as to the real problem itself, it is surely one
relating to the origin, to the nature and to the variations, of
a certain important collection of mental habits. What are
these habits ? How do they arise ? I insist, a mere catalogue
of the contents of self-consciousness helps us little, unless we
can interpret the facts in terms of the known laws of habit.
For a man is self-conscious in so far as he has formed habits
of regarding, remembering, estimating, and guiding himself.
And now whenever these habits are in play, they all of them,
as I must next insist, have a common and noteworthy character.   If a man regards himself, as this individual Ego, he
always sets over against his Ego something else, viz. : some
particular object represented by a portion of his conscious
states, and known to him as his then present and interesting
non-Ego.   This psychological non-Ego, represented in one's
conscious states, is of course very seldom the universe, or
anything in the least abstract. And, for the rest, it is a very
varying non-Ego. And now, it is very significant that our
mental habits are such that the Ego of which one is conscious
varies with the particular non-Ego that one then and there
consciously seems to encounter. If I am in a fight, my consciously presented non-Ego is my idea of my opponent. Consequently, I am then conscious of myself as of somebody
fighting him.   If I am in love, my non-Ego is thought of as
my beloved, and my Self, however much the chord of it pretends, trembling, to pass in music out of sight, is the Self of
my passion. If I strut about in fancied dignity, my non-Ego
is the world of people who, as I fondly hope, are admiring
me.   Accordingly, I then exist, for myself, as the beheld of
all beholders, the model. If I sink in despair and self-abase-
ment, my non-Ego is the world of the conceived real or ideal
people whose imagined contempt interests, but overwhelms
me, and I exist for myself as the despised Ego, worthy of

their ill will.   When I speak, my non-Ego is the person or persons addressed, and my Ego is the speaker.   If I suddenly note that, though I talk, nobody marks me, both the non-Ego and my Ego dramatically change together in my consciousness.   These two contents of consciousness, then, are psychologically linked.   Alone, I am so far not myself. My consciousness of my Ego is a consciousness colored by my conceived relations to my endlessly changing consciousness of a non-Ego.   And notice, I speak here as little of any metaphysically real non-Ego as I speak of any metaphysically real Ego.   The whole question is here one of mental states and of the actual habits of their grouping, not of relative, nor yet of real existences outside of consciousness.   I point out merely the fact that, according as one chances to conceive thus or thus the non-Ego of his strongest current interest, even so, on the other hand, he conceives his Ego thus or thus, viz., as something related to this non-Ego, opposed to it, concerned in it, possessor of it, crushed by it, desirous of winning it, or however the play of habit and of interest makes the thing seem.   Here, I think, lies the real key to all the variations of Self-consciousness, whether their conditions involve the common sensibility or not.

The psychological problem of self-consciousness reduces itself, then, to the following form.   One must ask : How has one come to form all these habits of drawing a boundary, in one's consciousness, between mental states that represent a non-Ego, and mental states that clump themselves together into the central object called the Ego ?   One must also ask : Whence comes all this material for variation, whereby the content called the Ego shifts endlessly as the content called the non-Ego alters ?   And one must further inquire : How do the constitution and the variations of the Ego get that intimate relation to the sensations of the common sensibility upon which we have laid stress from the start ?

Now to all these questions, as I hold, the recent study of

childhood has tended to suggest at least a plausible answer. The substantial basis for the answer that I shall suggest has been reached, pretty independently, by my friend Professor Baldwin, of Princeton, and by myself. Professor Baldwin has given to some aspects of the matter, so far as concerns child life, a much fuller working out than I have done, both in his earlier papers and in his recently published book called Mental Development in the Child and the Race. But the application of these theoretical considerations to the study of the pathological variations of self-consciousness in the present paper is, I think, new.

The early intellectual life of the child is lost to us in obscurity, despite numerous recent observations. But we are clear that the infant, in the first months of life, has nothing that we should call self-consciousness. The first clear evidence that we get of the presence of a form of self-consciousness intelligible to us comes when the infant begins to be observantly imitative of the acts, and later of the words, of the people about it. In other words, the first Ego of the child's intelligible consciousness appears to be, in its own mind, set over against a non-Ego that, to the child, is made up of the perceived fascinating, and, to its feeling, more or less significant, deeds of the persons in its environment. From this time on, up to seven or eight years of age, any normal child remains persistently, although perhaps very selectively, imitative, of deeds, of habits, of games, of customs, and often of highly ideal and perhaps quite imaginary models, such as are suggested to it by fairy-stories and other such material. As one follows the growth of these imitative tendencies, from their initial and quite literal stages, through those stages of elaborate impersonation and of playful, originally colored, often enormously insistent games, in which the child follows all sorts of real and fantastic models, one is struck by the fact that any normal child leads, relatively speaking, two lives, one naïve, intensely egoistic from our point of view, but relatively free from any marked self-consciousness in the child's own mind, while his other life is the life in which he develops his conscious ideas and views of himself as a person. The relatively naïve life is the life of his childish appetites and passions; the relatively self-conscious life is the life of his imitations and dramatic impersonations, of his poses and devices, of his games, and of his proudly fantastic skill, and of the countless social habits and attitudes that spring up from this source. The two lives mingle and cross in all sorts of ways. But the child who merely eats, cries, and enjoys his physical well-being, is not just then self-conscious as is the child who plays horse, or hero, or doctor, or who carefully tries to follow a model as he draws, or to invent a trick as good as one that he has seen. The latter child, however, is essentially imitative, first of persons, then of ideas, then of the facts of the physical world as such. But the former child is simply the creature of natural impulses and passions, and would never come to self-consciousness, in our sense, if his life were not gradually moulded by the elaborate habits which the imitative child constantly introduces.

Now the psychological importance of imitation lies largely in the fact, that in so far as a child imitates, he gets ideas about the inner meaning or intent of the deeds that he imitates, and so gets acquainted with what he early finds to be the minds of other people. The child that repeats your words, slowly learns what they mean. The child that uses scissors, pencil, or other tools after you, learns, as he imitates, what cutting means, and what drawing, or other such doings. And as he thus learns, he gets presented to his own consciousness contents, which he regards as standing for those of your mind. The experienced interesting outcome of an imitated deed, is for the child the obvious meaning of that deed, for you, as you did it. But he does not get these contents—these glimpses of your meaning—he does not get

them, at first, very easily. He gets them by persistently
watching you, listening to you, playing with you, trying to
be like you—all activities that for him involve muscular sensations, emotional concerns, and still other variations of his
common sensibility. These efforts of his to grasp your meaning are marked and often delightful incidents of his consciousness. He returns over and over to his favorite games
with you. He encounters every time your meaning, and
he sets over against it those experiences of his own doings,
whereby he comes to participate in your meaning. Here
now the child always has present to him two sets of contents,
both fascinating, each setting the other off sharply by contrast, while the contrast itself establishes the boundary between them. The first set of contents are his perceptions of
your deeds, and his representation of your discovered meaning in these deeds. The second set of contents are his own
imitative acts themselves, as perceived by himself, these acts,
and his delights in them. The first set of contents depend,
upon you. The child feels them to be uncontrollable. As
perceptions, and as representations, these contents do not
get closely linked to the child's common sensibility. They
stand off as external although welcome intruders. On the
other hand, the other set of contents, the child's own newly
discovered powers, due to his imitation, are closely centred
about his common sensibility, are accompanied with all the
feelings which make up the sense of control, and get remembered, thenceforth, accordingly. The first set of contents
form the psychological non-Ego of this particular phase of
consciousness. The second set of contents form the psychological Ego corresponding thereto. One sees why the Ego-
part of this sort of consciousness includes the common
sensibility, and the sense of voluntary control, and why the
non-Ego here involves contents that are set off by the contrast as uncontrollable, and as not closely linked to the common sensibility. And it is in this contrast that the source

of true self-consciousness lies. We do not observe a given group of mental contents as such, unless they are marked off by contrast from other contents. One could have all the common sensibility you please, and all the feelings of voluntary control, without ever coming to take note of this totality of united or centralized mental contents as such, and as clearly different from the rest of one's field of consciousness. Even now we all of us tend to lose clear self-consciousness so soon as we get absorbed in any activity, such as rowing, hill-climbing, singing, whistling, looking about us at natural scenery—any activity I say, whose object does not, by the sharp contrast between its own external meaning and our efforts, call our attention to our specific relation to some non-Ego. Yet in lonely rowing and hill-climbing the common sensibility is as richly present as it is in many of our most watchfully self-conscious states. On the other hand, when I work hard to make my meaning clear to another man, or to make out what he means, I am self-conscious, just in so far as I contrast my idea of his ways and thoughts, with my own effort to conform to his ways and thoughts. And just such an effort, just such a contrast, seems to mediate the earliest self-consciousness of the imitative child, and to secure the tendency of the self to be built up about the common sensibility, while the not self gets sundered therefrom. So then one sees the rule : If one is keenly self-conscious, the common sensibility must be central. But, on the other hand, one may have a rich common sensibility without any keen self-consciousness. It is the contrast of Ego and non-Ego that is essential to self-consciousness.

But of course the child's relations to the varying non-Ego of consciousness do not remain merely imitative. When once he has other minds in his world, the function whose essence is the contrast between his conceptions of these minds and his view of his own response to them, can take as many forms as his natural instincts determine. His naïve life of appetites gets gradually infected by his conscious relations to other people. He wants good things, and perhaps must feign affection or show politeness, or invent some other social device, to get what he wants. Here again is an activity depending upon and bringing to light, the contrast between his own intention, and the conceived or perceived personal traits and whims to which he conforms his little skill. He learns to converse, and gets a new form of the contrast between the sayings of others (which he interprets by listening), and his own ideas and meanings. He reaches the questioning age, and now he systematically peers into the minds of others as into an endlessly wealthy non Ego, in whose presence he is by contrast self-conscious as an inquirer. Here, every time one has the essential element of contrast upon which all self-consciousness depends. Argument and quarreling later involve similar contrasts. As to the external physical world—what the child shall most care for in that, is largely determined for him by his social relations. Whatever habit he has acquired by social imitation, he can, therefore, in the end, apply to things as well as to persons. As a fact he is notoriously often animistic, directly transferring social habits to physical relations, and regarding things as alive. And here again he becomes self-conscious, by contrasting his own activities with the conceived natures and meanings of external things. I do not at all suppose that the child regards all natural things in an animistic way ; but I am of opinion, for reasons which I have set forth elsewhere, that our whole tendency to distinguish as sharply, as we all now do, between the self and the external physical world, is a secondary tendency, due in the child's case, to social influences. It is language, it is the accounts that people give to us of things, it is the socially acquired questioning habit—it is such things that extend the contrast between Ego and non-Ego, at first mainly a social contrast, to the relations between one's own mind and one's physical environment. Even now, as I just pointed out, if we forget that nature is full of thinkable mysteries, of meanings, of laws, of other ideal contents whose significance we do not comprehend—if we forget this, and lapse into mere busy and absorbing physical experience, as when climbing hills alone, or rowing, or cheerily whistling as we walk, we forget to be self-conscious, just because we lose sight of the sharper contrasts of Ego and non-Ego.

III.

But, to return to the explicitly social relations, there is still another factor to note in our early relations to our conceived social non-Ego. And this is the fact that, by our instinctive mental constitution as moulded by our social habits, we are early subject to a vast number of more or less secondary emotions, each one of which involves large alterations of the common sensibility, while all of these particular emotions arise under circumstances which make explicit the contrast between one's self, and one's idea of one's fellow's mind. Such emotions we get as children when people praise us, blame us, caress us, call us pet names, stare at us, call us by name, ask us questions, and otherwise appeal to us in noteworthy ways. Such emotions too we get again, in novel forms, in youth, when the subtle coloring of the emotions of sex begins to pervade our whole social life. Such emotions are shame, love, anger, pride, delight in our own bodily seeming as displayed before others, thrills of social expectation, fears of appearing ill in the eyes of others. Such emotions involve blushing, weeping, laughter, inner glow, visceral sensations of the most various kinds, and feelings of the instinctive muscular tensions related to our countless expressive social deeds. These experiences are, however, aroused by situations all of which essentially involve the aforesaid contrast between our own ideas, wishes, or meanings, and the conceived states of other minds.

Hence these emotional states associate themselves, as variations of the common sensibility, first, with social situations, i. e., with cases where Ego and non-Ego are sharply contrasted ; and then especially with the Ego-member of the relation of contrast. And so, altogether by the force of habit, these emotions, which if primarily aroused would be mere content, belonging neither to Ego nor to non-Ego, come to be the specific emotions of self-consciousness, so that now whenever we have just these emotions, from any cause whatever, we are at once keenly self-conscious—and that merely because the emotions in question faintly or keenly suggest particular social situations. Emotions that have had no such constant relation to social situations, involve no such marked states of self-consciousness. Fear of physical dangers tends to diminish our self-consciousness ; shame intensifies it. Yet keen physical fear, as the more primitive emotion, involves vaster commotions of the common sensibility than does shame. Were then the marked presence or variation of the common sensibility in consciousness the sole and sufficient cause of the presence or of the variation of one's immediate or sensory Ego, physical terror would make one more self-conscious than does shame. But panic fear, in its intensest conscious forms, involves rather a destruction than a positive alteration of self-consciousness ; while the most abject shame grows the more intensely self-conscious as it gets the more marked. Why ? Because shame, habitually associated only with social situations, suggests them even where it is pathological and is not due to them ; and so it brings to consciousness the contrast of Ego and non-Ego.

Thus, then, it is that I propose to explain what the current theories of self-consciousness usually seem unable to deal with, viz., the before-mentioned fact that certain pathological variations of the common sensibility profoundly alter the tone or constitution of a patient's self-consciousness, while others, equally intimate and vast, either leave self-consciousness relatively intact, or simply put it wholly out of sight without first tampering with its integrity. When a man has the colic he does not say, "My Ego is deranged." His account of the case is far less metaphysical. But when, as in the depression after the grippe, he has certain very much dimmer and more subtle alterations of the common sensibility, he may complain of precisely such a sense of alienation from himself. Why? Well, as I should say, the colic suggests no social situation; the vague depression after the grippe may dimly suggest, by habit, situations of social failure, or confusion, or powerlessness, such as, from sensitive childhood until now, have played their part in one's life. The suggestion may be very faint, and utterly abstract. No particular failure, no special case of social helplessness, comes to mind. But our nascent associations can be present in all degrees of faintness; and here I maintain are associations dimly involving social contrasts between Ego and non-Ego. Here, then, are conditions for the function of self-consciousness.

Since the emotional alteration of the common sensibility has thus the most various habitual relations, now with our unsocial physical states as such, now with social activities, one sees how it is possible for a nervous sufferer to say, on one day, that he personally feels his very being wrecked, and his self-hood lost or degraded, while on another day he may simply declare that he suffers keenly, but regards the affair as a mere physical infliction, external to his central self-hood. In the physical sufferings of sensitive women this shifting of the enemy's ground from the region of the physical or psychical pain felt as a mere brute fact, hateful but still bearable, to the region where the sufferer complains of an intolerable loss of self-possession, is notoriously a common and, to the sufferer herself, a puzzling incident. Both times the common sensibility is deeply affected, often in

ways not subjectively localizable; the difference, I think,
must be due to the nascent associations of the common sensibility now with ideas of social situations, now with ideas of
unsocial bodily events.   There are some chronic neurasthenic sufferers who, despite headaches, spinal pains, and other
distorted sensations innumerable, preserve for years a marvellous self-possession in face of their disorder ; very many
other such nervous sufferers, of the same general type, are
throughout self-consciously cowardly and abject.   One cannot assert that the latter class are more deranged in common
sensibility than are the former.   But many a neurasthenic
man has really little to complain of, *except* the unspeakable
wretchedness of his deranged self-consciousness.   How can
one explain such phenomena without resorting to the principles of habit and association ?   The social habits, however,
of the type now defined, at once furnish a *vera causa* for the
interpretation of some sensory disturbances as alterations of
self-consciousness, while other disturbances, equally great
and vague, get interpreted by the sufferer as merely external
events.   To be sure we cannot yet give an exhaustive classification of the variations of the common sensibility into
those closely associated with social situations, and those not
associated, or but slightly associated, yet the contrast of
physical fear and of shame has already shown us that such
a classification might, with care, be more or less worked out.
We know, for instance, that the sexually tinged emotions
normally have very complex social associations.   Consequently, we may expect to find self-consciousness especially
deranged in disorders involving the sexual functions.   This
expectation seems to be abundantly verified, even in ordinary
cases of disorder, such as the teacher of youth may sometimes see as well as the doctor ; and if one wants more verification, one may get it at will from the monumental records
that fill Krafft-Ebing's too well-known and ghastly book.
On the other hand, a sufferer from the emotional states

accompanying ordinary physical exhaustion, or from some
forms even of grief, or from a severe cold that does not give
the form of depression now associated with the grip, or from
some forms of even violent headache, often wonders how
much pain and emotional alteration he can endure without
any proportionate alteration of self-consciousness. And
these states are precisely such forms of consciousness as
are not so closely associated with social situations. Finally,
the emotions connected with laughter furnish an almost perfect natural experiment for our purpose. There are three
principal sorts of laughter : the laughter of mere physical
gleefulness, such as appears much in children, less in adults;
the laughter of scorn, and the laughter of the sense of humor. The first is not an especially self-conscious affair ; but
the laughter of scorn and of a sense of humor are both of
them always keenly self-conscious, involving what Hobbes
called "sudden glory in him that laugheth." The emotions of the two latter types involve social situations, present or suggested. I shall find no time to point out at any
length the application of the foregoing analysis to the study
of the associative alterations of the socially tinged self-consciousness in true melancholia, in mania, or in the exaltation of general paralysis. But the mention of such alteration of the self brings us at once to the next and final stage
of our inquiry.

IV.

I have so far spoken of self-consciousness as it appears
in more or less explicitly social relations. But, one may
reply, " Are we not, at pleasure, self-conscious when we are
quite alone ? Does not one reflect, does not one judge one's
self ? Is lonely meditation free from self-consciousness ?
Is not conscience a self-conscious affair ? And yet in such
cases does one contrast an Ego with any literal non-Ego ?
In such processes is not the Ego explicitly related to just
the Ego, alone by itself ? And are there not, in the phe-

14

nomena of insanity, many alterations of this sort of purely internal self-consciousness?" I reply at once that my theory is precisely *that habits once acquired in social intercourse can and do hold over when we are alone, and can then apply within the content of one's own mind.* The transition is simple. First, I can dramatically remember my actually past imitative deeds, my quarrels, my successful social feats, my chagrins, my questionings, my criticisms of others, and the bearings of others towards me. In all such cases I am self-conscious over again in memory, by virtue of our now familiar contrast-effect. Further, as just seen, my emotions can vaguely suggest social situations indefinite in character to any degree. By coalescence, a vast group of social habits of judging others, and of feeling myself judged by them, can get woven into a complex product such as is now my conscience. Conscience is a well-knit system of socially acquired habits of estimating acts—a system so constituted as to be easily aroused into conscious presence by the coming of the idea of any hesitantly conceived act. If conscience is aroused in the presence of such a hesitant desire to act, one has, purely as a matter of social habit, a disposition to have present both the tendency to the action, and the disposition to judge it, standing to one another in the now familiar relation of Ego and non-Ego. Which one of them appears as the Ego, which the non-Ego, depends upon which most gets possession, in the field of consciousness, of the common sensibility. If the tendency to the estimated act is a passionate tendency, a vigorous temptation, and if the conscientious judgment is a coldly intellectual affair, then the situation dimly reminds me of cases where other people, authoritative and dignified rather than pleasing, have reproved my wishes. Conscience is then the colder non-Ego, the voice of humanity, or of God. My common sensibility merges with my passion. The reproof perhaps shames me; yet I want to have my way; only that other, that authoritative inner non-Ego, my conscience, will not let me go free.   But if, on the other hand, the conceived act is less keenly desired, and if my conscientious plans are just now either fervently enthusiastic or sternly resolute in my mind, then it is my conscience which merges with my common sensibility, and I myself am now, in presence of the conceived act, as if judging another.   I feel then secure in my righteousness, and I look with disdain upon that which would tempt me if I were weaker, but which now is a mere non-Ego.   It is in a similar fashion, by a dramatic imitation not of actual, but of abstractly possible social relations, that I can question myself, and wait for an answer, can reflect upon my own meaning, can admire myself, love myself, hate myself, laugh at myself, in short do or suffer in presence of my own states and processes whatever social life has taught me to do or to suffer in presence of the states and processes of others.   In every such case the central Ego is so much of my conscious process as tends more to merge with the common sensibility.   My inner, but more peripheral, relative non-Ego is so much of my conscious process as tends more to resemble, in interest, in general tone, or in uncontrollable unexpectedness, the experiences which, in ordinary social life, are due to other people.   Yet since all these inner contrasts are constantly corrected by my habits of external perception and of memory, which remind me all the while of a literal non-Ego outside of all these processes, this inner sundering normally remains only, as Professor Ladd has called it, dramatic—a sort of metaphor, which I can correct at pleasure, saying at any moment, "but all this is merely Ego, after all.   The real non-Ego is the world of live other people yonder."

Thus the normal inner life of reflection, of conscience, of meditation, and of the so-called "spiritual Ego" in general, is simply, in us human beings, an imitation, a brief abstract and epitome, of our literal social life.   We have no habits of self-consciousness which are not derived from social habits, counterparts thereof. Where the analogy of our relations to our fellows ceases, reflection ceases also. And this is precisely what constitutes the limitation of our reflective processes in philosophy and in psychology.

But surely, if this summarizes the conditions of our normal self-consciousness, when we are thinking alone, it also gives room for indefinitely numerous abnormal variations. Suppose that there appear in the conscious field hallucinations of the muscular sense, of the sort so well described in Cramer's noted monograph. Let these be motor speech hallucinations. Then the patient may observe the puzzling phenomenon that, whenever he thinks, there is some mysterious tendency present that aims to objectify his thoughts, in spoken words. Somebody or something either takes his own thoughts away from him and speaks them, or forces him, willy-nilly, to speak them himself. The thoughts are his own. The sounding of them forth, in this way, is not his. His thoughts run off his tongue, get spoken in his stomach, creak out in his shoes as he walks, are mockingly echoed or in the end commented upon by another power. This other power, this stealing of his thoughts, involves of course a deep disturbance of his self-consciousness, which tends gradually to pass over into a regular system of delusions. Yet what does the process mean ? It means, at first, merely the appearance of uncontrollable elements of consciousness, which by virtue of the habits connected with the uncontrollable in general cannot get merged in the common sensibility, and which are yet in a problematic and painfully intimate relation to what he does recognize as his own. This foreign power need not for a good while behave *enough* like the true voice of another to become a genuine hallucinatory comrade or enemy, as it would do and does if the patient hears his voices without of himself recognizing their close relation to his stream of thought. But in this uncontrollable hallucinatory thinking aloud there is enough suggestion of the foreign to make the patient feel that his own thoughts are getting somehow estranged from him. That these are his own thoughts he at first knows, by virtue of the general contrasts between real Ego and real non-Ego still present to him. That they are getting estranged he knows, for that is to any one a relative non-Ego which behaves more or less as one's original social non-Ego, one's fellow in society, behaves. His behaviour is relatively uncontrollable; and so is here that of the patient's thoughts.

Or again, suppose that one's depressed emotional condition, as in melancholia, or at the outset of a delirium of suspicion or of persecution, contains emotions resembling the normal emotions of conscientious guilt, or the feeling of social dread. Then these feelings tend to assimilate in one's actual surroundings, or in one's memories, data which suggest, to one patient an actually believed social condemnation of his deeds, or an actual judgment of his inner conscience passed upon his sinfulness, while to another patient his own sorts of emotion suggest an especially hostile scrutiny of his appearance by the passers-by, or an inner sense that he must hide from possible scrutiny. On the other hand, feelings quite the reverse of these suggest to the exalted general paralytic whatever remembered or fancied social relations, expressing his vast powers. the fragments of left-over social habits which still survive in his chaos permit him, in passing, to express.

Or, once more, another patient has present to consciousness two or more streams of feelings, impulses, thoughts, which are sharply contrasted with one another, while the portions of each stream more or less hang together, by virtue of common contents or tone. All of these streams belong to his general Ego—this he recognizes by the normal contrast with the actual external world. But meanwhile they have their inner contrast, which is no longer, like the just mentioned contrasts in normal consciousness, a source of merely dramatic metaphor. This abnormal contrast is intense, uncontrollable, continuous. Now let the reflections, or the context of these streams be such as in any fashion to remind the patient of any social relation, contest, rivalry, quarrel, criticism, pity, questioning, discussion ; and then the patient can only say : " There are in me two or more selves, I am divided." If one of the streams involves more of the common sensibility than does the others, or more of the sense of control, the patient may speak of the less favored streams as other selves, or as the "Other Fellow" without having any full-fledged delusion of a real outside oppressor. And in all this there will be mere associations of ideas, mere socially acquired habits—no new mysteries of self-hood whatever.

I conclude with a summary of the main theses of the foregoing paper.

1. Self-conscious functions are all of them, in their finite, human, and primary aspect, social functions, due to the habits of human intercourse. They involve the presentation of some contrast between Ego and non-Ego. This psychological contrast is primarily that between the subject's own conscious act, idea, intent, or other experience, and an expereince which is regarded by him as representing the state of another's mind. By means of habits gradually acquired, this contrast early comes to be extended to include that between one's inner states and the represented realities which make up the physical world.

2. In the primary cases of contrast between Ego and non-Ego, the former—the Ego—always includes (for reasons which have been explained in the foregoing) the present modifications of the common sensibility, and the feelings of the sense of control, where these are present at all. The latter, the psychological non-Ego, is a colder,

a more localized, and less controllable mass of mental contents.

3. Emotional states, and in general all those modifications of the common sensibility which uniformly accompany any of our social reflexes, become, by association, linked with our memories and ideas of social situations, and cannot be repeated without more or less clearly or vaguely reminding us of our social situations in an individual or in a summary form.

4. When social situations involving particular contrasts of Ego and non-Ego are remembered or imagined, we become self-conscious in memory, or in idea. When emotions, associated by old habit with social situations, dimly or summarily suggest such situations, with their accompanying contrast of Ego and non-Ego, our self-consciousness gets colored accordingly. Finally, when the varied contents of our isolated consciousness involve in any way, as they pass, contrasts which either remind us of the social contrast between Ego and non-Ego, or excite us to acts involving social habit, such as questioning, or internal speech, we become reflectively self-conscious, even when quite alone with our own states.

5. The anomalies of self-consciouness are (1) primary alterations of the common sensibility, or of the other contents of passing consciousness, such as dimly or clearly suggest anomalous social situations, contrasts and functions ; or else they are (2) primary anomalies in one's social habits themselves. The two forms can be of course to any degree combined.

SELF-CONSCIOUSNESS, SOCIAL CONSCIOUS-NESS AND NATURE.

THE ultimate purpose of the present paper is to reach, and, in closing, to sketch some views as to the relation of Man to Nature. By way of introduction, I must first define the place of my inquiry in the general catalogue of philosophical questions, and must then state the theses that I mean to defend.

There are two great divisions of philosophy—theoretical and practical. The present paper concerns itself with a matter belonging to theoretical philosophy. Within the range of theoretical philosophy, however, one may distinguish between the discussion of the ultimate problems of knowledge and of truth, and the treatment of the more special theoretical problems suggested by our human experience. General Epistemology and general Metaphysics have to do with what can be made out about the deepest nature of our knowledge and the final constitution of the universe. But there are, within the scope of theoretical philosophy, other problems relating to the constitution of our finite world—problems which are often grouped together as the questions of special metaphysics, or of the Philosophy of Nature—a doctrine to which has also sometimes been given the name Cosmology. The problems of Cosmology

---

* A paper read before the Philosophical Club of Brown University, May 23, 1895, and later considerably enlarged and supplemented.

are such as the questions : What is the truth behind what we mortals call Nature, or the physical world ? What are finite minds, and how are they related to physical reality ? What, if any, is the philosophical interpretation to be given to the doctrine of Evolution ?

Now the present paper, as I just said, is an inquiry within the region of theoretical philosophy. Within that region my investigation, however, here concerns itself only secondarily with the ultimate problems of general metaphysics. I shall chiefly aim to reach, before I close, light as to a certain problem of philosophical cosmology. Here about us, as we all admit, whatever our ultimate metaphysical views, is the natural world, the world that appears to our senses—a world manifesting some sort of finite, and obviously, as we mortals see it, some sort of highly fragmentary truth. Now man, as we phenomenally know him, appears as a part of nature, a product of nature, a being whose destinies seem to be the sport of purely physical laws. The problem that this paper aims in the end to approach is : What is the meaning of this phenomenal relation of man to nature ?

Now, as I need not say, a real answer to this question must lead us past, if not through, the realms of the most ultimate and general sort of metaphysical inquiry. Nor will this paper wholly escape the responsibility of considering to some extent, as we proceed, such ultimate matters. But on the other hand, all philosophical students are used to the fragmentary, and I shall not here attempt completeness. Such general metaphysical views as come in sight in this paper will remain, after all, of rather secondary importance. I shall attempt only to clear some of the way that leads from the study of man as we ordinarily know him towards the regions where general philosophy attempts to grapple with the ultimate issues of life, and with the rational constitution of the universe.

The relation of man to nature—this, then, is our immediate topic. But why, you may ask, if such is the purpose of this paper, have I chosen my actual title? Why does a study of the relations of Self-consciousness and Social Consciousness seem adapted to throw light on the cosmological problem of the relation of human beings to natural processes? To this preliminary question let us at once address ourselves.

I.

The philosophical examination of man's social consciousness has been left, rather too exclusively, in the hands of the students of ethics. Even the psychologists, until very recently, have paid a very inadequate attention to the distinctively social aspects of their science. It is far too customary, in consequence, for the ethical philosophers themselves to begin their study of the duties of man with a very abstract view of the nature of the social consciousness, and of its original relations to our self-consciousness. We hear nowadays, for instance, in popular philosophy, a great deal about the supposed primal and natural conflict between Egoism and Altruism. Egoism, so we are told, is the original human tendency—the natural and innate bias of any one of us mortals. And it is so because, as soon as one becomes self-conscious, i. e., aware of one's Ego, one finds one's self, as an animal, instinctively selfish. The practical tendency of the self-preserving animal organism, translated into the terms of self-consciousness, becomes deliberate Egoism. Hence the moral problem is to make a man altruistic. The philosophical problem of ethics, on the other hand, is to show a man why he ought to be altruistic, i. e., why Egoism, which is naturally prior and apparently self-evident, ought rationally to be subordinated, upon reflection, to its derived and slowly acquired natural opponent, Altruism.

But now, I insist that, as a fact, this far too customary notion of a natural and fatal opposition between self-consciousness, Egoism, and our socially determined and derived Altruism, is also far too falsely abstract a notion. There are evil tendencies in plenty in human nature, and common sense has a very wholesome meaning in mind when it condemns our natural selfishness. But when one defines in philosophical terms our evil tendencies, or undertakes to analyse in an ultimate sense what common sense knows as our selfishness, one does ill if one merely substitutes abstract distinctions for our concrete and passionate life-conflicts. As a fact, the abstract opposition, Ego and Alter, or Egoism and Altruism, ill suggests the meaning of the opposed ethical aims that struggle in us. This whole customary popular and philosophical opposition between a man's self-consciousness, as if it were something primitive and lonely, and his social consciousness, as if that were something acquired, apart from his self-consciousness, through intercourse with his fellows, is false to human nature. As a fact, a man becomes self-conscious only in the most intimate connection with the growth of his social consciousness. These two forms of consciousness are not separable and opposed regions of a man's life; they are thoroughly interdependent. I am dependent on my fellows, not only physically, but to the very core of my conscious self-hood, not only for what, physically speaking, I am, but for what I take myself to be. Take away the Alter from consciousness, and the conscious Ego, so far as in this world we know it, languishes, and languishing dies, whatever may become of the organism in whose fortunes this Ego, while it is known to persist, seems to be involved. Hence, I am not first self-conscious, and then secondarily conscious of my fellow. On the contrary, I am conscious of myself, on the whole, as in relation to some real or ideal fellow, and apart from my consciousness of my fellows I have only secondary and derived states and habits of self-consciousness. I cannot really will to preserve the Ego,

then—this derived conscious creature of the habits of my
social consciousness; I cannot really will to preserve the
Ego, without also willing to preserve and to defend some
sort of Alter, and some sort of relation to my fellow who is
this Alter, and upon whom my conscious Ego depends for
its very life. It is only in abstraction that I can be merely
egoistic. In the concrete case I can only be egoistic by
being also voluntarily altruistic, however base may be the
sort of Altruism that I chance to prefer. I can aim, for
instance, to be a political " boss." That appears to be a very
egoistic aim. But the political " boss " exists by the suf-
frages of interested people, and must aim at their conscious,
even if illusory, sense of advantage in so far as he wills them
to be sincerely interested. I can will to be a flattering demagogue, admired for vain show by a crowd of fools. The end
is selfish ; but it also involves wishing to be agreeable in the
eyes of many people ; and even a saint might on occasion
wisely include so much of the demagogue's aim in his own
vastly different context of voluntary life. The tyrant wills
the lives and even the limited good fortune of his subjects,
for without powerful and numerous and even devoted subjects he would be no tyrant. The master wills his slave's
preservation, even in willing to preserve his own mastery.
Even the thief or the defaulter wills that the hoarding of
valuable property should be on the average sufficiently ad-
vantageous to others to make them willing and careful to
provide him with the wherewithal to win his thief's liveli-
hood. Even the murderer, although he directly aims to
destroy his fellow, does so, in general, and whenever the
act is deliberate and intelligent, for a social end—honor,
property, power—all of them ends which involve willing
the preservation, and even the prosperity, of many social
relations involving others than the murderer himself.
There is, then, much bad Altruism in the world, much base.
wishing of social relations which do involve the preserva-

tion, and even the relative private advantage of others besides the evil-doer. But bad Altruism is not mere Egoism, nor is it identical with a lower animal's unconsciously naïve selfishness. The mere instincts of the self-preservation of this organism have to be far transcended before one can become consciously egoistic. Vanity, pride, love of social power, the greed of mastery, covetousness, oppression —all these are tendencies that, just in so far as they are conscious and deliberate, involve not only Egoism, i. e., the love of the advantage of this individual, but also some more or less evil form of Altruism—the love of the preservation, and often of a certain limited advantage, of those of one's fellows who form the necessary other term of the social relation which satisfies one's vanity, one's greed, or one's love of power. In brief, speaking ethically, you cannot consciously be merely egoistic. For you, as a man, exist only in human relations. Your aims have to be more or less social, just so far as you clearly define them. The ethical problem is not: Shall I aim to preserve social relations ? but: What social relations shall I aim to preserve ?

But to return from these illustrations to the general topic : my first point on this occasion is that, just as there is no conscious Egoism without some distinctly social reference, so there is, on the whole, in us men, no self-consciousness apart from some more or less derived form of the social consciousness. I am I in relation to some sort of a non-Ego. And, as a fact, the non-Ego that I am accustomed to deal with when I think and act, is primarily some real or ideal finite fellow-being, in actual or possible social relations with me, and this social non-Ego, real or ideal, is only secondarily to be turned into anything else, as, for example, into a natural object that I regard as a mere dead thing. And I have dwelt upon these facts here for the sake of first introducing a matter towards whose final definition the whole of the following argu-

ment is to tend, viz., the assertion that what you and I mean
by Nature is, as a finite reality, something whose very conception we have actually derived from our social relations
with one another; so that, as we shall see, to believe that
there really exists a finite reality called Nature, is of necessity, when you rightly analyze the facts, to believe that
there is, in the real universe, an extra-human, but finite
conscious life, manifesting its presence to us by means substantially similar to those whereby we have become assured
of the presence of the inner life of our human fellows. As
it is not true that we are primarily and in unsocial abstraction merely egoistic, just so it is not true that we primarily
know merely our own inner life as individuals, apart from
an essentially social contrast with other minds. While it
is true, as all idealistic analysis has affirmed, that the object
of knowledge is precisely what it is known as being, it is not
true that you and I ever know our own individual inner
world of objects, without contrasting these objects with
others that we regard as present to some sort of conscious
life beyond our own. But primarily we learn to contrast
our own inner life with what we regard as the inner life
of our fellows in human society. It is by virtue of this
very contrast of our own inner life with a finite conscious
life beyond our own, viz., that of our human fellows, that
we become self-conscious. When later, for reasons that I
shall soon define, we learn to oppose to ourselves as finite
knowers, a world of relatively independent natural objects,
which we conceive as existent apart from any human insight, all the categories in terms of which we can learn to
think of these nature-objects are categories derived from
our social experience, and modified, but not really transformed, to suit the peculiar behavior of the relatively unsocial beings whose existence our experience seems to indicate to us in nature. Our relations with nature are thus
such as involve a more or less social contrast between our

life and the life of nature. And upon this principle every philosophy of nature must rest.

II.

I have begun our research, as you see, by some decidedly general and positive assertions. I must next try to show you more precisely and more in detail what these assertions mean, and why I find myself obliged to hold them.

The theses of the present paper, set forth in particular, run as follows:

1. A man is conscious of himself, as this finite being, only in so far as he contrasts himself, in a more or less definitely social way, with what he takes to be the life, and, in fact, the conscious life, of some other finite being—unless, indeed, he modifies his natural self-consciousness by contrasting his own life with the conceived fullness of the life of God. But except by virtue of some such contrast one cannot become self-conscious, and the result is that, as a matter of simple and necessary meaning, if any metaphysical argument is to prove than I am I, viz., this finite being, then at the same time this argument will prove that there is other conscious life besides mine. For otherwise my own finite life as this Ego cannot be defined or conceived.

2. The other conscious life that I must contrast with mine, in order to become self-conscious, is primarily, in our human relations, the life of my fellow in the social order. The original, as Hume would say, of the conception of a non-Ego is given to me in my social experiences. The real other being that I, as this finite Ego, can know is, at first, the human being. A man who had no social relations could form no clear conception of the reality of any finite non-Ego, and so could get no clear notion of the reality of the non-Ego now called Nature. Our conception of physical reality as such is secondary to our conception of our social fellow-beings, and is actually derived therefrom.

3. In consequence, any metaphysical proof that what we human beings mean by physical nature exists at all, must also be a proof that behind the phenomena of nature, just in so far as nature has finite reality, there is other conscious life, finite like our own, but unlike human life in so far as it, the nature-life, does not enter into closer social relations with us human beings. Yet all that manifests to us the external existence of nature, does so by virtue of a more or less definite appeal to the categories of our social consciousness.

4. But, as a fact, a probable proof, not amounting to philosophical demonstration, but capable of an indefinite degree of extension and illustration, does exist for the existence of a real finite world called the Realm of Nature. Hence, this very proof indicates that there is behind the phenomena of nature a world of finite life in more or less remote, but socially disposed relations to us human beings.

5. This proof of the finite reality of a conscious life behind the phenomena of nature is furnished by the whole mass of facts that in modern times have come to be conceived together as the basis of the doctrine of Evolution. And the doctrine of Evolution must in the end be interpreted in terms of this notion. In other words, the doctrine of Evolution seems to me the beginning of what promises to become a sort of universal Sociology, tending towards a definition of the social relations of the finite beings that together must make up the whole natural world, both human and extra-human.

6. Yet, on the other hand, the view of nature thus indicated ought to be very sharply distinguished, both from most traditional forms of Animism and of Hylozoism, and from the modern doctrine of Mind-Stuff. The view that I have in mind is not Schopenhauer's doctrine of the Will in Nature, nor Schelling's *Naturphilosophie*, nor von Hartmann's theory of the Unconscious as manifested in physical phenomena. From such theories mine is to be distinguished

by its genesis. It tries to avoid all premature dogmatism as to the inner aspect of the life of nature. But it conceives the possibility of a gradual and, as one may hope, a very significant enlargement, through the slow growth of human experience, of our insight into the inner meaning of nature's life, and into the essentially social constitution of the finite world. Meanwhile this conception of the natural order as a vast social organism, of which human society is only a part, is founded upon no merely animistic analogies between the physical phenomena and the phenomena of our organisms, but upon a decidedly deeper analysis of the very nature of our conception of other finite beings besides ourselves. And further, if my conception is true, it quite transforms certain important aspects of our whole notion of the meaning of Evolution. For the process of Evolution, as I now view it, becomes, not the history of the growth of life from the lifeless, but the history of the differentiation of one colony, as it were, of the universal society from the parent social order of the finite world in its wholeness.

Such, in some detail, are my theses. They need, of course, both analysis and defense. I will take them up in their order, dwelling perhaps too long upon the first thesis, upon which all the rest depends.

III.

First, then, as to the thesis that one is conscious of one's Ego only by virtue of the contrast between this Ego and some consciousness which one regards as external to one's finite self.

Speaking in psychological terms, one can say that our finite self-consciousness is no primitive possession at all, but is the hard-earned outcome of the contact between the being capable of becoming rational and the rationally-disposed world in which he slowly learns to move. A child becomes self-conscious only by degrees. When, as infant,

15

he cries for his food, or even, when more intelligent, shows lively disappointment if his expectations are not met, he is not yet self-conscious. When later, as older child, he struts about, playing soldier, or shyly hides from strangers, or asks endless questions merely to see what you will say, or quarrels with his fellows at play, or shrinks from reproof, or uses his little arts to win praise and caresses, he is self-conscious. These latter conditions are all of them such as involve a contrast between his own deeds and meanings and the deeds and meanings that he takes to be those of other conscious beings, whom, just *as* his conscious fellows, he loves or hates, fears or imitates, regards with social curiosity, or influences by devices adapted to what he thinks to be their states of mind. In brief, then, I should assert here, as a matter of psychology, what I have elsewhere worked out more at length, that a child is taught to be self-conscious just as he is taught everything else, by the social order that brings him up. Could he grow up alone with lifeless nature, there is nothing to indicate that he would become as self-conscious as is now a fairly educated cat.

But in the present paper I am dealing, not with psychology, but with certain aspects of the constitution of our knowledge. Let us consider briefly our self-consciousness, now that it has developed. It is a familiar paradox of idealistic analysis that we can have true knowledge of ideas or other objects of consciousness only in so far as they have first been presented to ourselves in our own inner life. Whatever I know must be really known to me, one says, only in so far as it is in me. I know, or can conceivably come to know, my own states, my own presentations, my own thoughts, my own experiences. Things external to me can be known only in so far as they first appear inside my conscious world. When I pretend to know something about a far-off star, that something which I know proves, upon analysis, to be my own state, my experience, or my thought—nothing else. I cannot transcend consciousness. And consciousness is for me *my* consciousness, or, at least, can always come to be regarded as mine. "Das 'Ich denke,'" says Kant, "muss alle meine Vorstellungen begleiten können."

Now all this is, in one sense, quite true. There is an aspect of knowledge which is always dependent upon my presentations, my direct acquaintance with mental contents. Without such direct acquaintance, I have no knowledge. But, on the other hand, if one asks a little more closely about the implications of our inner consciousness, one comes upon another, a strongly contrasted, and a highly momentous aspect of our human knowledge. And this aspect is indicated by the well-known fact that if I can only really know my own inner states in so far as they are inner, still, on the other hand, I can never really define to myself just how much is actually presented at any one moment to my inner life. One can know the far-off star only by virtue of ideas and experiences that get presented in the inner life; but, on the other hand, this presentation, merely as such, is not enough. For if anything present in the inner life were, as such, at once and altogether known to me, I should always be able to know just what it is, just how much it is, that now constitutes the whole filling and meaning of my inner life. But alas, I never can find out in all my life, precisely the whole of what it is that gets presented to me in any one moment. Are you now conscious of all that is in your field of vision, e. g., of the head of every person who sits in this audience within this instant's range of your vision ? Obviously you are not, or at least are not equally conscious of all the possible objects of your momentary visual attention. You are now clearly aware only of what you are now attending to, and not of all the contents that are present but that you merely *might* attend to if you chose. But once more, what is precisely the whole of what you are now attending to—words, thoughts, sights, faces ? It is impossible just now exhaustively to tell yourself, unless—unless you first attend to your own process of attention, capriciously fixate its normal fluctuating attitudes, and so give an artificially prepared account of a deliberately falsified situation. The inner life, as we get it, is conscious, but normally very unequally self-conscious — possesses contents, but cannot precisely define to itself what they are ; seeks not to hold the present, but to fly to the next ; scorns the immediate, the presented, and looks endlessly for the oncoming, the sought, the wished-for, the absent, so that the inner eye gazes on a flowing stream of events, but beholds rather what they hint at than what they present.

Now it is this other, this curiously contrasted aspect, of our finite knowledge, that constitutes one of the deepest problems of the life of human reason. I can know only what can get presented to me. But, on the other hand, most of what gets presented to me always escapes my knowledge. I know not the merely presented, as such, but only that which in the presented facts I can hold, apperceive, contrast with other contents, and define as to the real meaning of this object which I am to know. But alas, the moment flits. What I now know turns into what I just now knew, even while I reflect upon it. The direct gets lost in the indirect, the instant in the imperfectly known series of states ; and my best approach to finite knowledge appears as only a sort of substituting of expectations and of memories for the desired presentations. If, then, on the one hand, I can know only my own ideas, states, thoughts, presentations, our present unhappy result seems to be that, as a fact, owing to the ceaseless flux of consciousness, I cannot fully know even these. For, once more, I can know only what I can examine with steadily fixated attention ; but while I fixate my attention upon the inner object, it changes even while I observe it. *Only the presented can be known :*

this idealistic proposition seems to be mockingly answered by the fairly tragic counter-assertion : *Not even the presented is, as such, known.*

In view of these paradoxes of our finitude, in view of the fact that only the presented can, as such, be known, while the presented never stays long enough in one moment of consciousness to allow us fully to know what it is, the actual situation of our human knowledge is simply this : What is always most clearly present to our consciously inquiring intelligence is the conceived relation between some content now immediately apprehended but very imperfectly comprehended, and that which, as we hope, believe, or expect, *will be* or *would be* apprehended, when we come more fully to know, or if we now more fully knew the meaning of this immediate datum. What I now experience leads me to expect another experience. My conscious knowledge is, then, mainly of this relation of transition from the immediate fact to the expected outcome. Or again, what I now experience leads me to believe that, were I otherwise situated, I should apprehend such and such other facts. My knowledge is here again consciously concerned with the relation between my actual and my conceived possible experience. Or, once more, I now have passing through my mind an assertion, a belief, an opinion. And I am thinking just what it is that I mean by this opinion. In this case, my meaning is partly presented to me, partly conceived as a more fully developed meaning, which I should get presented, or shall find presented, upon a further consideration of what I am aiming to do.

Thus, you see, the original paradox of our idealistic analysis gets corrected by this other paradox. To the unknowableness of whatever cannot get presented is now opposed the equal unknowableness of whatever merely gets immediately presented, without being held through a constant inner appeal from what *is* presented to what in future will be presented, or to what conceivably *would be* presented, were consciousness otherwise determined. I know only my own states and ideas ; but those I know only by virtue of their conceived relation to states and ideas that will be, or that would be, under other conditions, or in other moments, the contents of my experience.

But, from this point of view, the nature of the world of our knowledge gets transformed. Our only approach to that ideal of knowledge which complete and fixated presentation would involve if we *had* it, is afforded us by the imperfectly presented relation between fleeting actual presentations and conceived possible presentations. And therefore you will observe at once that my notion of my own Ego and of its contents depends upon a certain contrast between these contents and a conceived world of actual or possible experience beyond this Ego. For what I come nearest to knowing at any moment is the relation between imperfectly grasped immediate contents and the conceived experience beyond the moment. It is indeed true, as idealism is accustomed to say, that of a *Ding-an-sich*, out of relation to possible knowledge, I have and can have no sort of knowledge or conception. For, as soon as I try to tell what such a *Ding-an-sich* is, I turn it into actual or conceived possible experience, and conceive it only as in such experience. But, on the other hand, my whole knowledge of my inner finite Self and of its meaning is dependent upon the contrast between the immediate experiences of this self and a world of abstractly possible or of genuine experiences not presented to any moment of my inner self as such. Thus, all my finite knowledge involves as much mediation as it contains immediacy—assures me of fact only by sending me elsewhere for truth ; lets me know something, never the whole, of my actual experience, but through its contrast with possible experience ; verifies merely by presupposing experiences now unverified ; instructs me by suggesting further problems ; tells me who I am by indicating whither I am to go to look for my true self ; suggests fulfillment of insight, yet all the while sending me out to wander for more insight ; arouses the question, What do I mean ? at the very moment when I am attempting to answer the question, What is the experienced datum ?

Now this realm of contrasts, of the light of present experience and of the shadow of possible or of distant other experience, of presentation and of thought ; this dwelling in hope rather than in fulfillment, in search for a lost self rather than in enjoyment of a present self ; this realm, I say, and this dwelling constitute the inner finite life of every one of us, in so far as he lives rationally at all. My actual inner life is, then, always contrasted with experience other than is now mine ; and the problem of my intellectual life, whatever my worldly calling, is this : Where is the rest of my experience ? or, What is the content of the other experience with which mine is even now contrasted ?

But it is, of course, vain to regard my inner view of myself as constituted solely by the contrast between my individual presentation and a possible inner experience that I view as merely my own private, but still *individually* possible experience. My possible experience and the world of other experience than is now mine—these terms, in a wide but an essentially human sense, constantly include not merely the conceived experiences that I alone in my individual capacity am likely ever to have, or to find individually accessible, but also the whole world of experiences that other human beings either have had, or will have, or may have. The upper Nile valley is, in the general and abstract sense, a possible experience of mine; but I individually shall doubtless never come to get that experience. Yet the upper Nile valley is, and has been, a system of actual and of accessibly possible experiences for very many of my fellow-men. When I conceive the upper Nile valley. there are presented to my inner life words, images, map-experiences, and the like; and these I know as meaning something to me, in so far as I contrast these relatively immediate data with the conceived contents of the experience of other men who more directly verify what I only conceive as to that region. And, in fact, the whole contents of my individual experience get regarded as one conscious system of remembered and expected contents, in so far as, in conception, I contrast my own private inner life with the experiences which I attribute to my actual or conceived fellows. I often say that my own inner life, as a whole, past and future, actual and accessibly possible, is better known to me, is more immediate, is more accessible to me, than is your inner life. But what do I mean by saying this? Surely both my past and my future are now as truly and literally unpresentable to me as are your inner states. I have now only my memories of my past, as I have only my beliefs as to your inner states. Directly I can now verify neither set of ideas. What I mean by the relative intimacy and accessibility of my own individual past is, then, only the fact that my notion of my past has a "warmth," a definiteness, a sort of inner assurance, which contracts with the notion that I form of the past of any other man.

You see, whatever way I turn, I am definable to myself only in terms of a contrast with other experience which might, abstractly speaking, be conceived as mine, but which, as a fact, is viewed either as now inaccessible in comparison with my present experience, or else as the actual or possible experience of my fellow, and so as now more remote than even my own relatively warm and quasi-accessible, although actually unpresentable past experience appears to me to be. But to define any sphere whatever as the sphere of my own finite life, i. e., to define my life either as the sphere of my momentary finite life, or as the sphere of my whole human individuality, involves in each case a contrast between what is within my defined Ego, in the way of relatively realized, or warm, or accessible contents of experience, and what is beyond my defined Ego, as a sphere of experiences that, abstractly speaking, I regard as possibly mine, while, as a fact, I contrast them with mine, as being really somehow beyond me, and relatively inaccessible to me. These other experiences, which are not mine in precisely the degree in which what I call mine is viewed as belonging to me—these other experiences are, primarily, the actual experiences of other men. *My* opinion means, in general, my opinion as contrasted with opinions which I attribute to other men. *My* private experience means, primarily, whatever nobody else but myself has experienced, and is therefore defined by contrast with the conception of what everybody else has experienced. In brief, take away the concept of that world of abstractly possible other experience, which might be mine, or which would be mine, if I were you, or Cæsar, or any one else, or which would now be mine if I were once more my past self—take all this other experience out of my conception, and forthwith I lose all means of becoming conscious of my experience as mine, or of knowing what I mean either by my whole individuality, or by my present Ego.

IV.

So far, then, for our first thesis. To myself, I am I, not merely in so far as my inner contents get presented to me, but in so far as I contrast my experience present, or the sum total of my conceived individual experience, with an experience which is, in some sense, not mine, but which is conceived as other than mine.

But now what warrant have I, philosophically speaking, for assuming that there is any other experience than mine at all—any experience past or future, remote or warm, like my present experience, or unlike it ? Is this merely a practically warranted assertion of common-sense, or has it a deeper philosophical basis ?

The general answer to this question is simply that I know the presented experience as such, and in so far as, in passing it is imperfectly grasped at all, only by virtue of its contrast to the conceived other experience. Without knowledge that the other experience is, there can be then no meaning in saying that the presented experience itself exists. That the present is, he alone can say who regards the past and future as real. That I as this individual am, I can say only if I contrast myself with some conceived other experience. The judgment: "There is experience," can have meaning only if one defines some experience that is to be thus real. But the only way to define any finite experience is by its contrast with other experience. The total object of true knowledge is therefore never the immediate experience of my own state as such and alone, although there never is any knowledge without some immediate experience as one of its elements. The judgment : "There is experience" means, then, for any finite being, "There is my finite experience, known as somehow contrasted with other experience than what is here presented as mine." Thus, then, the conviction that there is other experience than what is presented to me here, has not only a common-sense value but a philosophical warrant. But if one says: "No, but the contrast is itself something given, and so is not the contrast between my experience and any experience that is really known to be other than mine, but is only a contrast between my presented experience and one that is not presented as other than mine, but that is merely conceived as other than mine "—then to this objection, once more, the answer is, that the very conception of other experience than what is now presented as mine either actually relates to such other experience, or else is a meaningless conception. But if it is to be meaningless, even while it takes itself, as it does, to have a meaning, then this conception that always shadows my presentations, this conception of other experience than mine, is itself an experience that is in fact other than it takes itself to be. For it always takes itself to mean something; although, unless it actually does refer to other experience than mine, it is meaningless. But to say that a conception, or any other presented content of consciousness, is other than it seems, and is, for example, really meaningless when it seems to mean something, this is already to distinguish between my erroneous experience of its nature, and another, a fuller experience of its nature which, if I knew it better, I should have. But thus to distinguish between what my experience really is and what it seems to be, is simply to distinguish between a presented and a not presented aspect of the very experience in question. For what can one say of an experience which is not what it seems to be, and which is yet only a presentation after all—a mere matter of the instant in which it happens to live ? If an experience, viz., here the conception of other experience than mine, presents itself as meaning something beyond the moment when it really means nothing beyond the moment, then this very experience itself is really other than the experience as it is presented, and once more one gets a real contrast between my experience as presented, and related experience which is not presented. The conception of other experience than mine must, therefore, in any case, have relation to a real experience which is other than my presentation.

Thus, then, that there is some experience not individually mine, is an assertion precisely as sure as the assertion that my own experience is. For neither assertion has meaning apart from the other. On the other hand, it is impossible to contrast my experience with any *Ding-an-sich*, existent apart from all experience, because the instant that I tell what I mean by a *Ding-an-sich*, I have converted it into an experience, actual or possible, and other than mine.

But finally, in this connection, one must still further insist that our now frequently illustrated contrast cannot ultimately be one between my presented experience and an experience other than mine which is *barely* a possible experience, and not an actual experience at all. A possible experience, not now mine, is a notion that has a very sound meaning in case it has some direct or indirect relation to a real experience not now mine. But bare possibilities, to which no actualities correspond, are indeed meaningless. Are there real facts or aspects of experience not now presented to me, then I can easily define these in terms of logical possibilities. But possibilities need realities to give them meaning. There must then be other experience than mine, not merely as possible experience, but as actual experience. Given such actual experience, there is not only convenience, but rational necessity in the attempt to define its nature in terms of all sorts of conceived possibilities; but unless you have some actual experience upon which to base your possibilities, then the possibilities themselves become mere contradictions. A barely possible experience is, as Mr. Bradley has well said, the same as an impossible experience.

v.

There is, then, an universe of other actual experience than my own finite experience, presented or remembered. Were this central truth not known to me, I should have no means of being conscious of myself as this finite Ego. The general constitution of this world of other experience, in its wholeness, I must here leave to metaphysics. We are now concerned with the finite aspects of the complex of experiences with which, as human beings, we have to do.

Concretely, we get information about the contents of experience not our own, when we communicate socially with our fellows. And the essence of social communication is this: My fellow does something in a certain situation—

deals with his environment so or so. He uses tools, utters
words, makes gestures. If these deeds of his are new to me,
they do not convey to me his inner experience. These deeds
are so far, for me, phenomena in my own experience. I
cannot directly view my fellow's experience at all. How,
then, is a word, or gesture, or other deed, which as yet con-
veys no meaning to me, to acquire a meaning, or to become
expressive to me of my fellow's inner life as such ? The
answer is, that, from infancy on, my fellow's expressive acts
get a meaning to me as the suggestion of his concrete inner
life, just in so far as I am able to imitate these deeds of his
by bodily acts of my own, brought to pass under conditions
like those in which he, my fellow, acts. For when I definitely repeat a bodily act that expresses any human meaning, the act, as I repeat it, under definite conditions, gets for
me an inner meaning which I could never grasp so long as
I merely observed such an act from without, as an event in
my perceived phenomenal world. But this inner meaning
which the act gets when I repeat it, becomes for me the
objective meaning of the act as my fellow performs it ; and
thus the meaning of the imitated act, interpreted for me at
the moment of my imitation, gets conceived as the real
meaning, the inner experience of my fellow, at the moment
when he performs the act which is my model. If you laugh,
I know what you mean just in so far as, under similar conditions, I can join with you and laugh heartily also, and
can thus, by fully imitating your deed, get a sense of your
meaning. But if I see you laughing under circumstances
that absolutely forbid me even to conceive myself as imitating your expression of mirth, then I have frankly to say
that I do not in the least know what you mean by laughing
at just this situation, and so cannot conceive in so far what
your inner experience is. If I see you playing cards, or
chess, I can only make out what your inner experience is in
case I learn the cards, the pieces, the rules, or the moves of

the game, and proceed to play it myself. If I want to know what the poets mean when they sing of love, I must myself become a lover. When I have imitated, in my measure, the lover's situation, and the lover's sincerely expressed devotion, then I know something of what love meant for the poet. In general, I believe in other human experience than mine in so far as I notice other people's expressive acts, and then gradually interpret them through social conformity. What I cannot interpret by imitation, I cannot definitely realize as another man's experience. Yet as my imitations always remain incomplete, and my interpretations correspondingly indefinite, I have constantly to contrast my fellow's experience, so far as I can realize it, with my fellow's experience so far as it attracts my efforts to interpret it, but also sets a limit to the success of these efforts. And thus I get a notion of a boundless world of human meanings which I can partially, but not wholly, grasp. In the effort, by social conformity, i. e., by imitation of expressive actions, to interpret such inadequately grasped human meanings, a great part of my social life consists. This effort is constantly supplemented by my efforts to convey my own meanings to others; and thus my self-consciousness and my social consciousness, each helped and each limited by the other, since each exists only in contrast with the other, get organized and developed in the endless giving and taking of social communications.

Thus far, then, we have been illustrating our first and second theses. Their application to our notion of Nature remains to be developed.

VI.

So far, then, a reality, external to my finite Ego, means a world of other experience with which my experience is contrasted. This world is concretely defined, in the first place, as the world of other human experiences than my

own. What these experiences actually are, I learn only by
myself repeating the expressive deeds of my fellows, and
by attributing to these deeds, when performed by my
fellows, an inner meaning similar to the one which I
more directly observe in the deeds when I myself repeat
them under conditions similar to those in which my fellows have already performed them. Of course, no such
interpretation of any human meaning is infallible; but I
am verifiably right in saying that, at every step, this social
process does really bring me into relation with experience
which, until I performed the deeds of social imitativeness,
was not mine. This concrete new experience, which was
not mine until I imitated, was then before my imitation,
at the very least, a possible experience other than mine.
The whole social world is full of suggestions of such actually possible experiences. If every real possibility must,
logically speaking, have a basis in actuality, I am philosophically warranted in saying that all these suggestions of
other human experience which social imitation interprets,
and which common-sense trusts, do as a fact stand not only
for a barely possible enlargement of my inner Ego, but for
real experience which, however fallible my private interpretations of it may be, has an actuality contrasted with,
and existent apart from, my finite individuality. The world
of my fellows' experiences may not be real just as I, in my
narrowness, interpret it. But this world is still, from the
philosophical as from the common-sense point of view, a
real world, a complex of experiences other than mine, and
more or less imperfectly communicated to me. And thus
it is that one in general defines the metaphysics of the
social consciousness. You observe once more the essential
relativity of the individual Ego and the social Alter.
Neither conception has any clearness apart from the other.

But now, in our human world of experience, there are,
yonder, the phenomena of physical nature. Our next

question is, in what sense are we to attribute reality to
them ?

J. S. Mill's answer to this question is well known, and
is, in one aspect, closely and instructively similar to Kant's
answer, despite all the differences between the two philosophers as to other matters. The phenomena of nature, e. g.,
the upper Nile valley, the other side of yonder wall, or of
the moon—these one conceives as systems of possible experiences, experiences which, in general, I now have not,
but could have under definable conditions. Nature, as
such, contains, apart from the bodies of my fellows and of
the higher animals, no objects that I conceive as communicating to me any now intelligible inner intents, meanings,
plans, or other socially interesting contents. Nature consists of masses of "possibilities of sensation." The problem
is, in what sense have these possibilities of experience any
inner or self-existent sort of reality ? Is nature a *Ding-an-
sich*, whose reality is absolutely inscrutable, but self-possessed ? The answer to this last and special question is
that such a notion is simply meaningless. I can contrast
my experience with other experience, and can regard myself as limited by facts of experience not now presented to
me. And such a way of regarding myself is, as we have
seen, absolutely essential to even my self-consciousness.
But I cannot contrast experience with what is no experience at at all. Even to say that there now exist certain
possibilities of experience which I do not realize, is to raise
the issue already several times touched upon in the foregoing. A bare possibility is a mere fiction. It cannot be
real. To my true definition of a given experience as merely
possible for me, there may correspond an experience which,
as it is in itself, is very unlike my private definition of the
real possibility. But if I am right in saying, " There is a
possibility of experience not now mine," then to such a real
possibility some sort of real experience, other than mine,

must correspond. The question arises: Is there any such real experience behind those nature-facts which we conceive is our own possible experiences?

But there is another aspect of natural phenomena which perhaps brings us nearer to our goal. The reality of the facts of nature, when we actually confirm their presence, is always viewed as capable of being submitted to social tests. The real nature-phenomenon is not merely conceived as the object of my possible experience, but in general as the object of my fellows' actual or possible experience as well. If the star that I see is a real star, then you, if you are a normal observer can see that star as well as I. This is the common-sense presupposition as to nature. Natural objects are viewed as phenomena that are, in some sense, public property, in so far as many different human observers could make them objects of possible inspection. The presupposition of common-sense is, that many observers could, on occasion, verify the *same* natural fact; so that the physical world will consist, for common-sense, not merely of possibilities of my individual experience, but of possibilities of common experience on the part of many observers.

Here surely is a well-known, but a paradoxical aspect of our nature-experience. I cannot observe your mind, but, as common-sense supposes, I can observe the same external natural fact that you observe. This presupposition is, in effect, a basis in terms of which we often define the facts of nature. What I alone experience, belongs to my inner life. What you can experience as well as I, is as such a physical fact, and, mind you, this means that, when we deal with nature-phenomena, common-sense supposes us, not merely to have similar inner states, but to refer to actually the *same* fact. If you as finite being count ten, and I as finite being count ten, we perform similar inner acts, but our objects are so far *not* the same; for the ten that you count is not

16

the ten that I count. We can in this case be referring to the same truth only if there is, as a fact, some sort of extra-human reality possessed by the truths of arithmetic, and actually referred to by both of us. But just such extra-human reality common-sense actually attributes to the facts of nature. If ten stones lie on the highway, and you and I count them, common-sense supposes that though your counting of ten is not my counting of ten, though your perception of the stones is not mine, though your inner life is in no fashion, here noteworthy, identical with mine, still the real stones that I count are identically the same as the real stones that you count. Now any natural fact, as common-sense conceives it, could, without losing its identity, be made the common object of as many observers as could come to get the right hints of its nature through their inner experience. All these possible observers, so common-sense holds, would really refer to the same natural fact.

The nature-things, then, are not merely possible experiences for me; they pretend to be possible objects of common experience for many observers.

Now when the nature-facts make such puzzling demands upon us as this, there are only two ways of viewing the situation thus created. One way is to say that in truth, all this common-sense notion of nature is illusory. As a fact, one might insist, it is impossible for two finite observers of nature to have the same external fact actually referred to by both of them at once. What one means is, that, as our social consciousness indicates, human beings have many similar experiences, and can socially convey to one another this similarity of their inner lives. When I rejoice, you may rejoice too; yet our rejoicings are not the same, but only similar. Just so, one might insist, when I point at my star, you may point at your star also. But what happens is that your experience then resembles mine; but has not the same outer object at all. Nature is the sum-total of those facts of our various experiences, concerning which our perceptual experience seems most easily to agree. But this agreement means merely a certain social communicable similarity of our experiences—not unity or sameness of natural object.

This, I say, is one possible hypothesis as to nature. But observe at once : There is *one* class of nature-objects in case of which just this negative and sceptical hypothesis simply cannot be carried out without destroying the very basis of our social consciousness itself. And this class of seeming outer objects is made up of the very bodies of our human fellows whom we observe, and with whom we socially communicate. The social consciousness, upon which, as we have seen, our very self-consciousness itself depends for its definition in finite terms, involves, as an integral part of its unity, the observation of certain natural phenomena definable as the expressive movements, the gestures, words, deeds, of our fellows. Now these phenomena are not merely to be viewed as reducible to the possible similar experiences of the various people who may observe their fellows from without. For these phenomena, on the contrary, have, whoever observes them, their identical and inner aspect ; for they indicate the inner life of the social fellow-being who thus expresses himself. Many of you are now observing me. Are all of your various inner experiences of me now actually referring to the *same* fact, external to you but having for me its presented internal aspect, identically the same whoever it is that regards himself as observing my movements ? The answer is here, at once : Yes. If I am I, and am communicating to you through deeds which are represented in you by systems of similar experiences, then, when you experience, in your inner lives, the observable phenomenal aspects of these my deeds, you are all at once meaning, referring to, listening to, the same genuinely real object.

Paradox though it be, the social consciousness insists that the same fellow-man can phenomenally manifest his presence to as many observers as can get some experience of his expressive deeds. All these observers can agree, with due care, as to their accounts of his deeds. These deeds, then, are so far nature-phenomena, like any others. My movements appear to any one of you in space, even as does this desk. So far, one could say, the fact is that the observers have experiences that are similar in one man's case to the experiences of his observing fellow. The observed deeds are merely such similar perceptions in the various observers. The various observers do not see the same real deeds; but they do possess similar perceptions, which they call perceptions of expressive deeds.

But no, this conclusion the social consciousness declines to accept. All your various but similar individual perceptions of my deeds really refer to the *same* genuine object, precisely in so far as I am I, and in so far as it is my inner experience that is manifested in these deeds. Thus, then, you could say that, if this desk were alone here, you could indeed so far talk sceptically of phenomenal experiences, in various observers, which only seemed to be experiences relating to the same object, but which as a fact do not demand the real sameness of their object. But it is no longer so if, in terms of the social consciousness, you consider not the desk, but me as your nature-object. For I am to you not only nature-phenomenon, represented in you by comparable and merely similar perceptual experiences of your various private worlds; but I am, as communicating fellow-man, the same outer object for all of you.

Now a similar proposition holds true of any fellow-man. Any man you please has for you his phenomenal aspect. In this aspect he is viewed as object of possible experiences, and the real facts corresponding to this view are, so far, expressible by saying that all of his observant fellows have

similar experiences whenever they come into certain definable groups of relations to their own inner worlds. But
this man has another˙existence than the existence of certain
images that his fellows form. All of these images refer to
him, to the same man, to his manifested inner experience,
and so to one reality. And this is what the social consciousness insists. Give up that insistence, in any general form,
and you have no social consciousness, no fellow-men with
similar experiences, no definable self-consciousness—yes,
nothing but an inexpressible immediacy of inner presentations. But hold by that insistence, and what can you say ?
I answer : You can and must say that to one portion of phenomenal nature, viz., to the observed bodily movements of
your fellows, there corresponds an inner life which is the
same in essence, however many may be the phenomenal
images that observers form of it when they refer to it as
a reality.

The first view of nature, viz., that nature consists of a
total of possible experiences, similar in various observers,
thus fails as to all those nature-objects that present themselves as our expressively moving fellows. Our fellows are
real beings, phenomenally observable from without by as
many observers as you please, but self-existent as masses of
inner experience, contrasted with one another, and with our
own experiences.

But now how can you separate the phenomenal fellow,
the originally real finite being, the original of your notion
of your non-Ego, from the phenomenal nature of which he
appears as a part, and with whose existence he appears to be,
in all his life, absolutely continuous ? For at this point
there returns to help us our whole knowledge of human
nature as such. A man's phenomenal expressive movements, objects of possible experience for all observers, stand
for, and phenomenally accompany, his inner life. They
then are real manifestations of a real interior finite life.

But his movements cannot be thus regarded as real unless his limbs, his muscles, his nerves, his brain, his circulatory and nutritive processes, the food that he eats, the desk from which he speaks, the air that he breathes, the room where he speaks, the ancestors from whom he descended—yes, in the end, the whole phenomenal nature-order with which he is phenomenally continuous, unless all these things be also regarded as real in the same general sense, viz., as inner finite experience. In short, you cannot separate your phenomenal fellows from the order of phenomenal nature. The continuity between man and nature, known to us first as the absolute inseparability of the expressive movements of our fellows from the nature-processes in which these movements appear to be imbedded, and of which they are phenomenally a part, has now become, in the light of our whole experience of natural phenomena, an all-embracing continuity, extending to cerebral and to general physiological processes, and to the ancestry and evolution of the human race, so that the highest in expressive human nature is now phenomenally linked by the most intimate ties to the simplest of physical processes. If, then, one's fellow is real, the whole of the phenomenal nature from which his phenomenal presence is continuous must be real in the same general fashion.

But observe, *this* deduction of the reality of the natural objects implies something very significant as to what nature is. The only possible way to get at the existence of a finite non-Ego is through some form of the social consciousness. What a finite non-Ego is, your fellow teaches you when he communicates to you the fact that he has inner experience, and is the same object, however many observers view him. Now if his continuity with the phenomenal nature of whose processes his observed expressive movements are an inseparable and continuous part, impels you to say that if he is real his whole body, and so, in the end, the whole nature of which that body is an inseparable part and an evolutionary product, is also real, in an inner and finite sense, then the only possible way to interpret this relation is to say: "Nature, by itself, is a system of finite experience which, on occasion, and by means of perfectly continuous evolutionary processes, passes over into, or differentiates from its own organization, the communicative form of socially intelligible experience that you and I call human."

VII.

The force of this proof is limited, of course, by the fact that it is precisely an argument from continuity. It is capable of endless development and illustration; and I take it to be the only possible proof that nature exists in any way beyond the actual range of our more or less similar human experiences of nature's observable facts. Yet no argument from any continuity of apparent processes has absolute force. It does not follow that every hypothetical conception which you and I now form of this or that natural process, e. g., of the atoms, or of gravitation, corresponds to any distinct form of the inner nature-experience. As a fact, I take it that our scientifically conceived laws of nature are largely phenomenal generalizations from very superficial aspects of the inner life of nature, and that very much indeed of what we now call nature has existence only for human perception and thought, as a matter of the similarities of the experiences of various human observers. But my point is here not a detailed theory, but a general conception of nature. And my general conception is this:—There is a vast system of finite experience, real as our socially communicative fellows are real, and manifesting its existence to us just as they do, viz., through the phenomena which appear to our senses as material movements in space and time. What this inner experience is we know, in case of our human fellows, by social communication. What the rest of the nature-experience is, we can only make out very indirectly. But the continuity proves that the nature-experience passes over, on occasion, by unbroken although vastly complex processes, into the form of human experience. All the facts grouped together as the doctrine of Evolution, make this continuity seem the more elaborate, minute, and significant, the better we know it. In consequence we have no sort of right to speak in any way as if the inner experience behind any fact of nature were of a grade lower than ours, or less conscious, or less rational, or more atomic. Least of all have we a right, as the Mind Stuff theories do, to accept our hypothetical atoms as corresponding to real nature-entities, and then to say that inorganic nature consists of a mass of scattered sensations. Of the reality of organized experience we all know; but scattered sensory states are mere abstractions, just as the atoms of physics are. There is no evidence for the reality of nature-facts which is not defined for us by the very categories of the social consciousness. No evidence, then, can indicate nature's inner reality without also indicating that this reality is, like that of our own experience, conscious, organic, full of clear contrasts, rational, definite. We ought not to speak of dead nature. We have only a right to speak of uncommunicative nature. Natural objects, if they are real at all, are *prima facie* simply other finite beings, who are, so to speak, not in our own social set, and who communicate to us, not their minds, but their presence. For, I repeat, a real being can only mean to me other experience than mine; and other experience does not mean deadness, unconsciousness, disorganization, but presence, life, inner light.

But it is customary to say, by way of getting rid of any sort of animism, that we have no right to reason by mere analogy from our inner experience to anything resembling life in inorganic nature. To this I answer that, were the foregoing argument one from analogy, it would be open to

the same objections as could be urged against any form of
animism. But the whole point of the foregoing analysis
has been that you do not first find nature as something real,
and occult, and *then* proceed to argue from analogy that
this occult reality is alive. On the contrary, I have first insisted that occult realities, things in themselves, in the abstract sense, are absurd ; that the social consciousness gives
us the only notion of finite reality that we can have ; and
that the social consciousness recognizes, as real, beings having conscious experience. After this point was reached, and
only then, could we turn, in our argument, to the phenomena
of nature to ask if they must be regarded as conforming to
just such a concept of finite reality, since, as a fact, this is
our only possible concept of what a real being is. Now a
phenomenon of nature, on the face of it, is solely something
suggested to us by the agreement between the series of experiences present in various men. And no purely physical
experience can possibly prove that nature has other reality
than this, viz., reality as a series of parallel trains of experience in various people. So far we had not to interpret
nature, but only to wonder why nature gets taken to be
real at all, apart from these parallel series of experiences.
Then it was that there came to our aid the argument from
continuity. Certain of the phenomena of nature do stand
for real inner experience, viz., the expressive movements of
men. It is impossible to separate these latter phenomena,
however, from the rest of the natural world, whose phenomenal unity the doctrine of Evolution is now daily making more manifest. Hence—so we reasoned—the rest of
phenomenal nature must be regarded as standing for systems
of finite experience, whose inner unity has to be defined in
the way that human experience illustrates. And it is thus,
not by analogy, but by the very process whereby nature
comes to be defined as real at all, that natural facts get
conceived as like other finite experience. Of the relation

of this " other experience than ours " in the cosmos, to our
human type of experience we can then at once say, that, in
the process of evolution, our human experience has become
differentiated, by long and continuous processes, from the
whole, so that relatively continuous intermediate stages now
probably link us to the rest of the cosmical inner life.   Of
" unconscious " experience in nature we have no right to
speak, precisely because consciousness means the very form
and fashion of the being of experience itself, as we know it.
Of transformations of conscious experience, with a preservation of continuity through the whole process, our own
inner life gives us numerous examples.

Meanwhile, let us lay aside, once for all, the petty human
Philistinism that talks of the evolution of humanity out of
so-called "dead nature," as if it were necessarily a vast
progress from "lower" to "higher," or from the meaningless to the world full of meaning.   What value human
life may get we in a measure know.   But we certainly
do not know that the nature-experience whose inner sense
is not now communicated to us is in the least lower or less
full of meaning.   Our human evolution is, as it were,
simply the differentiation of one nature-dialect, whereby
a group of finite beings now communicate together.   We
have no right to call the other tongues with which nature
speaks, barbarous, because, in our evolutionary isolation
from the rest of nature, we have forgotten what they mean.

VIII.

A few concluding considerations seem to be still in place
in view of the most cogent positive objection that is likely
to be urged against the foregoing interpretation of nature.
The hypothesis advanced in the foregoing transcends our
direct as well as our scientifically mediated experience of
nature, just in so far as our view supposes that the nature-
phenomena are hints of the existence of a finite experience

continuous with ours, but such that its extra-human contents are not communicated to us. And this transcendence of our human experience is indeed a perfectly obvious objection to my notion. Yet the objection is so far only negative. In admitting, as I do, all that such an objection can urge so far as regards the fact that our hypothesis transcends the limits of present human verification, I still answer that this objection is precisely as cogent against every theory which attributes any sort of genuine inner reality to nature, as it is against our own theory. The objection, in fact, contends only against the attribution of relatively independent reality to nature, just as such attribution, and not against our special view as such. No human verification, made as it is under social conditions, can of itself do more than prove (in the social sense of the word " proof ") that various human experiences, existent in different men, have certain actual agreements. To believe that nature has any reality apart from these, our intercommunicable parallel series of human experiences of what we call the nature-phenomena, is, therefore, to transcend the actual data of the social consciousness, so far as they are presented to us mortals. The present objection, then, is equally valid against all cosmological doctrines. The only question really at issue, however, is : What reason forces us to transcend the data of our literal social consciousness at all ? Why are we led to assume a nature outside of the various reports that men give of their parallel trains of describable physical experience ? To this question, as I conceive, the only fair answer is the argument from continuity, as it has now been stated. But the argument from continuity is an argument for the existence of finite realities whose ultimate type the social consciousness in general predetermines for our conception, while the nature of their specific relations to our experience is such as to preclude our filling out this general conception of " other experiences than ours " with any particular contents such as we attribute to the communicative minds of our fellows. My argument, then, is not for one concept of the reality of the facts of nature as against contrasting, and equally possible, concepts of the reality of beings other than ourselves. My argument is, that, from the nature of our human consciousness, with its primal contrast of inner Ego and social non-Ego, we can have just one general concept of a finite non-Ego, viz., the concept of "other experience than our own." The only real question, then, is: Shall we attribute this concept, in its most generalized form, to nature, or shall we not? There is no answer to this question except the one derived from our foregoing argument from continuity. That to attribute any reality whatever to nature is to "transcend our own experience," in the human and socially concrete sense of the word "experience," ought to be especially remembered by those who, while glibly attributing to nature a reality which they profess to regard as utterly inscrutable, are still accustomed to insist that one must never venture to transcend human experience in any fashion.

But it is not this negative argument that I myself regard as the most cogent. I am, as I have just said, more interested in a positive objection which will occur to many of you.

The nature-experience, so our hypothesis supposes, is, in at least a considerable degree, relatively continuous with ours. That is, there is experience in nature which closely resembles human experience; there is other experience which less resembles ours, but which need not be lower; there is conscious experience still more remote from ours; and so on. All this experience hints to us its presence, but only in case of our human fellows communicates its inner meaning to us. But one may now answer: "It is true that the phenomena of our bodies are, physically speaking, continuous with the phenomena of physical nature in general.

It is not true, so soon as we leave man, that we get any direct signs of the existence of an inner life, or nature-experience, at all corresponding, in its inner resemblance to, our own, to the physical continuity of its phenomenal processes with our own expressive physical life. The higher animals manifest their inner experience, apparently similar to ours, by expressive activities which resemble ours, but which certainly do not stand in any close physical continuity with ours. Our own organic processes, on the other hand, stand in very close relations of physical continuity with our most intelligent conscious and voluntary deeds. Yet if there is any inner experience connected with those of our organic activities which have no conscious equivalents in our own inner life, it is hard to show any sufficient body of evidence to bring this ' subliminal ' experience into any relatively continuous *inner* relations with our own, despite the numerous, and decidedly interesting, recent efforts which have been made to connect our individual consciousness, by empirical links, with some such ' subliminal ' processes." What my theory seems to lack, then, is a definition of any way in which our human consciousness *can* be in relations of inner continuity with a world of experience which, although thus actually in close continuity with ours, gives signs of its presence only through physical phenomena whose inner meaning, even in case of our own organic processes, quickly escapes any interpretation in terms now intelligible to our socially limited minds. An objector may well urge that this is a positive fault of the theory. Our theory, he may say, need not undertake to tell precisely what the supposed nature-experience contains. But it ought to show how physical processes continuous with those of whose inner meaning we are conscious, may involve, as their own inner aspect, types of experience more or less continuously related to our own, and yet now quite inaccessible to us.

As a fact, there is a very obvious way of hypothetically accounting for this presence and inaccessibility of types of experience closely related to ours, whose presence is hinted to us by physical processes such that we now wholly fail to interpret their inner meaning. This supplementary hypothesis is suggested by one of the most interesting and best known principles governing the correlation of mental processes and their phenomenal accompaniments.

Mental processes, in human beings, are correlated to physical processes whose phenomenal or externally observable basis is known to be the functions of nervous systems. Now the best known principle governing the physical fortunes of any nervous system is the principle of Habit. This is the rule that a nervous system tends to repeat its former functions, when once these have become set through series of repeated stimulations. Whatever function has frequently been accomplished under the direction of nervous centers, tends to be the more readily accomplished again. This principle tends, of course, to the production of stability and uniformity of conduct in us all. And the analogy between the results of this special tendency to the formation of nervous Habits, on the one hand, and the existence of the observable processes of Natural Law in general, on the other hand, has often been noted. The phenomenally observable conduct of a being with a nervous system is always, as a fact, and in proportion to the elevation of this being in the scale of life, a very irregular sort of conduct. Yet it tends towards regularity, because of the principle of Habit. Now, however, the regularity of outwardly observable conduct towards which, as towards an asymptote, the conduct of a being with a nervous system tends, is a sort of regularity which physical nature, especially in the inorganic world, continually shows us, only in a highly perfected form, in those extremely regular processes which we define, not, to be sure, as the ideally ultimate laws of the universe, but as

the observable routine of phenomenal nature (such routine
as is exemplified by the tides, the seasons, etc.). That nature's observable Laws might even be interpreted, from an
evolutionary point of view, as nature's gradually acquired
Habits, originating in a primal condition of a relatively
capricious irregularity, is a conception to which several recent writers, notably Mr. Cope, and, with great philosophical
ingenuity, Mr. Charles Peirce, have given considerable
elaboration. I do not myself accept this notion that the
laws of phenomenal nature, where they are genuinely objective laws, and not relatively superficial human generalizations, are the evolutionary product of any such cosmical
process of acquiring habits, as Mr. Peirce has so ingeniously
supposed in his hypothesis of "Tychism." But I mention
the analogy between these regularities of physical phenomena which are called the observable laws of nature, and the
gradually acquired regularities of conduct which slowly appear in the lives of beings with nervous systems, in order to
introduce another consideration, of equal importance for
the definition of the place of conscious experience in the
cosmical order.

If it is the rule that our nervous systems tend to form
habits, and that habits mean uniformities of phenomenal
behavior, it is equally true that our human consciousness
tends to grow faint just in proportion as our habits become
relatively invariable. Our human and conscious experience
is the inner accompaniment of what appears, when viewed
from without, as an irregularity of phenomenally observable conduct. Or, in other words, our conscious life is the
inner aspect of a physical process of what is called our adjustment to our environment. This adjustment tends to become, in proportion to the perfection of our habits, a matter
of predictable routine. But whenever this routine becomes
relatively perfect, our consciousness grows fainter, and in
the extreme case of an almost entirely invariable physical

routine, our consciousness ceases, while the perfected nervous habit remains, for human experience, only as an externally observable phenomenal process of a physical nature.
A young man consciously and proudly twirls his moustache. The acquisition of this new mode of conduct constitutes a novel adjustment, and so involves change of
routine behavior. This change is accompanied, at first, by
a decided sense of personal importance. In time the habit
may become set, so that it gets an entirely reflex perfection,
and then, as in a well-known reported case, a man struck
senseless by a street-accident, and suffering from severe
cerebral injury, is seen, as he is carried to the hospital, auto-
matically twirling his moustache, from time to time, in
what, from our human point of view, appears as absolute
unconsciousness, since we are unable, either then or later, to
get into any sort of communication with the conscious
experience, if such there be, that forms an inner aspect of
this nervous habit. Just so, if one's nervous habits were so
well formed, and if one's environment were so changeless,
that one's whole physical life were a settled series of rhythmically performed activities, recurring with the regularity
of breathing, or of the tides, the empirical evidence is that
one would have no conscious life of the sort now communicated to us by our social fellows. Consciousness, as we
know it in man, and interpret its presence in animals, is an
incident of an interrupted adjustment to our environment—
an interrupted adjustment which, seen from without, expresses itself in conduct that involves *alteration of old
habits to meet new conditions.* As Romanes well asserted,
the signs of mind, in any animal, are best to be defined as
just such relative *novelties of conduct in the presence of
new situations.* Not routine, then, as such, but irregularity, gives the physically interpretable sign of mind.
Habit is always present, in the actions of the obviously
conscious being; but, whenever he shows interpretable

signs of consciousness, habit is always undergoing alteration.

If one considers these various groups of facts together, one gets, at first, an impression of the place of consciousness in nature which seems quite unfavorable to our hypothesis. Inorganic nature seems to be, as we view it, a realm where physical routine is, at present, obviously much more nearly verifiable, in an exact degree, than is the case with organic nature. In the inorganic world, then, what might be called, by analogy, the habitual process of the cosmos, the observable routine of physical phenomena, seems to be especially fixed, and open in its fixity to our human observation. In the organic world, whether or no the same ultimate natural laws would, if we knew the whole truth, ideally explain the facts, it is obvious that, at present, we *see* less regularity—less perfected observable habits, so far as our present imperfect experience goes. But, just where we now see least regularity, there we get the only signs of finite minds that we can at present definitely interpret. The ordinary generalization from this whole situation is, that, phenomenal irregularity being characteristic of the physical processes which indicate mind, phenomenal regularity must, by contrast, indicate the presence of the Unconscious—whatever that may mean.

But now this generalization is open to many objections. The unconscious, as such, is, as a fact, a mere *Ding-an-sich*, a meaningless abstraction. And, on the other hand, if one leaves out the ultimate presupposition that *all* of nature's processes, organic and inorganic, are, in some fashion still unknown to us, absolutely and equally uniform—if one, I say, leaves out this ultimate metaphysical presupposition, which I intend to examine in another place, and which does not here concern us—and if one confines one's self simply to the phenomenal, and the to empirical differences between organic and inorganic nature, then one must say

17

that the observable or the scientifically computable and verifiable routine of rhythmic repetition in inorganic nature is nowhere concretely known to us as phenomenally invariable. The rhythm of the tides, at any given point, or over the surface of the globe at large, is invariable only if you do not take account of long periods of time. The same holds true of the regularity of the earth's revolution on its axis, and of the change of the seasons. The planetary orbits undergo secular variations, which are, within certain long periods, relatively rhythmic; but if you take a period sufficiently long, these variations are doubtless no longer rhythmic.

As a fact, then, the permanence of the phenomenally obvious "habits" of inorganic nature is only relative. It is true that, if you pass from such observably regular rhythms, whose actual degree of regularity is itself only a varying function of the time taken into account, and if you consider the ultimate and ideal "laws of nature," upon which all such approximate regularities are conceived to be founded, you do, indeed, reach systems of "force functions" conceived as absolutely independent of time. But thus to pass to the ultimate is to substitute a metaphysical conception of rigid causation for the empirically observed uniformities. And this conception which we here omit from consideration, must apply, if true at all, to organic nature quite as much as to inorganic nature. If, however, you cling to the observable "habits" of nature, then the difference between the organic and the inorganic is one only of the length of time required to make a given alteration of habitual sequence in the phenomena manifest. Our solar system is "adapting" itself to an environment of seemingly limitless extent by the well-known dissipation of its energies. This adaptation involves, in varied ways, slow processes of phenomenal change which must, in the end, alter every known phenomenal rhythm of regularly repeated nature-habits. When read backwards, the same tendencies indicate that the present phenomenal order must have been reached by processes whose phenomenal manifestations would have been, in past times, enormously different in their routine from any process now manifest. Even if ultimate laws exist, then, and involve absolutely ideal regularities, which hold for all phenomena, organic and inorganic, it still follows that the observable and relatively rhythmic regularities of inorganic nature must be as truly cases of constantly altered " habits," continually adjusted to numerous conditions in the environment, as are the seemingly so irregular expressive acts of our socially expressive fellows. The difference lies in the enormously different times required to make manifest the alterations of phenomenal conduct in question. A business man in a great commercial crisis, or a great general, directing his army during a battle, adjusts his regular routine to the new conditions by changes of conduct that occur within very brief periods. A planet or a solar system alters the routine of its rhythmic processes in ways that it may take millions of years to make manifest. But in both cases the essentials of adjustment are present, viz., variations in the rhythm of characteristic movements occurring in correspondence to changing situations.

If, thus viewed, the difference between the larger phenomenal alterations of inorganic and of organic nature appears mainly as a matter of the time-span involved in each alteration, it remains to consider a little more carefully the relation which we all experience between the inner processes of our conscious experience and those expressive alterations of habit to suit environment which accompany our conscious life.

What appears to our fellows from without as habit altered to meet circumstance, appears from within, in the experience of each of us, as the apperception of relatively new elements of experience by virtue of their relations of similarity and contrast to relatively old or familiar or established masses of inner states. The old, the familiar, the established in consciousness we have always with us whenever we experience. It is the element of our consciousness which corresponds, at any moment, to the established nervous habits just then aroused—to the routine of our lives so far as it is just then repeated. The novel, the puzzling, the intruding element in our consciousness corresponds to the alteration which the environment is at the moment producing in our established physical routine as at that moment represented. We breathe regularly, and are not conscious of the fact. But an alteration in breathing, produced by a novel physical situation, gets represented in consciousness as a shock of surprise. Thus the alteration of our physical routine, at any moment, corresponds to the degree of our conscious experience. The greater the masses and the contrast of the opposing new and old elements, the sharper is our consciousness, and, externally viewed, the more marked is our adjustment. If either mass of mental contents tends utterly to overbalance the other, consciousness becomes dim. The effacement of either element means the temporary or final cessation of our whole stream of conscious experience. In sleep one's physical routine is nearly regular, and one's conscious experience vanishes.

Meanwhile, our human experience is subject to another and very important limitation, which we may call *The Limitation of our Apperceptive Span.* This limitation, so far as we can see, is something purely arbitrary—a mere fact, which we have to accept like the rest of our finite situation. The existence of all such arbitrary limitations is, like the existence in general of any form of finitude, a proper problem for a general metaphysical inquiry. But a merely cosmological study has to be content, in such cases, with accepting the arbitrary fact as such. What is meant, however, by this apperceptive span is the fact that what we call a present moment in our consciousness always has a brief but still by no means an infinitesimal length, within which the "pulse" of change, which that moment apperceives, must fall. Changes of mental content which occur either too swiftly or too slowly to fall within the span of the least or of the greatest time-interval which our human apperception follows escape us altogether, or else, like the slower changes occurring in nature, are only indirectly to be noticed by us. Since the momentary change in the contents of our consciousness corresponds, in a general way, to the externally observable alteration of our physical routine to meet new conditions, one may say, on the whole, that where our established habits are changed too slowly or too quickly, the change is inadequately represented, or is not represented at all, in our individual experience.

Yet a change in our routine which is so slow as to escape our own apperceptive span, is still a fact in the phenomenal world, a fact capable of being recorded and verified. *Why may not just such facts be represented by experience which accompanies our own, and which is just as real as ours, but which is characterized by another apperceptive span?* This supplementary hypothesis is worthy of special consideration.

No element or character of our human experience, in fact, appears more arbitrary than does the apperceptive span when we submit its phenomena to experimental tests. That the whole of the contents of a finite series of temporal instants should, despite the fact of this temporal succession, form one moment of our consciousness—that, for instance, a rhythmic phrase, made up of a number of successive beats, should constitute one presented whole, and stand before our consciousness as such, is in itself a remarkable fact. That, when once this is the case, the length of such a single and presentable rhythmic phrase or other presentable conscious moment should be as limited as it is, is an entirely arbitrary characteristic of our special type of human experience. When once we recognize this aspect of our conscious life, we can conceptually vary indefinitely this temporal span of consciousness, and can so form the notion of other possible experience than ours whose essence, like that of our own, should consist in the contrast between relatively familiar or changeless contents and relatively new contents, but whose apperceptive span should differ from our own in such wise that for such experience a " present moment " might be, when temporally regarded, as much longer or as much shorter than ours as one pleases. A millionth of a second might constitute the span of one such conceivable type of experience. In that case changes of content far too subtle to mean anything to us would be matters of immediate fact to the experience in question. A minute, an hour, a year, a century, a world-cycle might form the apperceptive span of some other possible type of consciousness. In that case inner changes of content which utterly transcend our direct apperception might be matters of presentation to such another type of experience.

Now, however, imagine a system of finite series of experiences, agreeing, in a great measure, in their contents, but differing in some graded fashion, in their apperceptive span. Let each of these series be characterized by the fact that everywhere there were present, in the inner world of each experience, changing groups of contents A, B, C, D, the rate of change, however, differing in all the series alike for each group of contents, so that in every one of the series in question the group A changed at some rapid rate r, the group B at some slower rate r', the group C at a still slower rate r'', and so on. Now suppose it arbitrarily agreed that if, for any one of these series, a given change of contents Δ took place within the span of one of the presented moments of

that series, then this degree of change should mean a clear
consciousness of the nature of just that change from older
to newer conditions, whereas, in so far as contents changed
either much less or much more than Δ during such a presented moment, then these contents and their changes should
be relatively obscure for the experience in question, forming
only the background upon which the clearly apperceived
changes stood out. It would then become possible, in one
of these series of experiences (whose apperceptive span was
so related to the rate r that the required change Δ took place
in the group A during one presentable moment of this series),
that the changes of A should stand out clearly, as definite
facts, on a dimly apperceived background of the contents
B, C, and D. In a second series, whose contents we may
suppose the same as those of the first, but whose apperceptive span has relation to the rate r', the changes of A
would become obscure, while the changes of B were clear,
and so on. Thus what for one of these series of experiences
was the clearly apperceived relation of new and old, would
be, in another series, represented only by bafflingly swift
and confused tremulousness of contents, or by apparently
changeless contents. What one experience might indirectly come to regard as a conceivable secular variation of
the content which, so far as its own direct apperception
went, is found unalterable, another experience, substantially agreeing with the first in all but the apperceptive span,
would have presented to itself as definitely changing material. What one experience, therefore, viewed as seemingly unalterable, and consequently unmeaning routine,
the other would apperceive as significant and momentary
change.

Let one now further suppose, however, that through the
addition of still other elements to each of these series of
experiences, the presence of one series became communicated to the others by phenomenally observable manifes-

tations. Then surely one can conceive each series of experiences as aware, more or less indirectly, of the presence, and even of the inner reality of its neighbors. But of the meaning of this other life each series could form a directer sort of appreciation only in so far as the apperceptive span of one series agreed with that of another. Socially definite communication could occur only between types of experience of substantially the same apperceptive span. Finally, if one supposes the phenomenally indicated contents of the various series to involve many unlikenesses, as well as many agreements in the different series themselves, one approaches the conception of a system of series of experiences whereof any one series might manifest its presence to its neighbors, while the inner life and meaning of one series could be concretely realized by another only in so far as, along with much agreement in their contents, there was also close agreement in apperceptive span. But if a series of slowly changing contents, and of vast apperceptive span, manifested its presence to a series of swiftly changing contents, and of brief apperceptive span, then the only representative of the first series in the life of the second would be a group of changeless, or of rhythmically repeated phenomena, which would seem to manifest no intelligible inner life as such, but only those habits which form, not the whole, but a single aspect of the phenomenal life of any being whose inner experience his neighbor can interpret—only such habits, but no significant variations or adjustments of habits.

If one again reviews, in the light of these considerations, the facts before considered, one finds a situation which our single supplementary hypothesis now enables us in general to understand. This hypothesis is that the apperceptive span of finite experience is a quantity relatively fixed for our social fellows, but very vastly variable in the realm of cosmical experience in general. The "other experience than ours," of which we suppose the inner life of nature to consist, is everywhere an experience of new contents viewed on the background of old contents, of changes arising on a basis of identity, of novelty contrasted with familiarity. In order that such streams of gradual change should be inwardly appreciable, the change must everywhere be present, to a finite degree, within one presented moment of the series of experiences to which, in each case of conscious experience, this appreciation belongs. But a present moment does not mean a mathematical instant. It means, in any type of conscious experience, a period of time equal to the apperceptive span, and this period, in case of any given finite experience, might as well be a world-cycle as a second. Only, in case a type of changing experience whose apperceptive span is a world-cycle, hints its contents to a sort of experience whose apperceptive span is brief, like ours, then the phenomenal manifestation in question may, to any extent, take the form of an apparently final uniformity of contents, such as we seem to observe in the secular uniformities of physical nature. But, where uniformity alone is suggested, the element of change of contents, upon which every appreciation of any inner experience depends, is absent. One then seems to be apperceiving only fixed laws, absolute routine, settled habits of nature, and can detect no inner meanings, unless by the aid of the most fanciful analogies. Between experience of this august span and our human experience a relatively continuous series of types of experience may lie, whose presence gets manifested to us in processes of increasing phenomenal irregularity, such as those of organic nature. Nearest to our own type of human experience would doubtless lie masses of "subliminal" experience related to those changing habits of our own organisms which escape our apperceptive span. Below our own brief span there may lie types of experience of still briefer span, whose phenomenal manifestations have, like the hypothetical collisions of the molecules of a gas, an enormous irregularity, such as only the law of averages, as revealed by the doctrine of chances, enables us to conceive as resulting, by virtue of the vast numbers of facts that are concerned, in a secondary regularity of outward seeming when these facts are grouped in great masses.

But in itself, nature, as such, would be neither a world of fixed habits or yet a world of mere novelties, but rather a world of experience with permanence everywhere set off by change. For the rest, the problem which has been raised by Mr. Charles Peirce (to whose brilliant cosmological essays the foregoing discussion, despite the indicated disagreements, obviously owes very much)—the problem whether in nature there is any objective " chance," and whether all natural law is, in the last analysis, a product of evolution, has been in the foregoing, deliberately ignored. It is a problem, as above remarked, whose discussion belongs elsewhere than in this context.

IX

*ORIGINALITY AND CONSCIOUSNESS.**

IT takes but a small experience of men and of literature
to bring to our notice the fact that one of the most powerful enemies of effective originality, in conduct, and in artistic production, is the conscious wish and intent to be original.
Yet any man who means to do good work desires to be original. Hence there arises, for every such man, a problem—
a problem of self-conquest. It is easy to be commonplace.
One has only to follow the crowd, to drift, to live from day
to day. The ambitious man rebels at this destiny. He
wants to be himself. He realizes the force of the one
great command that the moral law addresses to the individual in regard to the individual's own self-cultivation.
This command is: " Be unique, as your Father in heaven
is unique." All other moral commands tell the individual
about the law of self-surrender. Such commands run:
Sacrifice yourself—be a servant—find your office and fulfill
its tasks—be loyal to your ties—in a word, give up your
separate life. There remains, side by side with all these
precepts, the other, the equally sacred commandment : Be
unique. That is : Render your service as nobody else can
render it ; do your work as you alone can do it ; fill the
place that nobody else can fill. There is no inconsistency
between these two aspects of the moral law. One supple-
ments the other. Some unique form of self-sacrifice re-

---

* From the Harvard Monthly, June, 1897.

mains the individual's inalienable privilege. Therein alone
can he fulfill his destiny. Well, all this the ambitious man
feels. And to feel this introduces the problem of every
noble youth: How shall I be original? Forthwith, however, the problem deepens. To wish to be original is, as we
have said, to come face to face with one of the principal
foes to originality. Conscious, deliberate, intentional effort
at originality is likely to involve one of two things: viz.,
either waywardness or self-imitation. Waywardness is
such trivial attempt at originality as depends upon following the passing mood of the moment. Self-imitation is the
well-known besetting sin of anybody who has once observed
himself saying or doing what he takes to be an uncom-
monly clever thing. Teachers, clergymen, and poets once
past their prime, all share with self-conscious children the
temptation to repeat their old successes by imitating their
own once novel, pretty deeds. Thus, in these two ways,
the will to be original tends to defeat itself. One must
begin one's self-assertion, even in this its most sacred undertaking, by an act of self-conquest. And meanwhile there
arises a certain purely theoretical question, namely: Why
this strange conflict between originality and consciousness? Why is the best human originality so largely an
unconscious product?

To this very natural theoretical question the present
paper suggests some answer. The answer, so far as it goes,
is founded upon a very simple analysis of our human type
of consciousness. It is easy to indicate that the narrow
field or span of conscious life in which you and I live is
not large enough to permit the source and essence of our
best and most individual processes to become directly present to us at all. Hence it is not so much the nature of
originality as the accidental limits of the human type
of consciousness which force us to admit that, for us
men, our originality, whatever be its grade, must in gen-

eral belong to the unconscious side of our life. On the
other hand, such a study of the reason why human consciousness and originality are related as they are, may help
us to suggest, in a measure, how to treat the practical problem with which we began, and how to show the way towards
that self-conquest upon which the successful effort of an
individual to mould himself to originality must depend.

Our conscious mental life is, as everybody knows, usually
classified under three heads, the Intellect, the Feelings, and
the Will. And one may raise the question : To which one,
if to any one, of these three aspects of our mental life, is
the originality of any given individual—say of a literary
artist—to be attributed ? This is of course an elementary
problem of mental analysis. I regard it as of essential
importance for the task before us.

In answer, I may first venture to point out one very
simple, but not infrequent popular mistake as to the region
of a man's mind in which we may most naturally look for
originality. It is customary for popular moralists to exhort
a man in a tone which presupposes that anybody can
accomplish essentially original acts of conscious Will.
The will is, in fact, often conceived as the most originative
aspect of mental life. "It lies with you," one says. "If
you will, you can be—this or that—within your limits, of
course, but still in an original way." It is thus supposed
to be especially the will that, in the course of my life, initi-
ates new fashions of conduct, and so transforms my destiny
by virtue of its own spontaneity. My will and my "power
of initiative" are often, in popular speech, identified. This,
one may suppose, is often what those have in mind who
identify genius with a "capacity for taking pains." Such
may mean, by this expression, that, whereas a lazy man
cannot invent and accomplish great and original things, a
painstaking man, by persistently exercising his power of
initiative, reaches results which, because they are the prod-

uct of his individual will, have a special right to be novel, and so to embody originality of some higher grade.

But it is a serious mistake thus directly to identify voluntary activity with origination. Every voluntary act, just in so far as it is voluntary, must for that very reason possess no originality whatever. For I cannot will to do anything unless I first know what I am to do. This, however, I must have learned by previous experience of precisely such acts. And this, again, implies that every voluntary act is essentially identical, in so far as it is voluntary, with an act that I have already performed before. Hence, every voluntary act depends upon previous acts whose origin, in the first instance, must have been involuntary. One can illustrate this principle indefinitely ; and it is of boundless importance for the practical training of the will. Voluntary acts come to be such only after they have first been involuntarily performed, their origin lying in the realms of instinct, of imitation, of chance experience, and of passing impulse. Inner, or psychological "power of initiative," so far as concerns the positive content of our actions, the will has none whatever. I cannot will to swim, unless I have first learned how to swim. I cannot learn, except by the gradual adjustment of inherited tendencies to environment, and of past habits to new situations. I can will to set about learning to swim ; but when I will that, I will merely old deeds, such as walking in shallow water—a process which I this time can choose to continue until I am beyond my depth. In that case the situation becomes at once novel enough ; but the novelty is not now in me, but precisely in the situation ; and what I thereupon do, namely, to struggle, to gasp, to try to obey the orders of the swimmer at my side, and so on, involves the reverse of conscious originality. If I at last learn to swim, that is because, after a time, I somehow involuntarily hit upon the right combination of movements, and get used to the strange situation.

It is just so if I try to write anything novel. My will can lead me into the deep waters of literary effort. It cannot teach me what to do there besides kicking and gasping, as many poor poets involuntarily do. We imagine the will to be originative merely because, very often, by repeating old deeds, we can get ourselves into unheard of situations. But it is life, in such cases, that contains novelties; it is not we who are original. The maiden says nothing original or novel when she says either No or Yes. Two lives happen just then to depend upon her word; but that has nothing to do with her originality. She is usually, in just such matters, an extremely unoriginal person, who behaves very much as the other women from time immemorial have behaved.

Volition, then—and that, too, without the least reference to the question whether the will is free or not—is, as to the contents of our voluntary acts, a wholly unoriginal process. As for Intellect—that, with respect to most of its factors and processes, constantly involves elements of novelty, but leaves at best a very sharply limited room, in all of its human *conscious* activities, for what can be called individual initiative. Why this has to be the case, it is easy to see. Novelty may be possessed to any extent by the facts of our external experience, or by the experiences due to our merely physical condition. But an experience of novelties in the outer world, or of novel physical states of our bodies, forms no part of our intellectual originality. A comet, an earthquake, an explosion, an attack of the grippe—all these are novelties. But the one who experiences these things does not thereby become original or " creative." In fact it is just such extreme novelties that, so long as they remain novelties, confuse us, and help the intellectual life least. We know best what we best recognize; and that, while it has some novel features, is essentially like what we have known before; and is in so far not a new thing. Learning means assimilating; and the rate of our learning of novelties has to be comparatively slow, because we need gradually to assimilate them to one another, and to our own past. Hence most intellectual processes are conservative in type; and essentially novel ideas enter the conscious intellect only gradually. Most rapidly we get possession of hosts of new ideas when, as in childhood, we acquire them by direct social imitation of the preëxistent ideas of others, or when, as in later years, we get them from our fellows by processes of reading, of listening, and of watching the world's ways. But all such externally acquired novelties are not our own in any originative sense. Moreover, in a large measure, the intellect is essentially and explicitly concerned in learning and imitating the truth of things—truth which we find, and which we do not make; so that there is a sense in which the normal intellect spurns many sorts of originality, even if they offer themselves, and professes itself as not merely by accident unoriginal and dependent, but also by choice devoted to submissive repetition of the truth. There is indeed, in all this, always room left for a certain sort of originality, but plainly, in the normal case, the possible range of conscious and fruitful intellectual originality is, psychologically speaking, very decidedly limited. The result so far is that it is at least very hard to define what constitutes the realm that is still left open, in the conscious intellectual life, for genuine and valuable originality.

But the realm of Feeling still remains as the one region of mental life not so far considered. Here the scope for possible originality is much larger; and, in fact, the most original literary men are obviously such, in a measure, by virtue of the strong individuality possessed by their characteristic emotions, interests, and tones of inner life. On the other hand, it must be insisted that mere novelty, or individuality of feeling, never by itself constitutes any independently valuable type of originality. The nervously degenerate, the "cranks," the acute, nervous sufferers, know of a great variety of feelings, both agreeable and disagreeable, both transient and lasting, which are often marked, in particular cases, by very decidedly individual and original shadings, and which therefore give their subject, upon occasion, a strong and often not unfounded sense that he is very "different from common men." But such originality of feeling constitutes something very remote from original genius, unless, indeed, the abnormity gets precisely that union with the life of the intellect which does distinguish true originality in great minds.   One is never a man of parts because of his novel feelings; genius implies knowing how to use feelings.

The result so far is that, as a matter of analysis, the most characteristic processes of the conscious intellect are, in the main, imitative, assimilative, and in so far uncreative.   The conscious will is similarly an unoriginal process.   On the other hand, the feelings are a possible source of very manifold and individual mental processes, but as mere feelings they are not an obvious source of what is valuable about originality, since a perfectly useless degenerate may have countless feelings of the most novel and intense character without any happy or creative result. The question then becomes : What union of intellectual and effective processes is responsible for valuable originality ?

A step nearer we come to the answer to this question when we observe in what senses a mental creation, such as a work of literary art, can possibly be novel at all.   The truth of things an artist finds, but does not make.   Even where a man of action creates new truth by voluntary processes, as a statesman or a conqueror creates, the activity, just in so far as it is voluntary, is, psychologically speaking, as we saw, decidedly unoriginal and unoriginative.   And as fact, the greatest artists, however original, are also imitators—imitators of artistic traditions, of the forms of their

18

mother tongue, of life, of human nature, of truth; and, unless they were thus in a due measure imitative, they would be lunatics. Their creative power is an extremely relative thing, which must be confined within strict limits. But there are three ways in which sane originality can display itself. They are these: (1) One can be original in the style or form which he gives to his work; (2) One can be original in the selection of the objects which he imitates; (3) One can be original in the invention of relatively novel combinations of old material.

The first of these forms of originality exists, in some very limited degree, in the activities of even the most unartistic and commonplace people, in so far as they possess individuality at all. The voice of your friend, by which you recognize him in a crowd, the step, the bearing, the little tricks of gesture, the handwriting, of any individual —these are features comparable in nature to those often indescribable characters which distinguish the style of one artist from that of another. In commonplace people these particularities of bearing, of manner, of personal quality, are of only domestic or neighborly interest. In great artists such features chance to appear extremely significant. One's individual style colors both one's purely physical activities and one's mentally significant ways of expressing one's self. Such a style may be modified by conscious self-observation, but no voluntary process can ever transform it. In its mentally valuable phenomena it is commonly rather the embodiment of one's ruling tones of feeling, one's prevailing moods, than of any consciously voluntary or intellectual process. Intellect and will may toil to improve it, but beyond certain limits they toil in vain. Its origin is in the unconscious realm. Its originality is due to hereditary factors. Its basis is something born and not made. It often constitutes, in artists, the most inscrutable aspect of their genius. Its value is due to our fondness of whatever most suggests fascinating individuality. Our æsthetic demands upon the individual are, like those of the moral law, paradoxical. We want an individual to do what his fellows do, to imitate, to follow custom ; and yet all the while we want him to *be* something unique, to give us a fascinating personality that nobody else can show us. Thus we object to everybody whose deeds are unconventional ; yet when a man is merely conventional, we despise him as a commonplace fellow. How then shall our neighbor please us ? One answer is : He must in a large measure do the thing that everybody does—he must follow the modes of the day, say the ordinary things, but he must do all this in his own unique way, in a style that is his own. Then, when he thus imitates inimitably, as a great actor does, we say, in case this his individual style chances somehow to touch our feelings, so that they surge up in sympathy with his own— we say : What a manner he has ! It is thus that the great artist impresses us, so far as concerns his literary style. Herein his personality gets an embodiment whose only directly conscious representative in mind is his prevailing way of feeling. But his way of feeling colors the form of all his intellectual work.

The second form of originality, named above, has a more obviously intellectual character. An artist's selection of his themes, of his ideals, of the characters, situations, and so forth, which he chooses to imitate, belongs of course amongst what we commonly call the labors of his intellect. Yet one must not misunderstand the true relations here. Consciously the artist may think, "What shall I choose ? What shall I write about ? What shall I depict ?" But the best choices of anybody's life are made for unconscious reasons.

The third form of originality, that of the larger combinations of one's ideas and acts, is the highest, and, in its best forms, the rarest of all. Yet no artist has ever been able to tell us, with conscious truthfulness, how such originality of combination is accomplished. Nor do we know in our own cases. The processes of combination are very slow. What it has taken you years to learn, may at last appear in its unity before you. At the moments when your mental combinations come to light, you may be getting what seems to be a bird's-eye view of an entire life. But how you came to get this view, your consciousness, which is of the moment, cannot tell you.

In sum, in case of all these three sorts of originality, you are dealing with a complex union of mental elements belonging to the feelings and to the intellectual life. But how the happy union takes place, how the valuable originality is acquired, your consciousness does not inform you —and that for two reasons. First, your consciousness never lights up the depths of your personal temperament—never shows you, at any moment, precisely why you feel as you do. And secondly, your originality, where it is important, has to do with the gradual organization of your life as a whole, while your consciousness, limited as it is to a very short span, flickers along from moment to moment, and never reveals the true meaning of your life-processes in their linkage, growth, and rationality. Hence your conscious moments show you little but dependent volitional and intellectual processes, which are powerless to reveal the secret of their own evolution. The feelings of the moment may be consciously original, but need not on that account be important. Your current consciousness interprets your true individuality, much as lightning at night shows the storm clouds. Whence the storm came, and whither it whirls, the lightning, like your passing moments of conscious life, is too brief to show. We men are always struggling to grasp eternity in a fleeting instant.

Yet of course our human type of consciousness, with all its flickering, is the best type that we have; and the practical problem remains: What shall I do consciously to direct myself towards my best type of originality in word and deed?

The answer runs thus: First, see why it is that your human sort of consciousness never can fully reveal to you, at any moment, what is best or most original about your own individuality. Seeing this, give up the vain desire to seem, at any instant, consciously original. You could only deceive yourself by following that vain desire. What seemed to you most inevitable, and perhaps most commonplace, your fellows would often find the most original and the best about you. What pleased you as your most original product, others would see to be a poor imitation, or else a trivially wayward mood. For the rest, consciously to aim towards originality in your whole development, and in your organized individual self-expression, is not to aim at the momentary consciousness: "Just now I see myself as an originator." Your self-conquest lies in saying, "I will serve as if I were nothing but a servant, but all the while I will not fear to be unique in my form and plan of service." The best thing, then, that one can consciously do towards attaining effective individuality is to put down one's paltry Fears of being as original, in style and in expression, as fate, despite all of one's loyalty to service, chances to make one. Think, then, thus: "I have a right to be unique; I will not fear to be unique when, as a matter of fortune, I find myself so; but I will not at any moment try to feel as if I were just then in the least an originator. I will consciously serve and efface myself; but when my individuality chances, nevertheless, to express itself, I will rejoice in the happy accident of having unconsciously done what vindicates my right to be this individual." With this in mind, with this assurance that the effectively best about you must grow up in its own way, and must grow, so far as your human mind goes, unconsciously, devote your conscious life to putting yourself into a serious office, where plenty of wholesome experience will come of itself; and then wait for the outcome with assurance. Whatever originality is yours will then come as a matter of life. For it is Life, and not Consciousness, that, in us men, is the originator. Yet the conscious purpose to become original is not unwise, if it only takes the form of choosing to accept that sort of devotion to life which ensures the conscious dependence of our will and of our intellect, but the actual freedom of our individual temperament.

X.

MEISTER ECKHART.

BROTHER ECKHART, later known as a Magister of the University of Paris, and accordingly called Meister Eckhart, was born about 1260, in the upper Rhineland, and died in 1327. The first in the series of German mystics, he was the direct teacher of the more popularly known Tauler, and the beginner of all the later German mystical movements. In the order of the Friars Preachers, or Dominicans, he was early a prior, later a provincial, and later again a prior. He held offices, in his order, in Erfurt, in Frankfort, in Strassburg, in Cologne; he was twice at the University of Paris, as learner and as lecturer; and won, in his time, no small fame as a preacher. In the annals of his Church and of his order, he appears as a man who, however devoted and loyal his purpose, taught, in addition to the faith of the Church, certain reputed errors that finally received, although not until two years after his death, the official condemnation of the Pope. In the history of German thought, occupying as he does the place of the first philosopher of mark to write in German, he has been given very various degrees of importance by the historians, according to the estimate that different writers have placed upon the originality of his ideas. As a fact, so far as his mere opinions are concerned, the most recent scholarly research

* A paper read before the Plymouth School of Ethics in the summer of 1894.

has come more and more to see in him, not so much the qualities of an independently constructive philosopher, but rather the character of a fairly representative Catholic mystic of the thirteenth or fourteenth century, whose religious career was, however, much modified by the really original personal temperament that led him in the end, although not by his own intent, to the verge of pronounced heresy.* And it is in this character, as a Catholic mystic, of no very novel philosophical opinions, but of a very marked individuality of personal character and influence, that I shall here try to portray Meister Eckhart. That reputation for startling originality of speculation which many writers have sought to give to this first in the long series of German philosophical writers, has been due largely to the very fact that Eckhart wrote and preached upon the profoundest speculative topics in the German tongue, with the deliberate intention of initiating the people into the deepest mysteries of their faith. He first thus translated into the vernacular speech of his land thoughts which were not new to scholastic philosophers, but which were sure to be startling to laymen, and which to us now, if we forget the earlier history of mysticism, have an air of uniqueness, which is increased by the skill of Eckhart's often marvellous German style, and by the sincere tone of personal experience which runs through all that he says. A mystic must always seem, when you consider him by himself, an original person, because it is not authority but intensely individual experience to which he constantly appeals. Before I am done, I shall especially indicate the practical side of Eckhart's life work. It is therefore at the outset enough to say that he was the first who translated speculative mysticism into the German tongue, in order to indicate how wide the range of his practical importance is, in view of what was to be the fu-

---

* Cf. Harnack, Dogmengeschichte, iii, 376.

ture of the German mind. Learn, then, from what follows something of how it felt about 1300 to be a Catholic mystic and at the same time to be a philosophical German missionary to the people.

I.

The order of St. Dominic, confirmed as an order of the Church in 1216, had grown by the end of that century to be one of the most important instruments of Catholic piety and learning. To this order had belonged Albertus Magnus, and his still greater pupil, St. Thomas Aquinas. In the care of these men, and of their immediate pupils, the scholastic philosophy had reached its most classic expression. St. Thomas died in 1274, when Eckhart was still a boy. Albert, who outlived his own pupil, died in 1280. The order of the Friars Preachers, according to the wording of its own constitutions,* " was principally and essentially designed for preaching and teaching, in order thereby to communicate to others the fruits of contemplation and to procure the salvation of souls." The triumphs that its great scholars won in the cause of philosophical and theological learning were therefore intended by themselves as a means to an end. The faith was to be defended; heresy was to be refuted; the world was to be taught. The fruits of contemplation were to be communicated to others.

Now Eckhart appears, in every recorded line of his writings, as one who understood the constitutions of the Dominicans in a very literal sense. He was very early trained to follow, and in time to administer, the discipline of his order; he received a thorough preparation in philosophy and in theology; he gave the closest attention to the art of preaching with effect in the vernacular tongue. All this was in the line of his education for his calling. The tech-

* Drane, History of St. Dominic (edition of 1891), p. 164.

nical finish of much of his preserved work reveals the expert veteran, who must have been made such by long and merciless exercise in harness. Mystics have often been essentially wayward and capricious persons, of sentimental nature and rebellious habits. Against just such waywardness, however, was the monastic training of the mendicant orders especially directed; and this man was thoroughly hardened to service; was of rigid life, and of well-knit, although gradually progressive ideas; and as far as possible his sentiment was kept under the control of his insight. So far you have just the monk. But his was withal, indeed, an extremely rich and individual temperament, and one in which the deepest emotion, when once it was permitted to go free, found ample room. Meanwhile he was rugged and manly, being impatient of mere formulas, fond of paradoxes, quick and original in expression. A very marked personal piety, too, inspired him. He was a faithful monk, but he must go beyond the mere formalities of his profession. He needed to restate everything in his own words. He could rest in none but absolute solutions of his problems. And he must, indeed, communicate to others the fruits of his contemplation.

Accordingly his experience, in its most general form, was this: He was throughout minded to preach the Catholic faith, and to move his hearers to live it in their daily lives. But the faith had now received, through the scholastic philosophy, an extremely elaborate formulation. And the Rhineland, in Eckhart's time, was a region where religious experience was intense and manifold, where individual intuitions of the highest truth abounded, and were often very waywardly followed out to heretical conclusions, and where more or less irregular efforts to found and to develop religious orders, and to save souls by extraordinary devices, were frequent and significant phenomena of social life. Practical mysticism, the ordering of the life of an individ-

ual upon the basis of the sensation of some form of immediate communion with God, was, in that time and region,
in the air. The communities known by the vaguely applied
names of Beghinen and Begharden—more or less irregular
unions of women and of men, as the case might be, devoted to some sort of religious separation from the world,
and to the pursuit of a piety that was not always free from
the well-founded accusation of heresy—these were familiar
phenomena along the upper and lower Rhine in the thirteenth century. The people in general longed for religious
guides. The previous ages of conflict between the Church
and the empire had left behind them, at the end of the century, a perplexed people and much confusion of faith. It
was in large part for the sake of meeting just such spiritual
needs as this, both in Germany and in other lands, that
the Church had so warmly favored that organization
of regular armies of her trained servants which occurred
through the rise of the two mendicant orders, the Francis-
cans and the Dominicans themselves. And so Eckhart
undertook, as his own special life work, the guiding of the
religious life of his hearers by means of the translation
of the philosophy of his Church and his order into the
language of the people.*

But for Eckhart scholastic speculation must now be
brought over from Latin into German, from the technical
speech of that most highly elaborated of philosophical
methods into words suited to all who looked to their own
highest good, who were submissive to God, who aspired,
and who had overcome themselves. For to all such Eck-

* For this general conception of Eckhart's life work, due in large part
to the recent researches of Denifle, but also in part maintained by
Preger, see (in addition to Harnack's book, above cited, and to Preger's
account in his Geschichte d. Mystik), Loof's Dogmengeschichte, p.
288, and Windelband's History of Philosophy (English translation), p.
334.

hart, as he tells us, addressed his speech.* And accordingly such speculation must tend from the outset to be modified as it was delivered. The truths of philosophy must be
linked to the actual experience of the faithful. Yes, what
were these truths but the outcome of learned reflection
upon such experience ? Eckhart must preach with the
understanding—ay, but with the spirit also. He had been
early trained to a sense of the importance of learning. But,
once more, these so precious fruits of contemplation must
be communicated to others ; yes, must be built up anew in
every hearer's mind, as the actual outcome, as the very form
and body of his own personal and religious life. For all
this meant the one great object—the salvation of souls, the
guidance of the perplexed, the portrayal of the truth. Such
popular translation of philosophy, in case a man's philosophy means to himself in any sense the mirror of human
life, the theory of passion, must always tend, in the man
who thus translates, to a continual renewal and refreshment
of his most fundamental thinking itself. The technical
weaver of philosophical theories may or may not bear in
mind the fact that had it not been for the vital perplexi-
ties of experience—the immediate issues of life—the problems of the schools would never have come into existence.
Accordingly, such a technical student may long neglect
the renewed examination of his own fundamental principles for the sake of devoting himself to the development
of their most remote theoretical consequences. But the
man who wants to make his philosophy immediately interesting to the serious-minded amongst the people, must
not dwell upon those remoter consequences so much as upon
principles ; for it is just the most fundamental principle of
life that the unlearned inquirer desires to get. People
naturally begin in philosophy with the most critical and

* Cf. Pfeiffer's edition, Deutsche Mystiker, ii, p. 2.

tremendous of its issues. But if you are to translate such
fundamental principles into the speech of your hearer's
spiritual experience, if you are to show him that the
most abstruse truth walks daily beside him, well, then,
daily you too must experience and must restate to yourself this abstrusely spiritual truth that lies at the basis of
your life, as of your hearer's. You must continually re-
initiate yourself into the mysteries of your own philosophical doctrine. It must become and remain a personal
as well as a technical matter with you.

Accordingly, we find Eckhart, although in many respects a Thomist, and also a sincere follower of the general
traditions of Catholic mysticism, still from the outset evidently disposed to be always afresh dependent upon his
own personal experience for the formulation and proof
of the philosophy that he expounds to his hearers. Learning is there and at his call, but while he preaches he keeps
it in the background of his mind. Authorities he can cite
in numbers, and, like Thomas, he is especially fond of cit-
ing, sometimes expressly, sometimes indirectly, Aristotle,
St. Augustine, and the Neo-Platonic Christian writer
known to the scholastics under the traditional, although
false, name of Dionysius the Areopagite. But after all Eckhart regards mere authority in itself as something principally serviceable in the deepest matters, by way of illustration. In physics he is, to be sure, altogether dependent
upon Aristotle. His psychology he gets in part from St.
Augustine, in part from the Aristotelian conception of the
Creative Intelligence as it had then been interpreted by recent philosophy. His technically theological concepts are,
up to a certain point, largely Thomistic. But the heart of
his doctrine, and so that group of conceptions which in the
end he comes most to love and to expound—these may
indeed be found more or less expressed in Augustine, in
Dionysius, in Thomas ; but Eckhart, for his own conscious-

ness, neither believes nor expounds these opinions precisely
as he there finds them, nor yet *because* the authorities in
any fashion support them.   On the contrary, he is conscious
of telling the truth as immediate religious experience,
interpreted by the light of reason, reveals this truth both
to himself and (for so he firmly holds) to every properly
guided soul amongst his hearers also.   Hence Eckhart's
philosophy, at first evidently a scholasticism, became, to his
own thoughts, as he actually preached, more and more the
record of a soul alone with God and with the absolute truth.
He wandered into strange regions in the spiritual world.
St. Thomas had sought to teach this age afresh, with great
elaboration of detail, the exact sense in which human reason can go only so far, and needs revelation from above to
guide it further.   The precise relation of natural to revealed
religion was accordingly one of the chief problems of philosophical discussion in that period.   But Eckhart, in his
own inner experience, erelong, both by the aid of Dionysius and by virtue of his own meditation, came to a certain wondrous place where not only human reason, but, as
he held, all reason, sees its own birth out of something beyond reason, out of something that is essentially a divine
mystery.   For at this point this birth of reason from a yet
deeper principle, this derivation of the light of insight from
a still diviner light that to us seems darkness—all this, I
say, appeared now in Eckhart's mind not as a mere accident, dependent only upon the chance that some things
have been hidden from our reason in this life, and have
been revealed only to our faith—not such an accident, but
an essential truth of things.   In God, too, there must be
something corresponding to just this failure of reason to
finish its own work.   The highest truth of religious experience, thinks Eckhart, is that the Godhead as such
simply cannot be absolutely revealed to any form of rational insight, human or divine.   On the contrary, it is of the

very essence of reason itself to be dependent upon something that is not reason. And this, I repeat, is not, for Eckhart, the mere mischance of our human reason, but the very nature of all reason. Knowledge of God, even when complete, and just because of its completeness, would see its own very self as essentially rooted in a certain central mystery, which Eckhart undertakes to define, so far as definition is possible. That this is true, Eckhart constantly seeks to verify afresh in his own experience. The conception in question, the conception of a principle to be called the One, or the Godhead, or the Absolute, above knowledge, yet the source and principle of knowledge, is old ; it is Neo-Platonic—yes, it is much older than that. It is almost identical with the conception of the Absolute Self or Atman of the earliest Hindoo speculation. But Eckhart, knowing nothing of course of the remoter sources or counterparts of his conception, and himself learning it in the main from Dionysius, discovers the everlastingly fresh and convincing verification of it in his own religious life. And now—this is just the essential feature of the man, in so far as he is a typical mystic—this conception of a central mystery at the very heart and source of the highest knowledge Eckhart treats not as a merely theoretical matter, but as an intensely practical concern. The salvation of the soul depends upon a certain act of rising above knowledge to what is beyond knowledge.

II.

I suppose that this central notion of Eckhart, as of most speculative mystics, will seem at first sight either a trivial commonplace, or an unnecessarily abstruse doctrine, according as it chances to strike you. That the world shall have something Unknowable at the heart of it is, in this age of Herbert Spencer and of the Agnostics, indeed a trivial enough observation of popular philosophy. But

Eckhart's Unknowable, the *wüste Gottheit*, or " wilderness of Godhead," of which he loves to speak, is not Spencer's Unknowable, but is rather the One above knowledge of Plotinus and of Dionysius. Eckhart's reason for asserting this as the final truth is not a vexation over the special limitations of human knowledge, but is a certain reflection upon what a mystic takes to be the absolute nature of all knowledge. It is the fullness, not the lack of insight that seems to bring the speculative mystic to this affirmation, that all insight must be rooted in mystery. In one of the preserved *Sprüche* of Meister Eckhart there is a striking passage whose parallel to the well-known burden of the angel's song in the Prologue to Faust is all the more remarkable, since of course Goethe can have known nothing of this word of Eckhart's. Goethe's angels sing:

> Der Anblick giebt den Engeln Stärke,
>   *Da* Keiner dich ergrunden mag.
> Und alle deine hohen Werke,
>   Sind herrlich wie am ersten Tag.

Eckhart says: " When God created the angels, the first glance that they took was, that they saw the Father's Essence, and how the Son burst forth from the heart of the Father, even as a green branch from a tree. This gladsome vision they have had more than six thousand years, and How it is, that they know this very day as much [i. e., as little] as when they first were made. And that is from the greatness of the knowledge. The more one knows, the less one understands." *

Now this principle, which is as old as mystical philosophy, has played not a little part, as I must at once assure you, in the discussions of modern Idealism. Here is no place to face the issue upon its own merits. But I want you

---

* Pfeiffer's Deutsche Mystiker, ii, p. 606.

to remember that here is no mere whim of the mystics, but a central problem of all philosophy. Readers who know anything of the modern forms of the doctrine of the Unconscious in philosophy are more or less acquainted with types of metaphysical speculation which have found the world in essence incomprehensible, not because it is unspiritual, but just because it shall be known to be spiritual, while the essence of spirituality shall be something beyond any transparently reflective definition, although it shall be productive of all the possible life of experience and of reflection, and shall be known, although never quite comprehended, as such, a supreme source of light. The motive of this special sort of recognition of mystery (of a mystery involved in the very light of the spiritual world), and the contrast between this and other shapes of the doctrine of the Unknowable, are not hard to indicate, if one may be permitted to speak for a moment in rather modern terms.

The common, the popular, if you like, the relatively trivial form of the doctrine of the Unknowable, runs thus: There is the world yonder, which goes its own way, and exists as a world of things in themselves. Here, however, is a creature called a sentient, or, by the grace of evolution, a more or less rational being. He wants to make out the nature of the things in themselves. He can do so only inasmuch as eyes and ears, smell and touch, permit him to get at the sense-data that his wits are to interpret. The things give him the sense-data. No further can he go than these data permit. Hence, in one way or another, as he reflects, he finds himself cut off by his limited senses from the real truth of the things. He has not data enough. No, he could not possibly have data enough. For a thing is never a sensation. The things never wander through your eyes. Only the sensations of color, of smell, of touch, somehow get awakened in you by the things. And so, too, with any other senses that one might have. We might
19

come to possess countless new senses added to our present ones. These would indeed indefinitely enrich our experience; but they would only show their various data, never the unconquerable external facts as such. *Das dort ist niemals hier.* Experience is never reality. Hence reality is unknowable.

This, I say, is the usual form of the doctrine of the Unknowable. Spencer indeed gets somewhat beyond this form, being himself a bit of an undeveloped mystic; but he never really reaches the other form, and so he remains in a region which does not now further concern us. Your genuine mystic, whether Neo-Platonic in his categories, or fashioned more like a modern idealist, takes a totally different view of the universe, and of the nature of truth; and accordingly he defines quite otherwise the nature of his mystery. Observe still closer the contrast.

The world, so our typical mystic holds, is not an Unknowable Reality, external to all knowing beings. It is in deepest essence a spiritual world, i. e., it is the world that exists in truth, not apart from any knowing being, but in and for, or else wholly by the ever-sustaining will and pleasure, of a being who is essentially omniscient, i. e., a being who knows whatever can logically become knowable, and what can logically become knowable is not a world of things in themselves, but of ideas, or of facts whose only reality is that they express or embody ideas. To exemplify by Eckhart's own case—our Meister, as a follower of Thomas, held that, in advance of the creation, the world of truth was represented in and so, in an inner sense, was eternally existent for the divine knowledge as a world of archetypal Ideas—Ideas, namely, of everything afterwards created, as well as of all that was never created, but that remains only possible. These divine Ideas are conceived as in nature similar to Plato's Ideas, except for the fact that they are explicitly to be defined as just content in the divine mind, while Plato's ideas existed apart from any mind. God foreknew all things; he saw all things in eternity. I, for instance, was there too, as ideal object amongst ideas—one of the objects that God knew—I in the inmost truth of me—not yet as created thing, but as thought of God. Then, God, of his goodness, choosing to impart himself, chose from his ideal world, the content of this world, and willed it to be. Its being—well Eckhart holds that such being is a sort of divinely supported shadow-being. "If God withdrew his own back to himself, all creatures would become nothing." * The things have no true being of themselves. God grants them the support of his own will as a sort of substitute for being; and in speaking of this shadow-land of created being Eckhart, who, as you remember, loves paradoxes, voices himself much more unguardedly than his master Thomas had done, whose gentle prudence had avoided, by means of finely shaded but sometimes rather suspiciously subtle distinctions, the conscious admission of any pantheistic interpretation of the dependence of the world upon God. For Eckhart, too, as for Thomas, the creation is unquestionably to be thought of as a real fact; but Eckhart has no great concern with what may have constituted this creation, beyond the consideration that God gave the created things nothing that they have any right to keep for themselves. Thus, then, for Eckhart, the spiritual order gets defined. In any case, the world preëxisted for God, in God's knowledge, and as a group of divine ideas. In existing now out of God, but solely by God's sustaining will, the world gets no such independence as makes the least atom of it otherwise than absolutely transparent to divine knowledge. And so, for God, both the ideal and the created world contain no unknowable elements. Their very *esse*, you see, is, from

---

* Pfeiffer, ii, p. 51.

the divine point of view, joined with what, for God's insight, would constitute their divine sort of *percipi*. There are, for God, no things in themselves at all—only ideas in God, and shadow creatures of his will without him.

This is the familiar Christian conception of the world as a spiritual order, only interpreted as a Thomistic mystic is disposed to view it. I use it here not only as an expression of Eckhart's own view, but also as an example of the general type of conceptions for which the reality is, first of all, a system of essentially ideal truth. But now to come nearer to the general reason why both Christian (and, as we shall later see, non-Christian speculative mystics also) have found, deep hidden at the very centre of this world of divinely spiritual transparency, another element, one of impenetrable mystery. For our Christian mystic, as you now see, the divine knowledge is not, from that divine point of view, engaged in the business of conforming to any such thing as an extra-divine reality, but depends solely upon the Godhead itself. God is not obliged to conform his ideas to things. On the contrary, the things are helplessly obliged to conform themselves to his ideas. Hence no external limits confine this divine knowledge to any imperfect sense that the things yonder are mysterious. There is for this view no Spencerian Unknowable outside of knowledge. The world of knowledge is a closed sphere, full of light. But now look within the conceived world of knowledge itself, not indeed at any part of it, but first at the structure and then at the root, at the source of it. There, within this world of the divinely transparent truth, is still the familiar distinction between Subject and Object, between knower and known, between the Self for which all this truth has being and that which has being for this Self. Now for God, as the mystic has thus far conceived him, the known object world, of eternal ideas and of temporally created things, is such that God as knower is absolutely adequate to it, while this world itself in its wholeness, as eternal and as temporal world together, is the full expression of God's necessary as well as of his freely constructed truth. But now, once more, whence this perfect adjustment of subject to object, of divine knowledge to divine truth ? Surely the answer must be : God's nature makes this so. There is, then, something to be called God's *Essentia*, or *Wesen*, his Godhead, his very being as God, his absolute self-control or self-possession, the very fullness of his life as the Absolute —there is something, I say, of this sort, which requires God's world of truth, distinct as it is from his knowledge of this world, to be still precisely the adequate correspondent to this his knowledge of it, as the latter is the adequate correspondent of the former. Suppose, if you will, to make this conception a little clearer, that one conceived God as being ignorant and as so far like our finite selves. Well, then, surely he would be, like us, of limited *Wesen* or *Essentia*. We know little because we *are* so little. Our essence is almost a naught. A stone or a brute has still less or lower being than a man ; hence it knows either nothing at all or less than a man. Just so God, if he were ignorant like us, would be of an undivine (i. e., of imperfect) essence. It is then his Godhead, his perfection, his limitless wealth of nature, that merely expresses itself in his omniscience. He is omniscient, if you choose so to express the matter, for two reasons : First, because his divine nature or essence, of its very fullness, begets from its own heart that distinction between known object and knowing subject whereon the divine knowledge itself is based ; second, because, since God's own nature or essence is supreme and limitless, the two members of this derived antithesis between knower and known, subject and object, cannot themselves be limited with respect to their own fulfillment, but must both, in their completeness, be adequate to each other, and so unlimited.

All this so far appears and is a revelation of the glory of God. But look still a little closer. Consider one fact more. God's *Essentia* thus appears as what Plotinus called the One, or the principle; while that distinction, that doubleness, upon which God's knowledge is based appears to our mystics to be itself a secondary derivative from this One principle. And here at length we reach the point where the genuinely divine mystery begins to appear, according to the opinion of the speculative mystics, as it is in itself—not beyond or external to the world of knowledge, but within, and at the heart of this world—not indeed as any part of this world, or as any one mysterious object there, but as the root and source of all knowledge and of all objects.

For God's life itself, his *Essentia*, his oneness that is above all distinctions—this, you see, is now the mystery, not for us, but *per se*. And it is the mystery because it is the source of that very distinction upon which the world of knowledge rests. Hence it can itself never enter into the world of knowledge, for that world is derived from it. Even the very omniscience of God cannot fathom this mystery, because this mystery is logically unfathomable. Nor would one really in presence of this mystery even wish to fathom it or treat it as a limitation to knowledge, for you are limited by unknown objects within the world of conceivable knowledge. But the source of the very world of knowledge is itself no object in that world. The divine knowledge is by the very power of the divine essence limitless as to all logically possible objects of knowledge; but just for that very reason this limitless knowledge, expressing itself through the distinction between knower and known, and so presupposing and depending upon this distinction, never gets as its own explicit object the divine *essentia*, in so far as the latter is source and foundation of the distinction upon which this very limitlessness of God's knowledge depends.

The One, the principle of the distinction, the source of God's omniscience, is deeper than the distinction, and so than the divine omniscience itself. If by truth you mean an object of knowledge, then the Godhead, as such, is the source of the world of truth, and so never becomes any part of the world of truth, which at best is the result and not the inclusive container of God's essence. Thus indeed the heaven of heavens—yes, the very wealth of the divine Word itself—cannot contain the Godhead. And omniscience itself presupposes, implies, involves, is based upon mystery.

I have kept so far fairly close to the relatively Christian categories of mystics such as Eckhart. Eckhart himself is never weary of going over and over this paradox of mystery in knowledge. The aforesaid remark about the angels was, to be sure, an assertion that moves altogether within the orthodox range of St. Thomas's own opinion.* But Eckhart far exceeds such expressions whenever he lets himself go free in the use of the mystical speech. " I say," so runs his word,† " who thinks of anything in God and names it with any name, that is *not* God. God [i. e., here the essential Godhead] is above name and above nature [i. e., above all derived distinctions, even the highest]. We read of a good man who prayed God in his prayer, and would give him a name. Then spake a brother : ' Be still, thou debasest God ' [' Swig, du underest Got']." Even this, to be sure, is still somewhat extravagantly paradoxically phrased Thomism. But Eckhart goes still further : " In the naked Godhead," he elsewhere says,‡ " there was never form

---

* See Summ. Theol. Quest., xii, art. vii, Corpus : " Quod comprehendere Deum impossibile est cuicumque intellectui creato." (Yet some created beings know, although they cannot comprehend, God in his essence.) On the other hand, Thomas, as Aristotelian, attributes to God complete self-knowledge, and so would reject Eckhart's absolute mystery of the Godhead.

† Pfeiffer, p. 92.   ‡ Pfeiffer, p. 468.

nor idea." The essential Godhead is often described as
wordless (*ungewortet*),* or by similar epithets, where Eckhart means by *Wort* the derived word, the world of Ideas,
the Son, who is indeed from eternity, but who is just the
derived. The Neo-Platonic and Dionysian expressions
about the divine Nothingness, as expressing the exaltation
of the divine essence above every "*iht*"—i. e., above every
even conceivable object that has predicates—are favorite expressions with Eckhart himself. "God is nameless, for of
him none can speak or understand. Therefore a heathen
master says : Whatever we understand or assert of the First
Cause that we ourselves are, rather than is the First Cause
any of these things ; for it is beyond all speech and understanding. If I say God is good, it is not true. Rather, I
am good, God is not good. . . . What is good, that can grow
better ; what can grow better, can grow best. Now God is
not good, and therefore it is that he cannot grow better ;
and since he cannot grow better, he cannot grow best ; for
these three things [good, better, best] are far from God, for he
is above all. . . . Therefore be still, and prate not of God—
for with whatsoever speech you prate concerning him you
lie and commit sin. . . . What, then, shall I do ? You shall
always sink away from your selfhood, you shall flow into
his self-possession, and your very thought of *Yours* shall flow
into his Mine, and become there his Mine so completely that
you with him eternally apprehend his birthless fullness of
being and his nameless nothingness." † The original here,
as often in its rugged skill, defies translation.

But yet further : Eckhart takes up an older and much
discussed scholastic terminology, which St. Thomas himself

---

* Pfeiffer, p. 319.

† *Loc. cit.*, p. 319 : Du solt alzemale entsinken diner dinesheit, unde solt
zerfliezen in sine sinesheit, unde sol din din in sinem min ein min werden
also genzlich, dass du mit ihm verstandest ewigliche sine ungewordene
istigkeit und sine ungenannten Nihtheit.

had, on the whole, either carefully avoided or very skilfully modified, but which Eckhart uses freely. Our mystic,
namely, is fond of making the already indicated technical
distinction between God as the developed Trinity and the
Godhead as the Essence or *Wesen* proper, a distinction of
central importance in his doctrine. Sometimes, to be sure,
he uses the words God and Godhead interchangeably. But
whenever he wishes to be especially exact he speaks of the
Godhead as the unrelated One, the first principle, or, as he
also calls it, the " unnatured nature," from which God himself, viz., the Trinity, as the sphere of the divine power,
knowledge, and love, is secondarily derived. The latter, or
God as the Trinity, Eckhart then calls the " natured nature "
of the divine. Of the divine persons as one in essence
but distinguished by their mutual relations St. Thomas
had elaborately treated, and in a great measure Eckhart
follows the angelic doctor's doctrine of the Trinity as
such in itself. But in the mystic's hands the scholastic
distinction between the divine essence and the divine persons is fearlessly exaggerated. It was Thomistic to make the
generation of the Son from the Father, a procession in the
divine "according to the emanation of the intellect," so
that the world of the divine Wisdom, or again that realm
of Ideas, before mentioned, so far as it is viewed, as pro-
ceeding from the originating nature of the Father, is the
Son. Then the Holy Spirit's procession is the *processio
amoris*, arising from a relation of a loving, and so volitional, type between the Father and the Son; and thus the
scheme of the Trinity is complete. All this Eckhart often
expounds, after Thomas. But, as we have now seen, the
very heart of this speculative mysticism lies in observing
that if, through what is called in Christian terminology
the procession of the Son, the divine omniscience gets a
complete expression in eternal terms, still there is even at
the centre of this omniscience the necessary mystery of the

divine essence itself, which neither generates nor is gener-
ated, and which is yet the source and fountain of all the
divine.   Eckhart is sure: If you really want to come into
communion with the absolute God, then even the holy
Trinity can never suffice you.   That—the Trinity—is the
revealed God.   The mysterious origin of this revelation—
well, that is the Godhead.   Who stops short of that knows
much, for he enters by the grace of God into the world of
the revelation of God, where God is omniscient.   But deeper
than God's omniscience is that which is the source of omniscience, the *essentia*, which, so far as it is considered in
itself, apart from the birth of the Word, is not yet even
the Father, much less the Trinity.   Yet in that Source, in
the Godhead, all that the Father begets, all that the Divine
Word reveals, all that the divine Love prizes, all that the
Trinity in its unity has created—all this is eternally hidden.   For thence—from that One, that Source—proceeds in
eternity the relational distinctions of the Trinity, in time
the whole created world.   Do you want the reality, the
soul of things, the absolute truth, then you must get past
God the Trinity, past the revealed God, past the God with
whom in the beginning was the Word.   For that God is in
his very existence only a being who is relative to the objects
of his omniscience.   Yes, you can say, as Eckhart often
says, that just as the Father were not, in case there were
not also the Son, so God would not be were there not the
world of God's ideas.   In God as the Trinity, in the revealed, in the omniscient God, all exists only relatively,
not absolutely : the Father exists as related to the Son,
both exist as related to the Spirit ; knowledge and its object
are relative ; yes, even the ideas of the created things are,
in God, just as real as he is himself.   Had not God thought
of me, he would not have been God ; so I am in a sense
cause of him as much as he is cause of me.   For God, as a
relative term, is relative also to even the creatures.   But the

Godhead—that is the source of sources—that is above all re-lations. And our true divine home is there, and there only, viz., in union with the incomprehensible depth of the God-head. God, says Eckhart, becomes and fades away, although not temporally. Only the Godhead has fullness of being.

"When," says Eckhart, speaking in a sermon of this difference between absolute and relative being—" when I stood in the depth, on the ground, in the fountain and source of the Godhead, no one asked me what I would or what I did. There was no one who should ask me. But when I issued forth—then all creatures, speaking, said: 'God!' If one asked me: 'Brother Eckhart, when did you go out of the house?' I should say: 'I must have been in it.' Well, just so all creatures speak of God." [I. e., God is a term relative to the term creature.] "But why do they [the creatures] not speak of the Godhead? All that which is in the Godhead—that is One, and thereof is not to be spoken. God acts. The Godhead does not act. It has nothing to do. There is no deed in the Godhead. Never did it look upon deed. God and Godhead differ as deed and non-deed. When again I come into God, if I form no image, my rewinning [of the Godhead] is nobler than was my issuing forth. I alone [viz., as thinking being in this world, conceiving of the true natures of created things] bring all creatures from their own reason into my reason, so that in me [i. e., in my conception] they become one. When I come to the depth, to the ground, to the fountain and the source of the Godhead, no one will ask me whence I come, or where I have been. No one had missed me when I vanished thence."

And hereupon, in this sermon, Eckhart, to whom all this has an intensely practical significance, closes with the following characteristic speech: " Whoever has understood this sermon, I wish him well of it. If nobody had been here then I still must have preached it—to this stick. There

are some poor folk who go home again and say : I will sit
in one place and eat my bread and serve God. I say by
the truth, such people must remain in darkness, nor ever
win or conquer what those others win who follow God in
poverty and in want. Amen." But of this practical aspect
further in a moment. It is enough so far to see that, as
Eckhart says in another sermon : " When a man turns
from himself and from all created things," . . . then the
central light, or, as Eckhart loves to call it, the "Spark," or
" Glimmer " of his soul, the highest form of rationality, the
creative reason of Aristotle, " takes no contentment in
Father, or Son, or Holy Ghost, nor in the three persons, so
far as each subsists in its own character. . . . I will say
still more," he goes on. " This light takes no contentment in
the simple movelessness of the divine essence, that neither
gives nor desires. But it longs to know whence comes this
essence ? It wants to go into the unity that is in the
depths, into the still wilderness, where never was seen
difference, neither Father, nor Son, nor Holy Ghost ; in that
absorption, where there is no one at home, there the Spark
of the soul is content in the light, and there is it at peace
more than in itself. For this depth is a simple stillness,
that in itself is moveless ; but from this movelessness all
things are moved, and all things have their life that live in
reason and possess themselves. That we may thus live in
reason, may God help us. Amen."

You have now before you the speculative basis of Eckhart's mysticism. Apart from the specifically Christian
and scholastic terminology, the central thoughts are simply
these : (1) The world of explicit being or of interrelated
being, both finite and infinite, is a spiritual, an ideal world,
where all objects are what they are only for a certain omniscient Subject, the Self of this world of truth. Hence
there is indeed no unknowable object ; and this divine
Self is so far omniscient. (2) But what even the knowledge

of this omniscient Self cannot word, or voice forth, or have for its own object, that is precisely the very selfhood, the highest nature or inner source of the divine Self in its own unity. Self-knowledge is notoriously a problematic thing. Well, this mysticism consists in saying that all the knowledge of even a divine Self is rooted in the impenetrable mystery of the existence, the nature, the inmost essence, of its own Selfhood. Whoever still obstinately and with divine love of the highest seeks to know this, must first lay aside the very conditions of knowledge, and pass into the still wilderness, where there is no longer either subject or object. But to do this is to reach the light above the light —is to touch the Absolute, and so to be in unity, and at peace, in the wilderness where no one is at home but the Godhead, and where even that is nothing determinate, and is yet the fountain of all things and determinations.

Now I have said that this sort of mysticism is something historically well and often known. As a fact, you can find in some of the posthumously published lectures of Fichte (e. g., the Wissenschaftslehre of 1804) almost the same essential thoughts as those at the basis of Eckhart's sermons, expounded upon the foundation of a post-Kantian idealism, by a man who himself revolted from many of the practical consequences of mysticism, who was far from pushing it to such consequences as Eckhart's, and who was as ignorant of Eckhart as he was of the Catholic middle ages in general. In the other direction, if you pass backwards from Eckhart, past Dionysius, past Plotinus, far beyond and before the Christian era, you find, as I have already said, in the very dawn of Hindoo thought, in the Upanishads, the same problem, with the same elements. There is, of course, no trace there present as yet of the doctrine of the Trinity ; but already one conceives the world as the world of the absolute Self. And in a famous legend, a sage, Yâjna-valkya, addressing his wife, Maitreyi, concerning immor-

tality, reasons that while we can attain to immortality by
union with this absolute Self, still we must not think of
this absolute Self as itself the prey of mere consciousness.
And the sage reasons substantially thus : Here, in this life,
one sees—*another*, one hears—*another*, one touches, smells,
tastes—*another*—yes, one greets, thinks, knows—*another*.
That is consciousness. That is explicit knowledge. That,
he apparently intends to suggest, might so far be conceived
as extended to omniscience without essential change. But
thus knowing subject and known object remain forever
apart; and therefore such knowledge would not yet be
union with the real Self. For, he goes on, if all had become
to one the Self, " Wherewith and whom should he then
see ? Wherewith and whom should he then hear, smell,
touch, taste ? Wherewith and whom should he then
greet ? " [" Da fragete mich nieman," says Eckhart, speaking of what one finds in the wilderness of the Godhead,
" da enwas nieman der mich fragete," or again, " There was
no one at home "]. " Wherewith," continues Yâjnavalkya—
" wherewith and what should he then think ? Wherewith
and what should he then know ? Wherewith should he
know him through whom he knows all things ? Wherewith, O Beloved, should he know the Knower ? "

In this mystic land, as you see, all roads lead to the
same eternal city, this conceived refuge of the ages, yet a
city that, alas, as Eckhart tells us, is after all the place *da
nieman heime ist.* Beyond eternity it shall lie—but the
way of glory is to be also the way of darkness.

So much then for the speculative aspect of our mystic's
thought. You may see now something of the magnitude of
the motives that have led human thought again and again
into this region, where the profoundest thinking comes at
times so close to a pathological love for a merely passive
rapture of inexpressible feelings. But in any case, I am
not here to criticise or to reconstruct ; but to portray. You

will be anxious to pass before we close to the practical aspect. Eckhart, who taught thus, expressing Catholic ideas in a form obviously so full of danger to his orthodoxy —why did he suppose that the people could possibly need to hear such things in their own vernacular ? And how did he escape that danger of the merely passive rapture ?

III.

Practically regarded, a mystic, as a public teacher, has in general two especially valuable characteristics : First, he is a man who believes himself to have faced absolute issues, and to have discovered absolute values. Hence he is not easily dismayed when he faces any lesser human problem. Suppose that there is something called union with God, which involves rising above the sphere within which even the assumed and unquestioned dogma of the Trinity is instructive. Then surely, if one knows the way to this union, or towards it, one who has in a measure transcended even the dogma of his infallible Church, is not likely to speak with an uncertain sound when he has to face the lesser problems of faith or of life. The little ones of his flock come to him with their sins. He says, Turn to God. There alone is peace. Forsake yourself. It is in your separation from God that lies the essence of sin. Turn from the creature. Forget the creature. There is but one good. There are not many ways to peace. There is one way. That is absolute surrender of all good but God. Others in our preacher's flock boast of their good works. Eckhart despises good works, unless—here is his often repeated formula—unless not the righteous man, but only God in him, does these works—i. e., they must be done without self-consciousness, without thought of merit, as the mere overflow of love and peace. Your righteousness must issue, like the Trinity, from the very Godhead itself; else all your striving is in vain. Or the afflicted in the flock lament their woes. Death and pain have come into their lives. They grieve and cannot be comforted. That, says Eckhart, is because you love creatures. Why do you not love God alone? There is no thing good but God. That is what sorrow teaches you. Hence sorrow is not to be lamented, but is to be prized. Do not think of your woes as a punishment, but as a call from God, a call to go home to his peace. From this point of view grief is itself something divine. "I say that after God there was never anything that is nobler than sorrow. For had there been anything nobler than sorrow, then surely the Father from heaven would have granted that nobler gift to his son, Jesus Christ. But we find that, except for his humanity, there was nothing of which Christ had so much of as sorrow. . . . Yes, I say, too, that were there anything nobler than sorrow, then therewith would God have redeemed man. . . . But we do not find that Christ was ever an hour upon earth without sorrow; therefore sorrow must be above all things." * The doctrine, you see, is not altogether new, but the absoluteness of the tone—this is one special privilege of the mystic.

The second general advantage of the mystic as a public teacher is that he speaks always upon that basis of direct experience of which we have already made mention. Other men are dependent upon their traditions, or their abstract formulas. The essence of the mystical doctrine is the recognition that all abstract formulas must fail in the presence of the highest truth, whose own innermost nature it is to be absolutely simple, and yet beyond words. Hence only religious experience can really touch this truth. Argument, tradition, authority—all these fail. When that which is perfect comes, that which is in part is to be taken

---

* Pages 337, 338. The suggested variation of the doctrine of the atonement is itself characteristic of Eckhart's type of mysticism.

away. And the perfect, according to the mystic, is reached
as soon as you abstract from all that is derived or explicit,
and return to the depth, to the source, to the fountain of
the Godhead. But that you apprehend only by an act of
inward surrender to the divine presence and absoluteness.
Other men hear of God, read about God, believe in God,
serve God. The mystic, in so far as he speaks with authority, declares that he has in some measure attained God.

Hence it is that Eckhart, like other mystics, speaks
always with the simple confidence of the man for whom
there are no alternatives. It is so. This he sees. He has
no doubt. To his followers (as the scribe of one of the
manuscripts of his sermons phrases it) he appears as
"Meister Eckhart, dem Got nie niht verbarc." For the
mystic this sort of assertion involves no vain pretense, no
unseemly pride. Of himself as this man the mystic makes
no account. But the simple revelation of God's unity and
consequent absolute mystery—has not one the right to
voice this revelation ? And if in this revelation lies the
whole secret of man's salvation, and one has experienced
that fact, must not one say so ?

These two advantages—(1) the fearlessness in the presence of all the lesser issues of life, because one has faced
once for all the central issue ; and (2) that assurance of
one's doctrine which is derived from the fact that all this is
a fresh report of one's own religious experience—these two
advantages, I say, Eckhart shares with many mystics. But
now, as the readers of mystical literature well know, the
practical danger, yes, the curse, of the doctrine, as taught
by many mystics, lies in that often fairly pathological
tendency towards dreamily passive emotions, and so towards what is well called Quietism. If God's central
Wesen is thus a voiceless mystery, a wilderness of un-
utterable Being, and if the highest union with God means
an absorption in the presence of this mystery—well, then,
20

is not the best, even in this life, a deedlessly passive and unspeakable rapture in God, a doing of nothing, a fascinated gazing towards the exalted Essence, which is to ordinary thought a mere Nothing, but that to the mystic is his All? To many mystics this indeed has seemed the whole solution. But is this so with Eckhart?

In answer to this question it must first be distinctly said that Eckhart is *no* quietist. I have spoken of his manly temper, of his rugged plainness of mood and manner. This man, so long as he is in this world, simply means business, viz., his life's business. Union with God is indeed his whole aim. But first he remembers that you cannot come into union with God until after you have learned to put off the creature, the world. Now you do not put off the world by pretending, in your private rapture, to have sentimentally forgotten it. You must, by the power of God, have overcome it; and overcoming is a matter of many years of growth, growth which Eckhart conceives as lying in a marvellously original combination of spiritual freedom and of rigid self-discipline. It is hard to sketch the precise picture of the true spiritual life as Eckhart presents it in his sermons, because the elements involved are so many. But still I can suggest a few things.

At all events, bear in mind that the soul of man, for Eckhart, has various higher and lower powers, or faculties, of which, of course, the intellect and the will are the most significant. These special powers do their work, and must continue to do their work, so long as we are in the body. What joins, or may in the end join the soul to God, is, however, no one of these powers, but the aforesaid Spark or Glimmer of the soul, the *Fünkelin* or *Ganster*, of which Eckhart often speaks. This, I say, is no power of the soul, though it is meant to correspond to Aristotle's Creative Reason. It is the uncreated essence of our created soul. Now this *Fünkelin* Eckhart conceives as something eternal and immortal, which has an inscrutable but real relation to the essence of the God-head. This Spark of the divine light it is in us which makes us eternally discontented with all but the Godhead, so that whatever we know or do, it is all naught to us whilst we still find ourselves out of union with God's essence. And so far you have the psychological basis of our human longing for salvation.

Now the soul's destiny it is to lay aside, in the higher life, all but this Spark of light, and by virtue of the Spark to be united to the Godhead. But next observe carefully, Eckhart never conceives that union with the Godhead as any utter absorption, wherein our individuality is to be really and substantially lost. Could the soul ever come to comprehend God's essence completely, then indeed it would be utterly absorbed into God, and would so become nothing but God. But, as a fact, except in a consciously hyperbolic speech, Eckhart never conceives the union of the soul with God as a process to be finally completed. Eckhart believes in individual immortality, and this he explicitly maintains. I said earlier that Eckhart held man's salvation to be dependent upon the very recognition that the divine essence involves an impenetrable mystery. How true this is you will perhaps now for the first time appreciate when I say that upon this very mysteriousness of God's own essence Eckhart, in a striking passage, founds his assertion that the union of our individual Spark of light with the Godhead can never be completed, and founds also his consequent affirmation of the immortality of the individual. Speaking of the state of the blessed, Eckhart says : * "In the exalted state the soul has lost itself, and flows all flowing into the unity of the divine essence. But, 'Ah !' one might ask, 'How is it with the soul thus

---

* Pfeiffer, p. 387.

lost, does it find itself or not ? ' And I will respond as it seems to me, namely, that the soul finds itself at the point where every rational being possesses itself in self-consciousness. Though it sinks all sinking in the unity of the divine essence, yet it can never comprehend its own source. And therefore God has left it a tiny point [*Pünctelin*] wherewith it returns again into itself, and knows itself to be a creature. And that is most of all the soul's essence, that she can never comprehend thoroughly her own Creator."

Here then already you see why Eckhart's mysticism, quite unlike that of the Hindoos, knows of the absorption in the Absolute only as something wholly relative to the preserved subsistence of the essence of the individual soul. And here you also see why he cannot become and remain a quietist. For a quietistic mystic, as such, simply ignores the individual. But Eckhart maintains individuality. The Spark or *Fünkelin* of the soul is itself something uncreated, and capable of the deepest and most mysterious union with the divine *Essentia*. But the created individual, shadowy as his creature existence in itself is, still accompanies, even through the ages of ages, this endless process of the union with the divine. Or, in other words, Eckhart means the individual soul to be absorbed by virtue of a self-surrender *in* the divine—i. e., in the contemplation of the Godhead—but never to be absorbed *into* the divine. Or, again, to try a familiar metaphor not used by Eckhart: Whatever you will, desire, know, think, or aim to possess, all that in the end, if you are saved, turns out to be, according to Eckhart's doctrine, nothing but the Godhead itself, towards which, as the absolute haven, all the winds of eternity are even now wafting the ship of your soul. But in that haven your bark will still float in the waters of mystery and peace—yes, and will eternally sail onwards, like a ship piloted forever through the landlocked fiords of some now far-off region of sky-piercing mountains. The mountains and the dark wa-

ters of the longed-for homeland will indeed be all in all;
but the little ship will still sail on these waves of eternity,
sustained and moved forever in an unresting peace amidst
the mountains of God.

Now here also appears another aspect of what is the
most important practical feature in Eckhart's teachings.
You have often seen in the foregoing how, like mystics in
general, he loves what one might call a nihilistic phraseology. The Godhead, as above all distinctions is, he has
told us, in a sense Nothing. It is equally true to say, in
our stammering human speech, that it is the creature
that is absolutely nothing, while God alone is the true
" *Iht*." And this also Eckhart says in countless places.
God then may be indifferently said to possess, as we have
seen, " *ungewordene Istigkeit*," or " *ungenannte Nihtheit*,"
unborn reality, or nameless nothingness. Now the noteworthy thing about all such nihilistic phraseology is that
it is explicitly founded upon the purely relative character
of all our human conceptions and speech. We live in contrasts, in relations, in a consciousness of light and shade.
Hence our every effort to express our relation to the simple
and ultimate mystery involves a duplicity of terms, and in
fact of mental attitudes. But this, I say, is itself a matter
of intensely practical import. Just as you cannot be in
union with God, unless, in the very union, you remain you,
just so your passivity, your self-surrender, your willing
nothingness, when you are absorbed in God, is something
that has also a very positive aspect. Unless your soul had
its special powers in addition to that central Spark already
mentioned—well, then, you could not surrender these
powers. *Master Eckhart, when did you go out of the
house ?* " *Do was ich darin.*" " I must have been in the
house." Well, just so, your absolute surrender to God, not
only in its beginning, but also in its continuance, means
that you in a sense keep your lower self in order endlessly

to surrender it. But this does not mean quietism; it means activity. In this life, at all events, the surrender to God is for Eckhart always as much a positive as a negative process. Begin anywhere you please. Say, " I as creature am nothing. I must forsake myself." What hereupon happens ? Escape implies first control. You must bind the strong man of your lower nature or you cannot spoil his house. Hence Eckhart condemns all the " wild " mysticism of his time, all merely antinomian tendencies. Your early training as mystic must mean self-control, such as the monks practise. And self-control means once more a prosaic business, which the love of God inspires, but which only minute daily discipline can accomplish.*

On the other hand, this daily discipline is itself only valuable in so far as it contributes to spiritual freedom. There must be an absolute union of spirituality and of daily activity. Eckhart has a manly contempt for all that is merely external, for mere penances, for formal good works as such, for all slavery to forms. All these external things are but means to ends. Not even vows need bind the free soul that once finds its former vows, in case they are not, like the marriage vow, public obligations, but are, like vows of penance, or of similar spiritual exercises, private affairs—in case, I say, the soul finds such vows to be a hindrance to the higher life. † The one rule is : Take the nearest way Godwards, but be always sure to keep in motion on that way, until God's rest comes of itself.

This preparatory self-discipline once in a measure fulfilled, and the next stage of piety reached, then what is for Eckhart the deep paradox of the spiritual life first really begins. Here is the soul in the body—a soul which has at its centre that uncreated Spark, whose life it is to rewin and retain union with the Godhead—but a soul also which has its special powers, some of these powers being spiritual, like intellect and will, some of them bodily, like sense and desire. How, in view of the persistent survival of these lower powers, shall the soul now find its earthly life ordered ? The situation is one of infinite complexity. Does the soul look Godwards, then that way lies a peace to be won, not by means of the life of the soul's special powers, but only through the virtue which Eckhart calls *Abgescheidenheit*, " departedness " of soul—absolute freedom from the bondage of the creature, rest in God, patient waiting for him, indifference to earthly fortune—a curious union of immovable stoicism in the presence of the finite, and of passionate love for the infinite.* *Abgescheidenheit* is the special virtue related to the centre or Spark of the soul. As so related it is a virtue higher even than charity. The man who has it is so far above not merely ill fortune, but even repentance for his past sins. He sees all as God's will. The Godhead is all in all to him, and the peace that passeth understanding. Is it God's will that of old he was a sinner, that concerns him not now. Let God's will be done in heaven ? And it is heavenward only, to the absolute home of mystery, that *Abgescheidenheit* looks. Nothing is good save what is yonder. And now you will say is not this once more Quietism ?

But no—all this is true, but it is not the whole story of virtue upon this stage of the religious life. *Abgescheidenheit* does not strive or cry, but it calmly and with absolute assurance, prays, or, what is the same thing, irreversibly determines and declares in its peace, that God's will shall be done on earth as it is in heaven. And "on earth," in the mystic language, means in the world of the soul's lower

---

* On *Abgescheidenheit*, cf. especially the ninth Tract of Pfeiffer, pp. 483–493.

powers. The lower powers continue here on earth to exist in their shadow land of created being. There, for instance, in the finite world, is the "outer man," of whom Eckhart often speaks. The outer man, as creature of finitude, is and must often be visited by pain and passion. Herein lies his very finitude. That indeed is his unalterable accident. That is his way—to be troubled. Did not Christ, who inwardly dwelt in absolute divine peace, say, "My soul is very heavy," and "My God, why has thou forsaken me?" Christ said all this in and with the outer man. Well, the outer man, as created shadow, defined through his very contrast to the divine, cannot possess *Abgescheidenheit*, but must be vitalized by it, as the body's members by the life of the heart. This is the only possible salvation of the lower man, and so in that lower world of the spiritualized materiality of the good man's nature there is indeed no quietism, but endless activity, even strife. For the inner man, in his *Abgescheidenheit*, stands as a sort of Aristotelian unmoved mover, beyond this tempestuous sublunary world of finite passion, never, during our earthly life, destroying but vitalizing the lower nature. The outer man has and must have temptations, and is better for having them if he only overcomes them. He overcomes them by outer strife; but the strife itself is inspired by the moveless peace of the inner man.*

It is with temptations as with sorrows. They are the nobler incidents of the life of the outer man, if only the inner man is at peace. "That a man has a restful and peaceful life in God is good. That a man endures a painful life with patience, that is better; but that man has his rest in the midst of a painful life, that is best of all." † And

---

* Cf. Pfeiffer, p. 551, *sq.*

† Pfeiffer, p. 221. On the whole relation of higher and lower, inner and outer nature, and on the whole doctrine of good works, cf. especially Sermon III, Pfeiffer, pp. 16–24, and the passages pp. 34, 35, 50–53, 183, 356, 607, 609.

therefore whoever as observer of the good man views from
without the soul thus constituted, such an outer observer
sees in general—for such is Eckhart's usual thought—a
person who appears to be not at all an ecstatic quietist,
but a strenuous, busy, virile, essentially practical being—
a man of hard sense, fearless of speech, vigorous in maintaining his cause, indifferent to the mere form of good
works, little disposed to fasting, to going barefoot, or to the
other non-essentials of the religious life, much disposed to
helping the brethren. "You should remember," says Eckhart in one passage,* addressing the formal penitents who
are proud of their own private good works, and who are devoted to petting and to admiring the personal beauty of their
own pious plumage—" you should remember that God is
the common Saviour of all mankind, and that much more
thanks are due to him therefore than would be due if he
had only undertaken to save you. And so you ought to
try to be a common saviour also." Nor need ·the man of
the higher life despise even the creature enjoyments, so far
as they nourish his outer man. The good man honors all
created things when he uses them by transforming their
lower forms into the higher form of his own nature. The
good men ought thus to help all lower creatures back to
God, namely, by subordinating them to his lower, and so
to his higher needs.† To be sure the perfect man prefers
in general poverty, but he would be indifferent if God sent
his outer man even wealth and pleasure. He leaves in
general the matters of fortune to God.

But if this inspiration of the strenuous outer man by
the passionless peace of the moveless inner man is, so far
as this world is concerned, the ideal, it must be remembered,

---

* Pfeiffer, p. 561.

† For this frequent thought of Eckhart's, see especially Pfeiffer, pp.
180, 183, 351, 474.

on the other hand, that the union in question is something essentially miraculous—the gift of God. Our striving may prepare the way for it, and without preparatory discipline and slow growth it comes not. But the victory is the gift of God. Hence, as I said before, a good man's works are not the direct result of his own will, but of God's power. Our will surrenders itself, then God acts on us.

Yet God has countless gifts. He might choose, even in this world, to grant the peculiar grace of mystic ecstasy itself. If he does so you can but accept it. In ecstasy the outer man, to be sure, does fall quite away, and no good works are done. As a fact, however, nobody has the power directly to produce the ecstatic experience by any effort. If God gives this his highest earthly revelation of his perfect peace, he himself undertakes the responsibility for the good works that are neglected while the outer man is silent. Hence the recognition of the existence of the mystic ecstasy does not make Eckhart a practical quietist. Ecstasy is like the heavenly state, something beyond this life, such as came to St. Paul.

Of a typical ecstatic mystic Eckhart has given an account in his marvellous tract, half-true portrayal of some real person or persons, half-free poetical invention, called Schwester Katrei. Schwester Katrei is a religious woman, although apparently not a woman of a regular order. She is turned to the higher life by her confessor (who represents Eckhart himself); but erelong she far transcends her teacher, rises superior to all formal obedience to him, or even to the Church, and follows God's secret leading into a life of uttermost unworldliness. She at length attains the place where she can say to her confessor, in the fearless mystic speech: "Rejoice with me, for I have become God." She, after years of merciless self-discipline and of saintly living, reporting her highest experience, can declare, in the words of typical ecstasy: "I have with angels and with saints nothing to do, nor aught to do with any creature, nor with anything that has been created . . . nay, nor with anything that has ever been conceived in words. . . . I have been confirmed in the naked Godhead, where never was form or idea . . . Where I stand no creature may come in created fashion . . . I am where I was before I was created. There is but God and only God. There are neither angels nor saints nor choirs nor heavens. Many tell of eight heavens and nine choirs. There is nothing of the sort where I am. You must know how all that one conceives thus in words and pictures thus to the people is but a hint to stimulate towards God. But in God there is naught but God, and no soul can come to God unless he becomes God as God was before the soul's creation." Yet Schwester Katrei, speaking at last as inspired wise woman to her now humbled and receptive confessor, who asks whether he too can come to such union with God, says plainly to him : " Ir sît ungetempert dar zuo." (For this you are not tempered). The way is long, she says. You must first learn not only to ascend but to descend the mystic road, year after year, till you know both the way and the heavenly company of the Trinity and the lonely place of peace, as a man knows his own courtyard. Then only can you finally remain at the threshold of the Godhead. This is not an affair of mere feelings, but of deeds, of grace, and of slowly won nearness to God. Till you have won all that you must cultivate your lower powers, take due pleasure in created things, and wait God's time.

And thus you see something of the fashion in which Eckhart conceives the unity of the Christian life, and the race that one must run toward the mystical glory.

XI

AN EPISODE OF EARLY CALIFORNIA LIFE: THE SQUATTER RIOT OF 1850 IN SACRAMENTO.

PRELIMINARY NOTE.

THE following paper was first prepared as a contribution to local history, and was addressed to an audience familiar with the traditions of the early days of California. The text still retains forms of speech due to this origin. The author here often speaks as a Californian to his fellows, refers freely to local issues, and presupposes an interest in a special region and group of people.

Yet if the affair here in question is one of local history, the passions, the social forces, and the essential ideas concerned, are of permanent significance. How often, even in some of our latest American conflicts, at Homestead, at Chicago, or at Hazletown, can we not recognize the same essential motives that were at work in the affair here described ? A lofty and abstract idealism, such as, despite the opinions of foreigners, is a permanent and potent force in our American life, appears, then, in this little story, as coming into contact with a very concrete problem of social existence—a problem about land ownership, about the rights and privileges of poor men, and about the good order of a new community. The Transcendentalist—a being who is, in one form, a characteristic American—imagines himself called upon to lead his fellows in a struggle for property and for bread. The Idealist gets into conflict with the sheriff; the Higher Law has to face the processes of the courts ; a company of homeless wanderers have to solve, in a moment, a critical problem of civilization. The philosopher (who is here also a man of the people) pretends, for the passing hour, to be, by popular choice, the king; and a crowd of men, who know not precisely what they mean, are forced to decide whether or no to follow this new king. Such incidents may well be studied in miniature as on a grand scale. They may seem petty, local, transient, accidental, but their meaning is permanent, and they will recur, over and over, and perhaps on a constantly grander and grander scale, as long as our national history lasts. In miniature we have then, in this case, a process of universal meaning.

As an example of the way in which the solution of the most practical problems of the daily life of a community may involve the ultimate issues of an idealistic philosophy, the present Study of Good and Evil seems to me to have its place in this volume. And I have deliberately left its locally determined form essentially unchanged.

The most general outlines of early Californian history are very commonly known, and may here be, for the most part, presupposed. California, acquired by the United States during the Mexican War, had long been under the irregular government characteristic of a remote and sparsely settled Spanish-American province. Land ownership, at the time of our conquest of the country, was legally founded upon Grants, which the various governments of the province had, from time to time, made to settlers. These "Spanish Grants," frequently in the region near the coast, both in the central and in the southern parts of California, did not extend (except in a single instance), into the mountain regions where, in 1848 and later, the great gold discoveries were made.   On the other hand, the portions of California nearer the coast, where the large towns soon grew up, and where the commercial interests of the new State, during the gold period, were principally centred, were especially affected by the controversies which soon began concerning the validity of the land-titles of Mexican origin.   By the treaty of 1848, between Mexico and the United States, the general validity of all such titles was guaranteed.   On the other hand, the precise definition of individual titles was often doubtful ; their authenticity could easily be questioned by unsympathetic strangers, unused to the simple provincial ways of a Spanish-American community ; and the rude surveys through which, in some cases, their supposed boundaries had been determined, had sometimes been carried out in a most primitive fashion.   Such titles needed a very considerate treatment, if they were to be recognized at all.

But the American newcomers were, in a goodly proportion of cases, men from the regions of our Middle West, where land ownership had very generally been determined either directly by settlement, or through conformity to easily comprehensible general laws.   The Oregon wilderness, from which some of the newcomers came to California, was similarly the natural paradise of the " squatter." In consequence, the settlers in California were ill-prepared to be patient with the Californian laws, and with mysterious sources of land ownership.   To add to the confusion of men's ideas, the lands of the gold region were, in general, actually free to all ; for they were, on the whole, untouched by the Grants. They were therefore now public lands of the United States. The National Government refused, for years, to part with the title, or to survey the gold-producing lands, and thus left the whole question of the practical ownership of claims to be determined, so far as mining was concerned, by the local " Miners' Custom " of each district. The result was, for California miners, a system of temporary land ownership, determined by the actual occupancy and use of the land itself, the limits of such occupancy being subject to local regulation by miners' meetings. The contrast between this simple and practical system of the mining districts, and the complex and mysterious problems of land ownership in the large commercial towns and in the coast regions, was especially vexatious for those who, in the course of their business, needed land in the portion of the State covered by the Grants, and who could not get such land by the process with which the mining life, as well as the customs common to all squatters, had familiarized them.

Social unrest and discontent immediately resulted. The remoter consequences, however, have been very far-reaching. The agrarian theories of Mr. Henry George (to mention one instance only) form a striking example of the later outcome, in certain minds, of this early Californian experience. The ideal of land ownership which Mr. George defends is simply the ideal suggested by the miners' methods in the gold districts of California. The ideal which he combats is the ideal of whose difficulties the weary history of the early litigation over the "Spanish Grants" in California was a peculiarly tragic example.

The present paper, in dealing with a single incident of the early struggle, is led to study, however, not so much the special problem as to the best form of land ownership, as the still more universal question of the conflict between abstract ideas and social authority, at a moment when the order of a new society, and the eternal conflict between the private and the universal Selves, had to be settled, for the time, by men of energy, of idealistic temper, and of very fallible intelligence, just as we to-day have, as men and as citizens, to solve our own analogous problems.

That the issues of the passing moment are also the issues of metaphysics, and that the eternal problems are met with in the midst of the temporal, is the familiar lesson for the sake of which I have ventured to introduce this paper into the present series.

So much by way of preliminary. Now follows the original discussion.

A prominent California pioneer, Doctor Stillman, published in the Overland Monthly for November, 1873, as one of the chapters of his since well-known book called Seeking the Golden Fleece, a contemporary record of his experiences at the time of the Squatter Riot of 1850 in Sacramento. In a note to this valuable reminiscence, Doctor Stillman remarked that no detailed account of the remarkable affair had ever been printed. So far as I know, the same thing can still truthfully be said. But the scenes of violence themselves form but a small part of the real story of the movement; and I shall venture in the following to try to present a somewhat connected account of the events that preceded the riot and that culminated therein. I draw my materials principally from the contemporary files of the Placer Times and the Sacramento Transcript; but I shall also seek to accomplish what has certainly so far been neglected—viz., to indicate the true historical significance of this little episode in our pioneer annals. For, as I think, the importance of the conflict was greater than even the combatants themselves knew; and most of us are not in a fair way to comprehend the facts, unless we remind ourselves of a good many long since forgotten details of the narrative.

I.

And now to begin the story with the moral, let us try to understand at once why this episode should seem of a certain more general significance. That a few lives should be lost in a squabble about land, is indeed a small thing in the history of a State that has seen so many land quarrels

as California. The Squatter Riot of 1850 was but a preliminary skirmish, if one will judge it by the number of killed
and wounded, while the history of settler difficulties in the
whole State, during the thirty-five years since, seems, by
comparison of number, a long battle, with killed and
wounded who would need to be counted, not by fives, but by
hundreds.

Not, however, for the number of lives lost, but for the importance of just that crisis at that moment, must we consider the Squatter Riot noteworthy. Just as the death of James
King, of William, by leading to the formation of the famous
Vigilance Committee of 1856, happened to seem of more importance to the California community than the death of
ninety-and-nine just miners and other private persons,
who were waylaid or shot in quarrels; just as that death
had many times the historical significance that it would
have had if King had been slain under the most atrocious
circumstances a few months earlier; even so the Squatter
Riot in Sacramento is significant, not because bloodshed
was unknown elsewhere in California land quarrels, but
because nowhere else did any single land quarrel come so
near to involving an organized effort to get rid, once for
all, of the Spanish titles as evidences of property in land.
Elsewhere and later, men followed legal methods, or else
stood nearly alone in their fight. Men regarded some one
title as fraudulent, and opposed it; or frankly avowed their
private hatred of all Mexican land titles, but were comparatively isolated in their methods of legal or illegal resistance to the enforcement of the vested rights; or they
were led into lengthy and often murderous quarrels by
almost hopelessly involved problems of title, such as so
long worried all men alike in San Francisco. Elsewhere
than in Sacramento men thus tried, in dealing with numerous questions of detail, to resist the enforcement of individual claims under Mexican titles; but in Sacramento in

21

1850 the popular opposition was deeper, and its chances of a sweeping success were for a moment far greater.

In form, to be sure, even the Sacramento squatters, like so many successors, pretended to be doubtful of the legal validity of Sutter's "Alvarado grant," and to believe that, if it were valid, the grant still did not cover Sacramento. But this pretense was here a very thin veil for an undertaking that was in its spirit and methods distinctly revolutionary. The squatters of that time and place were well led, and they meant to do, and contemporary friends and foes knew that they meant to do, what would have amounted to a deliberate abrogation by popular sovereignty, of Mexican grants as such. Had they been successful, a period of anarchy as to land property would probably have followed far worse in its consequences than that lamentable legalized anarchy that actually did for years darken the land interests of our State, under the Land-Law of 1851. Bad as that enactment proved, the squatter doctrine, as preached in 1850, came near proving far worse. To investigate how the people of Sacramento showed their weakness in letting this crisis come on as it did, and their strength in passing it when it at last had come on, is to my mind, in view of the dangers of that and of all times, a most helpful exercise in social science ; since it is such investigations that enable us to distinguish the good from the evil tendencies of the popular mind, and to feel the difference between healthy and diseased states of social activity. I want, in short, to make this essay a study of the social forces concerned in early California land difficulties.

Captain Augustus Sutter, the famous Swiss pioneer, whose name is closely connected with the gold discoveries of 1848, owned at the time of the conquest, and, in fact, since 1841, eleven leagues under a grant from the former Californian Governor, Alvarado. Moreover, as is again notorious, Sutter supposed himself to own much more than this grant by virtue of promises made to him by Governor Micheltorena, in 1845. In the latter supposition Sutter made a serious blunder, as was pointed out to him in 1858, by the United States Supreme Court. Micheltorena had made to him no valid grant whatever. In 1848, as soon as the gold seekers began to come, Sutter began to lose his wits. One of the pioneer statements in Mr. H. H. Bancroft's historical collection says rather severely that the distinguished captain thenceforth signed " any paper that was brought to him." At all events, he behaved in as unbusinesslike a fashion as could well be expected, and the result was that when his affairs came in later years to more complete settlement, it was found that he had deeded away, not merely more land than he actually owned, but, if I mistake not, more land than even he himself had supposed himself to own. All this led not only himself into embarrassment, but other people with him ; and to arrange with justice the final survey of his Alvarado grant proved in later years one of the most perplexing problems of the United States District and Supreme Courts.

One part of his land, however, seemed from the first clearly and indisputably his own, to deed away as he might choose. That was the land about his own " establishment at New Helvetia." Here he had built his fort, commanded his laborers, received his guests, and raised his crops; and here the newcomers of the golden days found him, the reputed possessor of the soil. That he owned this land was, in fact, by this time, a matter, so to speak, of world-wide notoriety. For the young Frémont's " Report," which, in various shapes and editions, had years before become so popular a book, and which the gold-fever made more popular than ever, had distinctly described Sutter as the notorious and indisputable owner of this tract of land in 1844. If occupancy without any rival for a term of years could make the matter clear to a newcomer, Sutter's title to his "establishment" seemed beyond shadow. Moreover, the title papers of the Alvarado grant were on record. Governor Alvarado's authority to grant eleven leagues to Sutter was indubitable, and none the less clear seemed the wording of the grant, when it gave certain outer boundaries within which the tract granted was to be sought, and then defined the grant so as to include the "establishment at New Helvetia." Surely, one would say, no newcomer could attack Sutter's right, save by means of some purely agrarian contention. A settler might demand that all occupied land in California should be free to every settler, and that Mexican land-ownership should be once for all done away with. But unless a man did this, what could he say against Sutter's title to New Helvetia ?

And so, when the town of Sacramento began to grow up, the people who wanted lots assented at the outset to Sutter's claims, and recognized his title. That they paid him in all cases a perfectly fair equivalent for his land, I venture not to say. But from him they got their titles, and under his Alvarado grant they held the lands on which the town grew up. Land-holders under Sutter they were who organized the town government, and their speculation was soon profitable enough to make them quite anxious to keep the rights that Sutter had sold them. The question, however, quickly arose, whether the flood of the new immigration would regard a Spanish land-title as a sufficient barrier, at which its proud waves must be stayed. The first safety of the Sutter-title men lay in the fact that the mass of the newcomers were gold-seekers, and that, since Sacramento was not built on a placer mine, these gold-seekers were not interested in despoiling its owners. But this safeguard could not prove sufficient very long. The value of land in the vicinity of a thriving town must soon attract men of small capital and Californian ambitions from the hard work of the placers ; and the rainy season would, at all events, soon crowd the town with discontented idlers.

Moreover, the whole question of California land-titles was a critical one for this new community. The Anglo-Saxon is, as we so often hear, very land-hungry. Many of the newcomers were accustomed to the almost boundless freedom of Western squatters ; the right to squat on vacant land had come to seem to them traditional and inalienable ; they would probably have expected to find it, with a little search, somewhere in the Declaration of Independence, or among the guarantees of the Constitution. Among these men some of the more influential pioneers were strongly under the influence of the Oregon tradition. In Oregon, squatter sovereignty, free and untrammelled, had been settling the land question, of a newly occupied wilderness most happily. The temptation to apply these methods to California was very strong ; in fact, during the *interregnum* after the conquest of the Territory of California, and before the golden days began, the discontented American settlers of the Sacramento Valley and of the Sonoma region had freely talked about the vexations caused by these Mexican land-titles, and had even then begun to propose methods of settling their own troubles. The methods in question would ultimately have plunged everybody into far worse troubles.

The dangerous and blind Americanism of some among these people is well shown by discussions in the California Star for 1847 and 1848, a paper which I have been able to consult in Mr. H. H. Bancroft's file. There is, for instance, a frequent correspondent of the Star in those days, who signs himself " Paisano." Although I have nobody's authority for his identity, I am sure, from plain internal evidence, that he is L. W. Hastings, then a very well-known emigrant leader, and the author of a descriptive guide to California and Oregon. Hastings was a very bigoted

American, at least in his early days on the Pacific coast, and his book had filled many pages with absurd abuse of native Californian people and institutions. Such a man was, just then, an unsafe popular leader, although he was a lawyer by profession, and later did good service in the Constitutional Convention of 1849. In discussing land-titles, in these letters to the Star, " Paisano " plainly shows the cloven foot. Let us insist upon a Territorial Legislature at once, he says, in effect; let us set aside this nuisance of military government by its own consent if possible, and let us pass laws to settle forthwith these land difficulties. All these " Paisano " cloaks under an appeal to the military government to call such a Legislature. But the real purpose is plain. The Legislature, if then called, would certainly have been under the influence of the squatter-sovereignty tradition of Oregon, since its leaders—e. g., Hastings himself—would have been, in many cases, Oregon men. It would, at all events, have been under purely American influence ; it would have despised the natives, who, in their turn, fresh from the losses and griefs of the conquest, would have suspected its motives, would have been unable to understand its Anglo-Saxon methods, and would have left it to its work of treating them unfairly. Unjust land laws would have been passed, infringements on vested rights would have been inevitable, and in after time appeals to the United States authority, together with the coming of the new immigration, would have involved all in a fearful chaos, which we may shudder to contemplate even in fancy. Yet " Paisano " did not stand alone among the pioneers of the *interregnum* in his desires and in his plans. That such plans made no appearance in the Constitutional Convention of 1849 is due to the wholly changed situation of the moment, and to the pressing business before the Convention.

But if things appeared thus to the comparatively small

group of Americans in the dawn of our life here, even before the gold discovery, how long should this complex spider web of land-titles, wherewith a Californian custom or caprice had covered a great part of the Territory, outlast the trampling of the busy newcomers ? Who should resist these strange men ? The slowly moving processes of the courts—how could they, in time, check the rapacity of American settlers before the mischief should once for all be done, and the memory of these land-titles buried under an almost universal predatory disregard of them, which would make the recovery of the land by its legal owners too expensive an undertaking to be even thought of ? The answer to this question suggests at once how, amid all the injustice of our treatment of Californian land-owners, our whole history has illustrated the enormous vitality of formally lawful ownership in land. Yes, this delicate web, that our strength could seemingly so easily have trampled out of existence at once, became soon an iron net. The more we struggled with it, the more we became involved in its meshes. Infinitely more have we suffered in trying to escape from it, than we should have suffered had we never made a struggle. Infinitely more sorrow and money and blood has it cost us to try to get rid of our old obligations to the Californian land-owners, than it would have cost us to grant them all their original demands, just and unjust, at once. Doubt, insecurity, retarded progress, litigation without end, hatred, destruction of property, expenditure of money, bloodshed : all these have resulted for us from the fact that we tried as much as we did to defraud these Californians of the rights which we guaranteed to them at the moment of the conquest. And in the end, with all our toil, we escaped not from the net, and it binds our land-seekers still. But how all this wonder came about is a long story, indeed, whereof the squatter riot of 1850 forms but a small part.

At all events, however, the critical character of the situation of Californian land-owners at the moment of the coming of the gold-seekers appears plain. That all the rights of the Californians should ultimately be respected was, indeed, in view of our rapacious Anglo-Saxon land-hunger, and of our national bigotry in dealing with Spanish-Americans, impossible. But there were still two courses that our population might take with regard to the land. One would be the just-mentioned simple plan of a universal squatters' conspiracy. Had we agreed to disregard the land-titles by a sort of popular fiat, then, ere the courts could be appealed to and the method of settling the land-titles ordained by Congress, the disregard of the claims of the natives might have gone so far in many places as to render any general restitution too expensive a luxury to be profitable. This procedure would have been analogous to that fashion of dealing with Indian reservations to which our honest settlers have frequently resorted. Atrociously wicked as such a conspiracy would have been, we ourselves, as has been suggested above, should have been in the long-run the greatest sufferers, because the conspiracy could not have been successful enough to preserve us from fearful confusion of titles from litigation and warfare without end. Yet this course, as we shall see, was practically the course proposed by the Sacramento squatters of 1850, and for a time the balance hesitated between the choice of this and of the other course. The other course we actually adopted, and it was indeed the one peculiarly fitted to express just our national meanness and love of good order in one. This was the plan of legal recognition and equally legal spoliation of the Californians ; a plan for which, indeed, no one man is responsible, since the coöperation of the community at large was needed, and obtained to make the Land-Act of 1851 an instrument for evil and not for good. The devil's instrument it actually proved to be, by our friendly coöperation, and we have got our full share of the devil's wages of trouble for our ready use of it. But bad as this second course was, it was far better than the first, as in general the meanness and good order of an Anglo-Saxon community of money-seekers produce better results than the bolder rapacity and less legal brutality of certain other conquering and overbearing races.

This struggle, then, resulting in the triumph of good order over anarchy, we are here to follow in a particular instance. The legalized meanness that was to take the place of open rebellion disappears in the background, as we examine the immediate incidents of the struggle, and we almost forget what was to follow, in our interest in the moment. Let us rejoice as we can in an incident that shows us what, amid all our folly and weakness, is the real strength of our national character, and the real ground for trust in its higher future development.

II.

In the winter of 1849–'50, that winter of tedium, of rain, of mud, and of flood, the trouble began. The only contemporary record that I know bearing upon this controversy in that time, I did not mention above, because it is so brief and imperfect. Bayard Taylor, then travelling as correspondent for the New York Tribune, had his attention attracted by the meetings of malcontents on the banks of the Sacramento. They were landless men, and they could not see why. These people, Taylor tells us,* " were located on the vacant lots which had been surveyed by the original owners of the town, and were by them sold to others. The emigrants, who supposed that the land belonged of right to the United States, boldly declared their intention of retain-

* Bayard Taylor, Eldorado (in his Works, Household Edition), chap. xxvi, p. 279.

ing possession of it. Each man voted himself a lot, defying the threats and remonstrances of the rightful owners. The town was greatly agitated for a time by these disputes; meetings were held by both parties, and the spirit of hostility ran to high pitch. At the time of my leaving the country, the matter was still unsettled; but the flood which occurred soon after, by sweeping both squatters and speculators off the ground, balanced accounts and left the field clear for a new start."

The papers of the following spring and summer refer a few times to these meetings. Taylor was wrong in supposing that the affair was to be ended in any fashion by the flood. More water does not make an Anglo-Saxon want less land, and this flood of 1850 itself formed a curious part of the squatter's pretended chain of argument a little later, as we shall see. Much more efficacious in temporarily quelling the anger of the landless men was the happy but deceitful beginning of the spring of 1850. Early fair weather sent hundreds to the mines, and put everybody into temporary good humor. Arguments gave place to hopes, and the landless men hunted in the mountains for the gold that Providence had deposited for the sake of filling just their pockets.

The intentions of Providence included, however, some late rains that spring. The streams would not fall, mining was delayed, provisions were exhausted in some of the mining camps, and a good many of the landless men went back to that city where they owned no land, abandoning their destined fortunes in the mountains, and turning their attention afresh to those ever-charming questions about the inalienable rights of men to a jolly time and a bit of land. And then the trouble began to gather in earnest; although, to be sure, in that busy society it occupied a great place in the public attention only by fits and starts. The growth of the evil seems to have been steadier than the popular notion of its character and magnitude. But let us turn for an instant to glance at the general social condition of the city that was to pass through this trial.

The Sacramento Transcript, in its early numbers in the spring of 1850, well expresses the cheerful side of the whole life of the early days. The New California world is so full of wonders, and the soul of the brave man is so full of youth and hope! Mr. F. C. Ewer, the joint editor with Mr. G. Kenyon Fitch, is a person of just the sort to voice this spirit of audacity, and of delight in life. " The opening of a new paper," he says (in No. 1 of the Transcript, April 1, 1850, *absit omen*), " is like the planting of a tree. The hopes of many hearts cluster around it. . . . In the covert of its leaves all pure principles and high aims should find a home." As for the city, he tells us in the same issue, everything is looking well for its future. The weather is becoming settled, business activity is increasing, substantial buildings are springing up, health " reigns in our midst." The news from the mines is good. There is Murderers' Bar, for instance. Late reports make " its richness truly surprising " ; two ounces per day's work of a man for from one hundred to one hundred and fifty workers. To be sure, however, there has been a great rise in the water, and a large portion of those holding leads have been obliged to suspend operations. But all that is a matter of time. When one turns from the contemplation of the mines to the contemplation of the general condition of the country at large, one is struck with awe ; for then one has to reflect on what the great American mind has already done. "Never has a country been more orderly, never has property been held more inviolable, or life more sacred, than in California for the last twelve or fourteen months."—(Editorial, April 20.) " Is it strange, then, that this feeling of self-reliance should be so strong and broadcast in the land ? With a country so rich in resources—so blest in a people to manage it—the future destiny of California is one of the sublimest subjects for contemplation that can be presented to the mind."—(*Id.*) All this sublimity is, of course, quite consistent with occasional items about affrays and robberies of a somewhat primitive sort here and there in the sublime country ; but such things do not decrease one's rapture. Surely " bliss was it in that dawn to be alive," and Mr. Ewer and Mr. Fitch were the generous youth to whom " to be young was heaven."

In such a good humor one finds, of course, time to write glowing accounts of the wondrously good society of Sacramento, of the great ball that those charming belles attended ; that ball whose character was so select that every gentleman had to send in beforehand to the committee his application for tickets for himself and for the fair lady whom he intended to take, and had to buy a separate, presumably non-transferable, ticket for her ; the ball, whose brilliancy and high character, when the great evening came, surprised even Mr. Ewer, in this delightful wilderness of the Sacramento Valley. Nor in such a period does one forget the fine arts of music and poetry. One's heaven-favored city is visited by Henri Herz, indubitably the greatest of living pianists, " every lineament " of whose face " marks the genius," and who is therefore comparable in this respect to Daniel Webster, to Keats, to Beethoven, and to Longfellow (see the Transcript of April 20). Herz plays the sublimest of music to an enraptured audience : "The Last Rose of Summer," " The Carnival of Venice," and, greatest of all, his own grand " Voyage Musicale," actually a medley of national songs, with passages of his own composition, illustrating the Rhine, the castles, the sunny vales of Bohemia, the Napoleonic wars, a storm at sea, and other similarly obvious and familiar experiences, even on unto his " California Polka," wherewith he concludes ! It is divine, this artistic experience, and the story of it fills columns of the generous little paper. Furthermore, one writes even sonnets, and having first printed them, one later finds occasion to quote them one's self, since, after all, one's own newspaper is a good place to be quoted in. The intellectual life of Sacramento is thus at the highest point. What shall such a community fear ?

As for the Placer Times, that paper, a little later, calls attention to the stability of Sacramento conditions. San Francisco is a restless place, but for Sacramento, the speculative era is past. Solid business, permanent and steady growth, now begin. All this, you must remember, is in the spring of 1850. The whole picture is really an enchanting one ; and only a churl could fail to feel a quickened pulse-throb when he reads these generous and innocent outbursts of splendid courage in both the newspapers. Here are energy, high aim, appreciation of every hint at things beautiful and good ; here is every element of promise, save any assurance of real steadfastness and wisdom. Are these qualities truly present ? For the trial is coming, and by another year these two papers will be as realistic and commonplace as you please. Will their purposes and those of the community gain in wisdom and in tried purity what they must lose of the bloom and beauty of a childlike delight in novelty ?

III.

On April 23, 1850, there appears in the Transcript, for the first time, an advertisement that announces as " just published," and now for sale, a " translation of the papers respecting the grant made by Governor Alvarado to ' Mr. Augustus Sutter,' showing that said grant does not extend any further *south* than the mouth of Feather River, and, therefore, of course, does not embrace Sacramento City." This document could be bought for fifty cents. I have never seen the pamphlet itself, which contained some comments that would now have much interest; but the course of its argument, at all events, when taken together, with the other popular squatter talk of the time, is made plain by subsequent discussions in the newspapers. John Sutter, the squatters intend to show, has no claim, save, of course, as squatter himself, to the land on which Sacramento is built. Frémont found him here; but then he was, for all that, just a squatter. For, behold, what becomes of his boasted grant, when you turn a keen American eye upon it? In the first place, it is incomplete, since no evidence is produced that the central Government in Mexico ever sanctioned it. Furthermore, it is informal, if you will insist upon legal technicalities at all. For we will let land speculators have all the law that they want, if it is law that they are talking about. The grant is to "Mr. Augustus Sutter." Is that the Sutter known to us as the great captain? Still more, the grant is within a tract that is to have Feather River for its *eastern* boundary. Is the Feather River east of Sacramento? Yet again, the grant is specially framed to exclude land overflowed in winter. Let the land speculators, who were lately driven off their precious possessions by the flood, read and ponder this provision. Can you float in boats over a grant that is carefully worded to exclude the overflowed tracts near the river? Best of all, however, is the evidence of figures that cannot lie. Sutter's grant is not only too informal and ill-defined, but it is also far too formal and well-defined to afford the speculators any shadow of excuse for their claims. For the latitude of the tract granted is limited by the outside boundaries, recorded in the document. The southern boundary is, however, expressly stated as latitude 38° 41' 32". And this parallel is some miles north of the city, crossing the Sacramento River, in fact, not far above its junction with the Feather. This is conclusive. The inalienable rights of man are no longer to be resisted by means of such a title as this one. The public domain is free to all. And Sacramento is obviously upon the public domain.

Such was the contention for which this pamphlet undertook to state the basis. Many a man has heard the old story repeated in lawsuits occurring years after that time. Early in the seventies the California Supreme Court Decisions contain a settlement on appeal of a suit in which the appellant, resisting a title in the city of Sacramento derived from the Sutter grant, had managed still, after all State and national decisions, to present as a forlorn hope the old argument about the latitudes. The argument was, of course, at that date promptly rejected ; but one watches with interest the reptilian tenacity of its venomous life. The whole case had received, as late as 1864,* the honor of restatement in the records of the United States Supreme Court, by the help of Attorney-General Black, who never missed an opportunity of abusing a Californian Land Grant title. The court, indeed, had failed to recognize the force of the argument.

And yet, even in 1850, this chain of squatter reasoning seems as one reads it to express rather a genuine American humor than any sincere opinion of anybody's. It is so plain that the squatter, annoyed by the show of legal right made by the other side, has determined in a fit of half-amused vexation to give the "speculators" all the law they want "hot and heavy." It is so plain, too, that what he really means is to assert his right to make game of any Mexican title, and to take up land wherever he wants it. For every item of his contention is a mere quibble, which would have been harmless enough, no doubt, in court proceedings, but which at such a moment, when urged with a view to disturbing the public mind of an established community, could easily become a very dangerous incitement to disorder and violence. Every Californian land-title had,

---

* United States Reports, 2 Wallace, 575.

of course, to be interpreted with reference to the conditions under which it was given. Substantial rights could not be left at the mercy of quibbles about matters of detail. A *bona fide* grant to Sutter, intended to include his "establishment at New Helvetia," could not be ignored because its boundaries were awkwardly described, nor because a surveyor, with poor and primitive instruments, had blundered about the latitude both of the northern and of the southern boundary, after Sutter's petition had described both of them with sufficient clearness, by the natural landmarks. Nobody, for instance, could have pretended that by Sutter's Buttes, the "*Tres Picos*" of the grant, must be meant some imaginary point out in the plains to the north, merely because the surveyor, Vioget, had erred about the latitude of the peaks, so that the grant put them just north of the northern outside boundary, while the line of latitude named for that boundary actually ran north of those familiar landmarks themselves. The *Tres Picos* formed an evidence of the true northern boundary of the tract in question, that was worth far more than Vioget's figures ; for the peaks are visible and the lines of latitude are "merely conventional signs," after all. The figures did in fact lie, and Vioget this time, so soon as the trouble had begun, frankly confessed his old error in an affidavit signed by him at San Francisco. There had been a constant error in latitude in his work, he averred, and by the southern boundary in latitude 38° 41′ 32″ he had meant "the estimated latitude of a point of land on the east bank of the Sacramento River, on the high ground south of the *lagunas*, below a town now called Sutter and distant about four and one half miles in a southerly direction from Sutter's fort."* As for the argument about the exclusion of the overflowed lands, that capped the climax of the squatter humor. The flood was,

* Transcript for June 8 ; see also Placer Times of the same date.

indeed, a land-speculator whom no one could gainsay, and to its writ of ejectment nobody made successful resistance. But then, if one calls his beloved tract of firm land swampland, because a great flood has driven him from it, one is understood to be amusing himself with hard words.

Here, then, was the outer armor in which the squatter doctrine encased itself. Its inner life was a very different thing. " Captain Sutter," said a squatter correspondent of the Placer Times, " settles this question himself, by plainly declaring with his own lips that he *has* no title to this place, but he *hopes* Congress will *give* him one." These words of the correspondent are false on their face, but they express truthfully enough the spirit of the squatter contention. Sutter "*has*," indeed, as yet no patent from the United States and he "*hopes*" that Congress will pass some law that will protect his right to his land. So much is true. But when a squatter interprets Sutter's position as this correspondent does, he plainly means that there are at present no legally valid Mexican land-titles in the country, since Congress, the representative of the conquering power, has so far passed no law confirming those titles. The squatter wants, then, to make out that Mexican land-grants, or at the very least, all in any wise imperfect or informal grants, have in some fashion lapsed with the conquest; and that in a proper legal sense the owners of these grants are no better than squatters themselves, unless Congress shall do what they "*hope*," and shall pass some act to give them back the land that they used to own before the conquest. That the squatters somehow held this strange idea about the grants, is to my mind pretty plain. The big Mexican grant was to them obviously an un-American institution, a creation of a benighted people. What was the good of the conquest, if it did not make our enlightened American ideas paramount in the country ? Unless, then, Congress, by some freak, should restore to these rapacious speculators their old benighted

22

legal *status*, they would have no land. Meanwhile, of course, the settlers were to be as well off as the others. So their thoughts ran.

Intelligent men could hold this view only in case they had already deliberately determined that the new-coming population, as such, ought to have the chief legal rights in the country. This view was, after all, a very obvious one. Providence, you see, and manifest destiny were understood in those days to be on our side, and absolutely opposed to the base Mexican. To Providence the voyagers on the way to California had appealed at Panama, when they called on General Persifer Smith to make his famous proclamation excluding foreigners from the Californian mines. "Providence," they in effect declared, "has preserved the treasures of those gold-fields all through these years of priestcraft and ignorance in California, for us Americans. Let the Government protect us now." * Providence is known to be opposed to every form of oppression ; and grabbing eleven leagues of land is a great oppression. And so the worthlessness of Mexican land-titles is evident.

Of course the squatters would have disclaimed very generally so naked a statement as this of their position. But when we read in one squatter's card † that "surely Sutter's grant does not entitle to a monopoly of all the lands in California, which were purchased by the treasure of the whole nation, and by no small amount of the best blood that ever coursed or ran through American veins," the same writer's formal assurance that Sutter ought to have his eleven leagues whenever they can be found and duly surveyed, cannot blind us to the true spirit of the argument. What has this "best blood" to do with the Sutter grant ? The connection in the writer's mind is only too obvious.

---

* See the Panama Star, in the early part of 1849.

† Transcript, June 21, 1850.

He means that the "best blood" won for us a right to harass great land-owners. In another of these expressions of squatter opinion I have found the assertion that the land-speculators stand on a supposed old Mexican legal right of such as themselves to take up the whole territory of California, in sections of eleven leagues each, by some sort of Mexican preëmption. If a squatter persists in understanding the land-owner's position in this way, his contempt for it is as natural as his wilful determination to make game of all native Californian claims is obvious.

But possibly the squatters would not have shown, and in fact would not have developed, their doctrine as fully as they in the end did, had not events hastened on a crisis. With mere argument no squatter was content. He was a squatter, not because he thoretically assailed Sutter's title, but because he actually squatted on land that belonged to somebody else. In order to do this successfully, the squatters combined into a "Settler's Association." They employed a surveyor and issued to their members "squatter-titles," which were simply receipts given by the surveyor, who was also recorder of the Association, each certifying that A. B. had paid the regular fee for the mapping out of a certain vacant lot of land, 40 × 160, within the limits of the town of Sacramento. The receipts have the motto, "The public domain is free to all." * The Association announced its readiness to insist, by its combined force, upon the rights of its members.

A member, who has already been quoted, wrote to the Placer Times, that "with the Sutter men there has been and is now money and power, and some of them are improving every opportunity to trouble and oppress the *peaceable*, *hard-working*, *order-loving*, and law-abiding settler, which, in the absence of the mass of the people in the mines, they

* Placer Times, June 7th.

do with comparative impunity." The italics are his own. The letter concluded with an assurance that the settlers were organized to maintain what "country, nature, and God" had given to them. The mention of the "absence of the people in the mines" is very characteristic of the purposes of the squatters; and the reference to "country, nature, and God" illustrates once more the spirit of the movement.

As for this "absence of the people," the squatters plainly hoped for much in the way of actual aid from the mining population, whenever it should return for another rainy season. That system of land-tenure which was so healthful in the mining districts, was not just the best school for teaching a proper respect in the presence of Mexican land grants. Colonel Frémont's later experience in the matter of the Mariposa grant proved that clearly enough. And not only the miners, but also the newly arriving emigrants, were expected to help the squatter interest, and to overwhelm the speculators. In an editorial on squatterism the Placer Times * expressed not ill-founded fears, as follows: "Reckless of all principle," it said, the squatters "have determined to risk all hopes upon the chances of an immediate and combined effort, as upon the hazard of a die." "They hope," the editorial continued, "to overcome all resistance for the moment, and to get the land. Then they will have a colorable show of title; surveys and associated action of other sorts will make the thing look formal; and there will be the law's delay. Then the immigration of strangers from the plains will come in with the autumn, undisciplined by our system, untutored by our customs, ignorant of our laws, and wholly actuated by a desire for rapid and enlarged accumulation." These will finish the mischief. "Through their thronging ranks the apostles of

---

* Weekly edition, June 29th.

squatterism " will " penetrate far and wide, disseminating
radical and subversive doctrines, and contending for an
indiscriminate ownership of property by the whole people,
qualified only by a right of possession in the actual possessor." The editor, of course, considered a conflict imminent when he wrote these words. And what makes me
think his notion of the significance of the squatter movement correct, is, in addition to what has been mentioned
above, the fact that the squatters continued to assert their
claims more and more violently and publicly from this
time till the end, but never took any pains to allay the
very natural alarm that they had thus aroused as to their
intentions. The movement was plainly an agrarian and
ultra-American movement, opposed to all great land owners, and especially to all these Mexican grantees.*

The appeal quoted above, to " nature, country, and
God," is also, as I have said, characteristic of the spirit of
the movement. The writer of the letter in question is very
probably no other than the distinguished squatter-leader,
Doctor Charles Robinson himself, a man to whom the movement seems to have owed nearly all its ability. And when
we speak of Doctor Robinson, we have to do with no insignificant demagogue or unprincipled advocate of wickedness, but with a high-minded and conscientious man, who
chanced just then to be in the devil's service, but who served
the devil honestly, thoughtfully, and, so far as he could,
dutifully, believing him to be an angel of light. This
future Free-Soil Governor of Kansas, this cautious, clear-
headed, and vigorous anti-slavery champion of the trou-

---

* One of the Tribune squatter correspondents (see Tribune for October
8, 1850) says, after the crisis, that, owing to the crowd in California, people
are much in one another's way ; but, he adds, " of necessity the rights of
the *majority* are most worthy of respect, and ought to be maintained."
This is the old story of robbers.

blous days before the war, who has since survived so many
bitter quarrels with old foes and old friends, to enjoy, now
at last, his peaceful age at his home in Lawrence, Kansas,
is not a man of whom one may speak with contempt, however serious his error in Sacramento may seem. He was a
proper hero for this tragic comedy, and "nature, country,
and God" were his guiding ideals. Only one must understand the character that these slightly vague ideals seem
to have assumed in his mind. He was a newcomer of 1849,
and hailed from Fitchburg, Massachusetts. He was a college graduate, had studied medicine, had afterwards re-
belled against the technicalities of the code of his local
association, and had become an independent practitioner.
His friends and interests, as his whole subsequent career
showed, were with the party of the cultivated New England
Radicals of that day. And these cultivated Radicals of the
anti-slavery generation, and especially of Massachusetts,
were a type in which an impartial posterity will take a
huge delight; for they combined so characteristically
shrewdness, insight, devoutness, vanity, idealism, and self-
worship. To speak of them, of course, in the rough, and as
a mass, not distinguishing the leaders from the rank and
file, nor blaspheming the greater names, they were usually
believers in quite abstract ideals; men who knew how to
meet God "in the bush" whenever they wanted, and so
avoided him in the mart and in the crowded street; men
who had "dwelt cheek by jowl, since the day" they were
"born, with the Infinite Soul," and whose relations with
him were like those of any man with his own private
property. This Infinite that they worshipped was, however,
in his relations to the rest of the world, too often rather
abstract, a *Deus absconditus*, who was as remote from the
imperfections and absurdities of the individual laws and processes of human society, as he was near to the hearts of his
chosen worshippers. From him they got a so-called Higher

Law. As it was ideal, and, like its author, very abstract, it was far above the erring laws of men, and it therefore relieved its obedient servants from all entangling earthly allegiances. If the constitution upon which our sinful national existence depended, and upon which our only hope of better things also depended, was contradicted by this Higher Law, then the constitution was a " league with hell," and anybody could set up for himself, and he and the Infinite might carry on a government of their own.

These Radicals were, indeed, of the greatest value to our country. To a wicked and corrupt generation they preached the gospel of a pure idealism fervently and effectively. If our generation does not produce just such men, it is because the best men of our time have learned from them, and have absorbed their fervent and lofty idealism into a less abstract and a yet purer doctrine. The true notion, as we all, of course, have heard, is, that there is an ideal of personal and social perfection far above our natural sinful ways, and indeed revealed to us by the agencies of spiritual life, and not by baser worldly means, but not on that account to be found or served by separating ourselves, or our lives, or our private judgments, from the social order, nor by rebelling against this whole frame of human error and excellence. This divine ideal is partly and haltingly realized in just these erring social laws—for instance, in the land laws of California—and we have to struggle in and for the actual social order, and cannot hope to reach the divine by sulking in the bush, or by crying in the streets about our private and personal Higher Law, nor by worshipping any mere abstraction. That patient loyalty to the actual social order is the great reformer's first duty ; that a service of just this erring humanity, with its imperfect and yet beautiful system of delicate and highly organized relationships, is the best service that a man can render to the Ideal ; that he is the best idealist who casts away as both unreal and unideal the vain private imaginings of his own weak brain, whenever he catches a glimpse of any higher and wider truth; all this lesson we, like other peoples and generations, have to study and learn. The Transcendentalists, by their very extravagances, have helped us towards this goal; but we must be pardoned if we learn from them with some little amusement. For when we are amused at them, we are amused at ourselves, since only by these very extravagances in our own experience do we ever learn to be genuine and sensible idealists.

Well, Doctor Robinson, also, had evidently learned much, in his own way, from teachers of this school. The complex and wearisome details of Spanish Law plainly do not interest him, since he is at home in the divine Higher Law. Concrete rights of rapacious land speculators in Sacramento are unworthy of the attention of one who sees so clearly into the abstract rights of Man. God is not in the Sutter grant, that is plain. It is the mission of the squatters to introduce the divine justice into California: no absurd justice that depends upon erroneous lines of latitude, and establishments at New Helvetia, and other like blundering details of dark Spanish days, but the justice that can be expressed in grand abstract formulæ, and that will hear of no less arbiter than the United States Supreme Court at the very nearest, and is quite independent of local courts and processes.

For the rest, Doctor Robinson added to his idealism the aforesaid Yankee shrewdness, and to his trust in God considerable ingenuity in raising funds to keep the squatter association at work. He wrote well and spoke well. He was thoroughly in earnest, and his motives seem to me above any suspicion of personal greed. He made out of this squatter movement a thing of real power, and was, for the time, a very dangerous man.

Thus led and moved, the squatter association might

easily have become the center of a general revolutionary movement of the sort above described. All depended on the tact of the Sacramento community in dealing with it. If the affair came to open bloodshed, the public sentiment aroused would depend very much upon where the fault of the first violence was judged to lie. The mass of people throughout the State looked on such quarrels, so long as they avoided open warfare, with a mixture of amusement, vexation, and indifference. Amusement they felt in watching any moderate quarrel; vexation they felt with all these incomprehensible land grants, that covered so much good land and made so many people trip; and indifference largely mingled with it all, at the thought of home, and of the near fortune that would soon relieve the average Californian from all the accursed responsibilities of this maddening and fascinating country. But should the "land speculators" seem the aggressors, should the squatters come to be looked upon as an oppressed band of honest poor men, beaten and murdered by high-handed and greedy men of wealth, then Robinson might become a hero, and the squatter movement, under his leadership, might have the whole sympathetic American public at its back, and the consequences we can hardly estimate.

How did the community, as represented by its generous-hearted papers, meet the crisis? Both these newspapers of Sacramento were, as the reader sees, editorially opposed to the squatters. They bandied back and forth accusations of lukewarmness in this opposition. But in July the Transcript, not formally changing its attitude, still began to give good reason for the accusation that it was a little disposed to favor squatterism. For, while it entirely ceased editorial comment, it began to print lengthy and very readable accounts of the squatter meetings, prepared, it is said, by a reporter who was himself a squatter, thus giving the squatters just the help with the disinterested public that they desired, and supplying for the historical student some amusing material.* By the beginning of July the arguments were all in ; the time for free abuse and vigorous action had come. Yet it is just then that this paper, whose motives were but yesterday so pure and lofty, shows much more of its good humor than of its wisdom, and so actually abets the squatter movement.

IV.

The reader needs at this point no assurance that the quarrel was quite beyond any chance of timely settlement by an authoritative trial of the Sutter title itself. Such a trial was, of course, just what the squatters themselves were anxious to await. It was on the impossibility of any immediate and final judicial settlement that their whole movement depended. Mr. William Carey Jones's famous report on California Land Titles reached the State only during the very time of this controversy. Congress had, .as yet, made no provision for the settlement of California Land Claims. The Supreme Court was a great way off ; hence the vehemence and the piety of squatter appeals to God and the Supreme Court. Regular settlement being thus out of the question, some more summary process was necessary to protect the rights of land-owners. In the first session of the State Legislature, which had taken place early in this year, the landed interest seems to have been fairly strong, apparently by virtue of those private compromises, which one can trace through the history of the Constitutional Convention at Monterey, and which had been intended both to meet the political exigencies of the moment, and to further the personal ambitions of two or three men. The result had been

---

* See the bitter letter to the editor of the Placer Times just after the crisis, published Aug. 16th. This letter may probably be trusted as to this one fact.

the establishment in California of a procedure already well known elsewhere. The " Act Concerning Forcible Entry and Unlawful Detainer" provided a summary process for ejecting any forcible trespasser upon the land of a previous peaceable occupant, who had himself had any color of right. This summary process was not to be resorted to in case the question of title properly entered into the evidence introduced in defense by the supposed trespasser, and the procedure was no substitute for an action of ejectment. It was intended to defend a peaceable possessor of land from violent dispossession, even in case the assailant happened to have rights that would in the end prove on final trial superior. The act, therefore, was well able to meet the case of the naked trespasser, or squatter, who, without pretense of title, took possession of land that was previously in the peaceable possession of anybody. The act provided for his ejection, with the addition of penalties ; and its framers had, of course, no intention to make it any substitute for a judicial determination of title.

To this act some of the land-owners of Sacramento now appealed for help. Moreover, as they were in control of the city council, they proceeded to pass, amid the furious protests of the squatters, a municipal ordinance, which in the end was indeed practically unenforced, forbidding any one, under serious penalties, to erect tents, or shanties, or houses, or to heap lumber or other encumbrances, upon any vacant lot belonging to a private person, or upon any public street. The land-owners also formed a " Law and Order Association," and printed in the papers a notice of their intention to defend to the last their property under the Sutter title. They began to drill companies of militia. A few personal encounters took place in various vacant lots, where owners tried to prevent the erection of fences or shanties. Various processes were served upon squatters, and executed. The squatter association itself plainly suffered a good deal from the internal jealousies or from the mutual indifference of its members. Only the ardor of Doctor Robinson prevented an utter failure of its organization long before the crisis. In the latter part of June, and for some time in July, the movement fell into the background of public attention. The Transcript helped it out again into prominence. But the squatters themselves longed for a newspaper of their own, and sent for a press and type. They were accused, meanwhile, of threats to fire the town in case their cause was put down. But, after all, their best chance of immediate success lay in raising money to resist the suits brought against them ; and to this course Doctor Robinson, although he had conscientious scruples about the authority of any California law, urged his followers as to the most expedient present device. It is at this point that the meetings of the squatters begin to receive lengthy reports.

At a meeting reported in the Transcript for July 2d, one squatter objected to going to law. It was unnecessary, he said ; for this whole thing of the Sutter title was illegal. He was answered by one Mr. Milligan, to the effect that the object was to keep their enemies at bay until the question could be brought before a legal tribunal, where justice could be done. Mr. Milligan was then sent about in the country to the "brother squatters," who were so numerous near Sacramento, for subscriptions. In a meeting narrated in the Transcript for July 4th, he reported imperfect success. Some of the brethren were not at home ; one told the story about the man who got rich by minding his own business ; few had money to spare. Doctor Robinson had some reassuring remarks in reply to this report, and Mr. Milligan himself then made an eloquent speech. "The squatters were men of firmness ; their cause had reached the States ; they had many hearty sympathizers on the Atlantic shores." His thoughts became yet wider in their sweep, as he dwelt on the duty of never yielding to oppression. "He saw, a few days ago, a crowd of Chinese emigrants in this land; he hoped to be able to send through these people the intelligence to the Celestial Empire that the Emperor don't own all the land in the world, and so he hoped the light would soon shine in Calcutta—throughout India, and Bengal, and Botany Bay, and lift up the cloud of moral darkness and rank oppression." This Oriental enthusiasm reads very delightfully in these days, and is worth preserving.

By the time of the meeting of July 24th, which was held in "Herkimer Hall," and was reported in the Transcript of the 25th, the talk was a little less world-embracing, and the feeling keener. Some land-owners had taken the law into their own hands, and had been tearing down a fence erected by squatters. Doctor Robinson announced that he would help to put up that fence next day, whereupon rose Mr. McClatchy.* He was a law-abiding citizen, but would submit to no injustice. He would rather fight than collect subscriptions any day. If land-owners wanted to fight let them fight, and the devil take the hindmost. "Let us put up all the fences pulled down, and let us put up all the men who pulled them down." This last suggestion was greeted with great applause and stamping.

Doctor Robinson introduced resolutions declaring, among other strong words, that "if the bail of an arrested squatter be refused simply because the bondsman is not a land-holder under Captain Sutter, we shall consider all executions issued in consequence thereof as acts of illegal force, and shall act accordingly." In urging his resolutions, he pointed out how the land speculators' doctrine about land grants would certainly result in the oppression of the poor man all over

---

* James McClatchy, author of the March 25th letter to the New York Tribune, had previously been associated with land-reform movements in New York State. He, too, knew the Higher Law by heart, and was a man of some ability.

California. "Was this right? Was it a blessing? If so, Ireland was blessed, and all other oppressed countries. Would any Anglo-Saxon endure this? The Southern slave was not worse treated." Doctor Robinson dwelt on the low character of these speculators. Look at the mayor, at the councilmen, and the rest. "There were no great minds among them. And yet these were the men who claimed the land. Can such men be men of principle?" He thought that "we should abide by all just laws, not unjust."

Mr. McClatchy now pointed out that God's laws were above man's laws, and that God gave man the earth for his heritage. In this instance, however, the laws of our own land, whenever, of course, we could appeal to them in the Supreme Court, were surely on our side, and so seconded God's law. "If the land-holders," he said, winding up his philosophic train of thought, "act as they do, we shall be obliged to lick 'em."

A Mr. Burke was proud to feel that by their language that evening they had already been violating those city ordinances which forbade assemblages for unlawful ends. "A fig for their laws; they have no laws." "Mr. Burke," says the report, "was game to the last—all fight—and was highly applauded." The resolutions were readily adopted, and the meeting adjourned in a state of fine enthusiasm.

In the second week of August a case under the "Forcible Entry and Detainer Act" came before the County Court, Willis, Judge, on appeal from a justice's court of the city. The squatters' association appealed, on the ground that the plaintiff in the original suit had shown no true title to the land. The justice had decided that under the evidence the squatter in question was a naked trespasser, who made for himself no pretense of title, and that, therefore, in a trial under the act the question of title had not properly entered as part of the evidence at all. The appeal was made from this decision and was promptly dismissed. The squatters were furious. Sutter had no title, and a man was a squatter on the land for just that reason; and yet when the courts were appealed to for help in sustaining the settler they thus refused to hear the grounds of his plea, and proposed to eject him as a trespasser. Well, the United States courts could be appealed to some time. One could well afford to wait for them if only the process under the State act could be stayed, and the squatter left in peaceable possession meanwhile. To this end one must appeal to the State Supreme Court. But alas! Judge Willis, when asked in court, after he had rendered decision, for a stay of proceedings pending appeal to the State Supreme Court, replied, somewhat informally, in conversation with the attorneys, that it was not clear to him whether the act in question, or any other law, permitted appeal from the county court's decision in a case like this. He took the matter under advisement. But the squatters present, in a fit of rage, misunderstood the judge's hesitating remark. They rushed from the court to excited meetings outside, and spread abroad the news that Judge Willis had not only decided against them, but had decided that from him there was no appeal. Woe to such laws and to such judges! The law betrays us. We will appeal to the Higher Law. The processes of the courts shall not be served!

Doctor Robinson was not unequal to the emergency. At once he sent out notices calling a mass-meeting of "squatters and others interested," to take place the same evening, August 10th. It was Saturday, and when night came a large crowd of squatters, of land-owners, and of idlers, had gathered. The traditional leisure of Saturday night made a great part of the assembly as cheerful as it was eager for novelty and interested in this affair. Great numbers were there simply to see fair play; and this general public, in their characteristically American good humor, were quite unwilling to recognize any sort of seriousness in the occasion. These jolly onlookers interrupted the squatter orators, called for E. J. C. Kewen and Sam Brannan as representatives of the land-owners, listened to them awhile, interrupted them when the thing grew tedious, and enjoyed the utter confusion that for the time reigned on the platform. At length the crowd were ready for Doctor Robinson and his inevitable resolutions. He, for his part, was serious enough. He had been a moderate man, he said, but the time for moderation was past. He was ready to have his corpse left on his own bit of land ere he would yield his rights. Then he read his resolutions, which sufficiently denounced Judge Willis and the laws; and thereafter he called for the sense of the meeting. Dissenting voices rang out, but the resolutions received a loud affirmative vote and were declared carried. The regular business of the meeting was now done; but for a long time yet various ambitious speakers mounted the platform and sought to address the crowd, which amused itself by roaring at them or by watching them pushed from their high place.

Next day Doctor Robinson was early at work drawing up in his own way a manifesto to express the sense of his party. It was a very able and reckless document. Robinson had found an unanswerable fashion of stating the ground for devotion to the Higher Law as opposed to State Law. There was, the paper reminded the people, no true State here at all; for Congress had not admitted California as yet, and it was still a mere Territory. What the Legislature in San José had done was no law-making. It had passed some "rules" which had merely "advisory force." These were, some of them, manifestly unconstitutional and oppressive. The act now in question was plainly of this nature. Worst of all, the courts organized by this advisory body now refused an appeal from their own decisions even to the Supreme Court of the State. Such a decision, thus cutting off an appeal on a grave question of title, that could in fact be settled only by the Supreme Court of the United States, was not to be endured. The settlers were done with such law that was no law. " The people in this community called settlers, and others who are friends of justice and humanity, in consideration of the above, have determined to disregard all decisions of our courts in land cases, and all summonses or executions by the sheriff, constable, or other officer of the present county or city touching this matter. They will regard the said officers as private citizens, as in the eyes of the Constitution they are, and hold them responsible accordingly." If, then, the document went on to say, the officers in question appealed to force, the settlers "have deliberately resolved to appeal to arms, and protect their sacred rights, if need be, with their lives."

The confused assent of the Saturday night torchlight meeting to a manifesto of this sort, an assent such as the previous resolutions had gained, would have been worth very little. Where were the men and the arms ? Doctor Robinson was man enough himself to know what this sort of talk must require if it was to have meaning. But what he did he can best tell. In his tent, after the crisis, was found an unfinished letter to a friend in the East. It was plainly never intended for the public eye, and may surely be accepted as a perfectly sincere statement. The newspapers published it as soon as it was found, and from the Placer Times of August 15th I have it noted down.

The date is Monday, the 12th of August. "Since writing you we have seen much and experienced much of an important character, as well as much excitement. . . . The County Judge on Saturday morning declared that from his decision there should be no appeal." Then the letter proceeds to tell how the meeting was called, as narrated above. The call " was responded to by both parties, and the speculators, as aforetime, attempted to talk against time. On the passage of a series of resolutions presented by your humble

23

servant, there were about three ayes to one nay, although the Transcript said that they were about equal. Sunday morning I drew up a manifesto, carried it to church, paid one dollar for preaching, helped them sing, showed it to a lawyer, to see if my position was correct *legally*, and procured the printing of it in handbills and in the paper, after presenting it to a private meeting of friends for their approval, which I addressed at some length. After a long talk for the purpose of comforting a gentleman just in from the plains, and who, the day before, had buried his wife, whom he loved most tenderly, and a few days previous to that had lost his son, I threw myself upon my blankets, and 'seriously thought of the morrow.'

"What will be the result? Shall I be borne out in my position? On whom can I depend? How many of those who are squatters will come out if there is a prospect of a fight? Have I strictly defined our position in the bill? Will the *world*, the *universe*, and *God* say it is *just*, etc.? Will you call me rash if I tell you that I took these steps to this point when I could get but twenty-five men to pledge themselves on paper to sustain me, and many of them, I felt, were timid? . Such was the case."

In the night we deal, if we like, with the world, the universe, and God. In the morning we have to deal with such things as the Sheriff, the Mayor, and the writs of the County Court—things with which, as we have already learned from the squatters, God has nothing whatever to do! One wonders, in passing, whether the church in which Doctor Robinson so lustily sang and so cheerfully paid his dollar that bright August Sunday was Doctor Benton's. If so, the settlers' leader surely must have noticed a contrast between his own God of the Higher Law and the far more concrete Deity that this noted and able pioneer preacher always presented to his audiences. That orthodox Deity, whatever else may have seemed doubtful about him, was surely conceived

and presented as having very definite and living relationships to all rulers who bear not the sword in vain. And nobody, whatever his own philosophic or theological views,
ought to have any hesitation as to which of these two conceptions is the worthier of a good citizen, however incomplete both of them may be for philosophy. And now, to
state this crisis in a heathen fashion, we may say that the
concrete Deity of the actual law, and Doctor Robinson's ideal
abstract Deity of the Higher Law, were about to enter into
open warfare, with such temporary result as the relative
strength of unwise city authorities and weak-kneed squatters might determine. For to such earthen vessels are the
great ideals, good and evil, entrusted on this earth.

What other squatters thought meanwhile is sufficiently
shown by two letters from their side, one written just after
the crisis, the other some months later, and published in
Eastern newspapers. The first says: "The cause of all this
[difficulty] is nothing more or less than land monopoly,"
and denies that the squatters could have done anything but
what they did. The second says, long after, be it noticed,
and when the lessons of the affair ought to have been clear
to every one, that the squatters have clearly shown their
intent to fight to the death against all "favoritism" shown
to old Californians. American citizens will never, the
writer of the letter says, submit to such outrageous injustice. He was himself present at the fight and speaks authoritatively.

v.

Morning came, and with it the printed manifesto. The
city, with all its show of care and all its warnings during
the last few months, was wholly unprepared for proper resistance to organized rebellion. The populace was aroused,
crowds ran to and fro, rumors flew thick and fast. Doctor
Robinson was found on a lot, at the corner of Second and
N Streets, where the Sheriff was expected to appear to serve

a writ. By adroitness in making speeches and by similar devices the doctor collected and held, in apparent sympathy with himself, a crowd of about two hundred, whom he desired to have appear as all squatters, and all "men of valor." * Meanwhile names were enrolled by him as volunteers for immediate action, a military commander of the company was chosen—one Maloney, a veteran of the Mexican War—and in all some fifty men were soon under arms. Mayor Bigelow now approached on horseback, and from the saddle addressed the crowd. It would be best, he said, for them to disperse, otherwise there might be trouble. Doctor Robinson was spokesman in answer. "I replied," he says in his letter, "most respectfully, that we were assembled to injure no one and to assail no one who left us alone. We were on our own property, with no hostile intentions while unmolested." The Mayor galloped off, and was soon followed to his office by a little committee of the squatters, Doctor Robinson once more spokesman. They wanted, so they said, to explain their position so that there could be no mistake. They were anxious to avoid bloodshed, and begged Bigelow to use his influence to prevent service of the processes of the Court. Doctor Robinson understood the Mayor to promise to use the desired influence in a private way and as a peace-loving citizen. They then warned him that, if advantage should be taken of their acceptance of his assurance, and if writs were served in the absence of their body of armed men, they would hold him and the Sheriff responsible according to their proclamation. The Placer Times of Tuesday morning declares that the Mayor's reply assured the squatters of his intention to promise nothing but a strict enforcement of the law.

Doctor Robinson's letter seems to have been written just after this interview. In the evening the rumor was preva-

---

* See his letter, after the passage quoted above.

lent that a warrant was out for his arrest and that of the other ringleaders. Many squatters, very variously and sometimes amusingly armed, still hung about the disputed lot of land. On Tuesday, possibly because of the Mayor's supposed assurance, the squatters were less wary. Their enemies took advantage of their dispersed condition,* and arrested the redoubtable McClatchy, with one other leader. These they took to the "prison brig," out in the river. In the afternoon the Sheriff quietly put the owners of the disputed lot in possession, apparently in the absence of squatters. The Mayor's assurance, if he had given one, was thus seen to be ineffective. There was no appeal now left the squatters but to powder and ball.

It seems incredible, but it is true, that Wednesday morning, August 14th, found the authorities still wholly unprepared to overawe the lawless defenders of the Higher Law. When the squatters assembled, some thirty or forty in number, all armed, and "men of valor" this time when they marched under Maloney's leadership to the place on Second Street, and once more drove off the owners; when they then proceeded down to the levee, intending to go out to the prison brig and rescue their friends; when they gave up this idea, and marched along I Street to Third in regular order, Maloney in front on horseback, with a drawn sword, there was *no* force visible ready to disperse them; and they were followed by a crowd of unarmed citizens, who were hooting and laughing at them.† Reaching the corner of Third,

---

* The letter in the New York Tribune of October 15, 1850, by a squatter, says that the young man who claimed possession as a squatter was absent from the disputed land on Tuesday by reason of his attendance at the examination of the arrested squatters in court. McClatchy is also here said to have given himself up.

† Transcript and Times of August 15. Compare Mr. Stillman's Golden Fleece, p. 172; New York Tribune of September 21, September 25, October 7, October 15, 1850.

Street, they turned into that street, passed on until J Street was reached, and then marched out J toward Fourth Street.

At this point, Mayor Bigelow, who had already been busily attempting to rouse the people near the levee, appeared in the rear of the crowd of sight-seeing followers, on horseback, and called upon all good citizens to help him to disperse the rioters at once. His courage was equal to his culpable carelessness in having no better force at hand; but to his call a few of the unarmed citizens replied (men such as Doctor Stillman himself, for instance) that the squatters could not be gotten rid of so easily by a merely *extempore* show of authority, since they surely meant to fire if molested. The Mayor denied, confidently, this possibility; the squatters were, to his mind, but a crew of blustering fellows, who meant nothing that would lead them into danger. He overtook the crowd of citizen followers, repeating his call; and the mass of this crowd gaily obeyed. Three cheers for the Mayor were given, and the improvised *posse*, led by Mayor and Sheriff, ran on in pursuit of their game. Only one who has seen an American street-crowd in a moment of popular excitement, can understand the jolly and careless courage that seems to have prevailed in this band, or their total lack of sense of what the whole thing meant. They were indeed not all unarmed, by any means; but it seems impossible that, acting as they did, they could have been expecting to draw fire from the squatters.

On J Street, Maloney of the drawn sword turned about on his horse to look, when lo! the Mayor, with the Sheriff, and with the little army, was in pursuit. The moment of vengeance for broken promises had come. Promptly the squatter company wheeled, drew into line across Fourth, and awaited the approach of the enemy, taking him thus in flank. Undaunted the Mayor rode up, and voiced the majesty of the law, by ordering the squatters to lay down their arms, and to give themselves up as prisoners. The citizen army cheerfully crowded about Bigelow, and in front of the armed rioters, curious, no doubt, to watch the outcome, anxious, it would seem, to enjoy a joke, incredulous of any danger from the now so familiar boasters. Armed and unarmed men seem to have been huddled together in confusion, beside the Mayor and the Sheriff. But the armed men displayed their weapons freely, and were ready for whatever might result. Thus everything was done to tempt a disaster.

The accounts of the scene that are written by the squatters themselves, pretend 'that they replied to the Mayor, refusing to surrender their arms, and even add that he himself first discharged a barrel of his own pistol before they began. But the newspaper reports, and Doctor Stillman's account, make it tolerably clear that the squatters had no intention of treating further at this moment with the Mayor, and make it doubtful whether they even replied to him. As the Mayor spoke, Maloney was heard giving orders. "Shoot the Mayor," he said ; and at the words firing began—a volley, Doctor Stillman calls it, who saw the whole from a block away—an irregular, hasty, ill-aimed, rattle of guns and pistols, most accounts make it.

Men standing further down the street saw the crowd scatter in all directions, and in a moment more saw the Mayor's horse dash riderless towards the river. Those nearer by saw how armed men among the citizens, with a quick reaction, fired their pistols, and closed in on the rioters. Maloney fell dead. Doctor Robinson lay severely wounded. On the side of the citizens, Woodland, the city assessor, was shot dead, the Mayor himself, thrice severely wounded, had staggered a few steps, after dropping from his horse, and had fallen on the pavement. In all there were two * squatters and one of the citizens' party killed,

---

* *Three*, says the Transcript, but never gives the name of this third. The other accounts name two.

and one squatter and four citizens * wounded. Like a lightning flash the battle came, and was done. The array of the squatters melted away like a mist when the two leaders were seen to fall; the confused mass of the citizens, shocked and awe-stricken where they were not terrified, waited no longer on the field than the others, but scattered wildly. A few moments later, when Doctor Stillman returned with his shotgun which, on the first firing, he had gone but half a block to get, the street was quite empty of armed men. He waited for some time to see any one in authority. At length Lieutenant-Governor McDougal appeared, riding at full speed, "his face very pale." "Get all the armed men you can," he said, and rendezvous at Foster's hotel."

"I went to the place designated," says Doctor Stillman, "and there found a few men, who had got an old iron ship's gun, mounted on a wooden truck; to its axles was fastened a long dray pole. The gun was loaded with a lot of scrap iron. I wanted to know where McDougal was. We expected him to take the command and die with us. I inquired of Mrs. McDougal, who was stopping at the hotel, what had become of her husband. She said he had gone to San Francisco for assistance. Indeed he was on his way to the steamer 'Senator' when I saw him, and he left his horse on the bank of the river."

In such swift, dreamlike transformations the experiences of the rest of the day passed by. In the afternoon, Caulfield, a squatter leader, who had fled from the scene of the fight, was captured, and brought toward the prison brig, his feet tied under his horse's belly, his face covered with blood and dust. He had been knocked from his horse with the butt of a pistol as he fought with his pursuers. So Doctor Stillman

---

* Of these four one indeed was a non-combatant, a little girl just then on the street, whose injury was not very serious.

tells us. From the newspapers we learn how people generally felt that afternoon. Rumors were countless. The squatters had gone out of the city; they would soon return. They were, it was asserted, seven hundred strong. They meant vengeance. They would fire the city. Yes, they had already fired the city, although nobody knew where. No one could foresee the end of the struggle. The city, men said, had been declared under martial law. Everybody must come out. The whole force of the State would doubtless be needed. If the squatter's failed now, they would go to the mines, and arouse the whole population there. One would have to fight all the miners as well. Such things flew from mouth to mouth; such reports the "Senator" carried towards San Francisco, with the pale-faced Lieutenant-Governor, who himself landed, by the way, at Benecia, to appeal for help to the general of the United States forces there placed. Such reports were even sent East by the first steamer, and there printed in newspapers ere they could be contradicted.

As a fact, however, the most serious danger was already past. The opening of the fight had made the squatters seem, in the public eye, unequivocally lawless and dangerous aggressors. They could expect, for the moment at least, no sympathy, but only stern repression. And so, in reality, the city was never safer, as a whole, than it was a few hours after the fatal meeting at the corner of Fourth and J Streets. A little flowing blood is a very effective sight for our public. Conscience and passion are alike aroused in the community. American good-humor gives way, for the instant, to the sternest and most bigotted hatred of the offenders. So, in Sacramento, there was just now no mercy for the squatters. Their late attorney was threatened with hanging. Their friends fled the town. And even while the wild rumors were flying, the most perfect safety from invasion had been actually secured in the city limits.

But yet neither the bloodshed nor the terror was wholly done. Outside the city limits there was yet to occur a most serious and deplorable encounter. The squatters were actually scattered in all directions; but the rumors made it seem advisable to prevent further attacks, by armed sallies into the country, and by arrest of leaders. Thursday afternoon (just after the funeral of Woodland), the Sheriff, McKinney, with an armed force in which were several well-known prominent citizens, set out towards Mormon Island, with the intention of finding and bringing in prisoners.* That the Sheriff had no writs for the arrest of any one, and only the vaguest notion of his own authority, seems plain. Panic was king. At the house of one Allen, who kept a bar-room some seven miles out, the Sheriff sought for squatters, having been informed that several were there. It was now already dark. Leaving the body of his force outside, the Sheriff approached the house with a few men and entered. There were a number of occupants visible, all alarmed and excited. The writless Sheriff's party were unaware that, in the back room of the house, Mrs. Allen lay seriously ill, attended by her adopted daughter, a girl of sixteen. To be seen at the moment were only men, and they had arms. McKinney called out to Allen to surrender himself to the Sheriff. Allen replied, not unnaturally, that this was his house, his castle. He proposed to fight for it. McKinney repeated: "I am Sheriff; lay down your arms." What followed is very ill-told by the eye-witnesses, for the darkness and the confusion made everything dim. At all events, some of the Sheriff's party left the house, perhaps to call for assistance from the main body; and in a moment more the occupants had begun firing, and McKinney was outside of

* See on this affair the Transcript and Times of August 16th and 17th, and Dr. Stillman's experiences, Golden Fleece, pp. 176, 177; also see the account in the New York Tribune.

the house, staggering under a mortal wound. He fell, and in a short time was dead. That the firing from without soon overpowered all resistance, that two of the occupants of the house were shot dead, that others lay wounded, and that the assailants shortly after took possession of the place and searched it all through, not sparing the sick room : these were very natural consequences. After about an hour the arresting party left, taking with them four men as prisoners. Allen himself, sorely hurt, had escaped through the darkness, to show his wounds and to tell his painful story in the mines.

The little dwelling was left alone in the night. Nobody remained alive and well about the place save the young girl and two negro slaves. The patient lay dying from the shock of the affair. For a long time the girl, as she afterwards deposed, waited, not daring to go to the bar-room, ignorant of who might be killed, hearing once in a while groans. About ten o'clock a second party of armed men came from the city, searched again, and after another hour went away. " Mrs. Allen died about the time this second party rode up to the house," deposes the girl. She had the rest of the night to herself.*

The city was not reassured by the news of the Sheriff's death. In the unlighted streets of the frightened place, the alarm was sounded by the returning party about nine o'clock. Of course, invasion and fire were expected. The militia companies turned out, detailed patrolling parties, and then ordered the streets cleared. The danger was imminent that the defenders of the law would pass the night in shooting one another by mistake in the darkness.

---

* Allen was a Missourian, who, like others, had brought his slaves to California at a venture. The State Constitution, when once the State was admitted, made slavery, as is known, impossible. Allen survived, and found his way back to Missouri in a year or so. I there lost sight of him.

But this was happily avoided. The families in the town were, of course, terribly excited. " The ladies," says Dr. Stillman, " were nearly frightened out of their wits ; but we assured them that they had nothing to fear—that we were devoted to their service, and were ready to die at their feet ; being thus assured, they all retired into their cozy little cottages, and securely bolted the doors." During the night, the Senator arrived from San Francisco, with reinforcements.   Lieutenant-Governor McDougal had already returned on Thursday from Benecia, bringing, according to the Placer Times, muskets and cartridges, but no United States soldiers. He had felt seriously the responsibilities of his position, and had accordingly gone to bed, sick with the cares of office.

But morning came peacefully enough. Quiet in external affairs was restored. In the city Sam Brannan and others talked mightily of law, order, and blood. There were, however, no more battles to fight. In a few days, quiet of mind also was restored ; people were ashamed of their alarm. Squatters confined themselves to meetings in the mining districts and in Marysville, to savage manifestoes, and to wordy war from a distance, with sullen submission near home. The real war was done. A tacit consent to drop the subject was soon noticeable in the community. Men said that the laws must be enforced, and meanwhile determined to speak no ill of the dead. There was a decided sense, also, of common guilt. The community had sinned, and suffered.

Of the actors in this drama little needs further to be narrated here. Doctor Robinson disappeared for the moment as wounded prisoner in a cloud of indictments for assault, conspiracy, murder, and what else I know not. Mayor Bigelow was taken to San Francisco, where he almost miraculously recovered from his three bad wounds, only to die soon of the cholera. The squatter movement assumed a new phase.

Doctor Robinson, indeed, was in little danger from his indictments, when once the heat of battle had cooled. He was felt to be a man of mark; the popular ends had been gained in his defeat; the legal evidence against him was like the chips of drift-wood in a little eddy of this changing torrent of California life. With its little hoard of drift, the eddy soon vanished in the immeasurable flood. After a change of venue to a bay county, and after a few months' postponement, the cloud of indictments melted away like the last cloudflake of our rainy season. *Nolle pros.* was entered, and the hero was free from bail, as he had already for a good while been free on bail to recover his bodily health, to edit the previously projected squatter newspaper, to run for the Legislature, and even to form friendships with some of the very men whom he had lately been assailing. In a district of Sacramento County, Doctor Robinson's friends managed, with the connivance of certain optimists, to give him a seat in the Assembly, that late "advisory" body, whose "rules," before the admission of the State, he had so ardently despised. The State was admitted now, and Doctor Robinson cheerfully undertook his share of legislation. But the Legislature cared more for senatorial election, and such small game, than for the Higher Law. Doctor Robinson was not perfectly successful, even in pleasing his constituents. Ere yet another year passed, he had forever forsaken our State, and for his further career, you must read the annals of the New England Emigrant Aid Society and the history of Kansas. I have found an account of his career in a Kansas book, whose author must have a little misunderstood Doctor Robinson's version of this old affair. For the account says that the good Doctor, when he was in California in early days, took valiant part for the American settlers against certain wicked claimants under one John Sutter, who (the wretch) had pretended to own "99,000 square miles of land in California." Alas, poor Sutter, with thy great schemes! Is it to come to this?

I cannot close this scene without adding that a certain keen-eyed and intelligent foreigner, a Frenchman, one Auger, who visited our State a little later, in 1852, took pains to inquire into this affair and to form his own opinion. He gives a pathetic picture of poor Sutter, overwhelmed by squatters, and then proceeds to give his countrymen some notion of what a squatter is. Such a person, he says, represents the American love of land by marching, perhaps "*pendant des mois entiers*," until he finds a bit of seemingly vacant land. Here he fortifies himself, "*et se fait massacrer avec toute sa familie plutôt que de renoncer à la moindre parcelle du terrain qu'il a usurpé.*" * This is well stated. But best of all is the following : "*Celui qui se livre à cette investigation prend dès lors le titre de* 'squatter,' *qui vient, je le suppose, du mot* 'square' (*place*), *et signifie chercheur d'emplacement.*" It is evident to us, therefore, that Doctor Robinson and all his party were "on the square." And herewith we may best end our account.

---

* Auger, Voyage en Californie, p. 154.

XII.

JEAN MARIE GUYAU.

JEAN MARIE GUYAU,* one of the most prominent of recent French philosophical critics, and one of the shortest
lived amongst those philosophers who have obtained,
whether by critical or by constructive work, any considerable
fame, was born October 28, 1854, and died March 31, 1888,
at the age of thirty-three years. To the pursuit of philosophy he was determined, not only by temperament, but by
his earliest home training. His education was directed by
Alfred Fouillée, the most distinguished constructive philosopher of contemporary France. Fouillée was the cousin
of Guyau's mother, and became, by second marriage, her
husband, and Guyau's step-father. The mother is known
in France as an author of educational works. The happy
intellectual conditions that resulted from this union show
themselves throughout our hero's brief career. His literary
skill, from the very first of his books, is that of the expert;
his scholarship, from this beginning on, is mature. His
eye is always set on the goal; he has but to run the
race, and no longer to learn the art, of the thinker, after
once he has begun to show his powers. His opinions develop; but the spirit of his work remains substantially the
same. His pace quickens, his feats of critical skill and of

---

* A paper prepared for the Cercle Français of Harvard University.

speculative imagination grow more remarkable as he proceeds. But what one sees is the progress of the man, and never the maturing of the boy. Yet Guyau's first book, a memoir of some thirteen hundred manuscript pages upon the history of Utilitarian Ethics from Epicurus to the present day, was crowned by the Academy of Moral and Political Sciences in 1874, and had been written in the previous year, when its author was nineteen years of age. Its two parts, the one on ancient Epicureanism, the other on modern English Ethics, were later published separately, and Guyau's youthful summary and criticism of the contemporary English ethical movement has received especial praise, and very serious consideration both in France and in England.

It thus becomes at once plain that we have here to deal with one of those cases of early promise and swift development of which the history of philosophy, like the history of poetry, shows us a number of instances. Amongst philosophers, Berkeley and Schelling readily come to mind, by way of comparison, as we consider Guyau's brilliant youth. To be sure, Guyau is not to be set beside either of these men as regards constructive ability. He is a critical essayist rather than an originator of systematic doctrine ; yet in native brilliancy of intellect he compares well with both. Of the two Schelling the more resembles Guyau in respect of the swiftness and manifoldness of literary production. Schelling was born in 1775, began to write for publication, like Guyau, just before he was twenty years of age, and was professor of philosophy at Jena by the time he was twenty-two. But Guyau has one trait that the young Schelling lacked, namely, speculative self-control. He constructs less originally, but he criticises more soundly. Schelling's early works followed one another like lightning flashes, each one striking in a new and unexpected place. Guyau is the product of a training as severe as it was kindly and stimulating. He has genius, but shows no way-wardness. He covers a wide range, and, as just said, his opinions develop. But he does not, like Schelling, alter essential features of his whole system at every new presen-tation. And, in fact, as just observed, Guyau, except in his Ethics, never had a system. On the other hand, by the tendency to determine all that he has to say through its relation to a few central and persistently elaborated prob-lems, Guyau reminds us of Berkeley. Like the young Berkeley, Guyau had been inspired by Plato. Like Berke-ley, Guyau had also to make use of this inspiration in deal-ing with problems and interests very far removed from those of Plato himself. But Guyau differs from Berkeley by the wider outlook and the far more complex character of his undertakings, as well as by the extent of his learning, although here too Berkeley is a more original and construc-tive thinker than Guyau.

Both Berkeley and Schelling lived far past the period of their youthful philosophical *Sturm und Drang.* Here Guyau differs from both. His is the philosophy not only of a young man, but also of a doomed invalid, who had indeed his intervals of physical vigor and his hopeful years, but whose eyes were, almost from the first, accustomed to look death in the face. His step-father, who has put on record a beautifully clear, faithful, affectionate, and yet per-fectly objective account of our thinker's philosophical de-velopment and career, until his death, is very sparing of biographical detail, and I do not happen to know of any account of the nature of our philosopher's maladies. It seems to be admitted, however, that his early intellectual labors involved a physical overstrain which certainly did not take away the acuteness of his intellect, but which added at all events to his constitutional or acquired burdens, and hastened the end. Yet when one considers what the man accomplished, despite his fatal maladies, one cannot
24

view this brief career without feeling, as the ancients would
have felt, that there are many ways of living well besides
merely living long. One hears much of overstrain. Guyau,
in his book upon Education, wrote himself upon the subject. Overstrain is a bad thing. It may have helped to
deprive us early of this remarkable man. Yet there are
young men, and even here at Harvard I have known
such, who, perhaps in order to add prudently to their
chances of intellectual efficiency in old age, are disposed to
sacrifice, in a restful way, nearly the whole of the intellectual opportunities of their youth. For my part, I regret
to see men throw away either end of life. But when one
observes that Guyau's permanently useful memoir upon the
history of Utilitarian Ethics was written in that year of life
which here in Harvard is dedicated, by most men, to the
work, and even, in a few instances, to the leisure of the
Freshman Class, it occurs to one afresh that, as Quintilian,
I believe, said, we ourselves are the ones who make our
lives short. At all events, death is not the only shortener
of life, and I venture to think that if more of our American
youth were to labor like Guyau, we as a nation could well
endure even a certain increase of the death-rate amongst
scholars. A man is but a man, and if you call a life wasted
that is passed in invalidism between twenty and thirty-
three, and then ended, still be willing to observe with me
for a little *how* our philosopher wasted away this his brilliant youth.

I.

Since 1870 France has been the centre of a philosophical
movement which as yet, to be sure, is not of the first grade
as to originality and constructiveness, but which certainly is
of great variety, liberality, courage, and fruitfulness. Our
first interest in Guyau is in his character as a representative
of the general tendencies of this whole French national
movement. To philosophize extensively and successfully,

whether as system-maker or as a critic of systems, such as
was Guyau, you must combine, first, a strong love of life
with a great deal of critical coolness; next, a considerable
range of intellectual vision with a keen eye for the unity of
things; and, finally, a cautious sense of human fallibility—a
power to doubt, with a courageous willingness to take your
risks, and even to make your blunders. Now the first two
of the three characteristics thus enumerated, namely, a combination of a strong love of life with a critical coolness in
observing life, appears to be very characteristic of the
French nature. A comparison with two or three other
philosophical peoples will serve to make the fact clearer.
The Hindoo, as a philosopher, has always been a keen critic
of human illusions, but since it chanced, by some accident
of race-development, that the Hindoo, from an early period
of his evolution, did not love life, Hindoo philosophy, extensive as are its literary monuments, is in essential doctrine always very brief and unfruitful. Life for the Hindoo
is an ill; one philosophizes to seek salvation. And salvation
lies in some sort of absolute contemplative abstraction
from life—an abstraction which you can define in many
ways; but the goal is always the same—a peace that passeth
understanding, and that flees from facts to the Absolute beyond life's illusions. The Greek, on the contrary, not only
criticised life, but loved it. His philosophy is accordingly
various, complex, and extremely fruitful. Well, Matthew
Arnold has declared the French to be the Greeks of modern
civilization, and Guyau himself, in a passage of his most
mature book, has gladly accepted the characterization.*
Something of the Hellenic willingness to live—to live however life comes—to live first and to be scrupulous only in
the second place—this we who are ourselves of a more hesitant and scrupulous race generally feel to be characteristic

of the French temperament. Meanwhile, if the Frenchman
seems to accept life with fewer preliminary scruples and
conscientious inhibitions than those to which we are early
trained, he always seems by nature more fearless than we
in dissecting life if ever he chooses the thinker's business.
In case of our English stock our consciences often seem to
make us fearful of thorough-going and deliberate reflection,
although, strangely enough, the very essence of our own
conscience is a sort of fatal and unpremeditated reflection.
If a man merely lives, and has not learned to think, he has
no conscientious scruples. But if thought about action
arises in him spontaneously and fatally, as a sort of obses-
sion, coming he knows not whence, then a man very generally becomes hesitantly conscientious, scrupulous, concerned about his motives and his future, disposed to inhibit
his instinctive acts. Guyau himself observed this tendency,
and expressed it in the psychological principle that the
consciousness of our various and separate instincts is, in
general, primarily opposed to the continuance and to the
strength of these instincts themselves. Think about your
pleasures too much, and they will please you less. Guyau
has very skilfully used this principle in his criticism of the
English utilitarian ethics. But the principle frequently
has, in case of our English temperament, this further ex-
emplification, that, although we are by nature and early
training fatally predisposed to conscientious considerateness and to consequent inhibitions of our instincts, so that
we get our native hue of resolution sicklied o'er with the
pale cast of thought, we often fear, for this very reason, to
let even our considerateness go free, in its own way. Very
common, in our race, even amongst those who philosophize,
is the sense that there are a good many things about which
you must not philosophize ; that there are questions which
you must not ask ; that there are topics which you must
not mention even in philosophy ; that, in short, reflection

and considerateness are only tolerable where they themselves come upon you, with the force of instincts, of obsessions, of God-inspired fate, and not when you make them a deliberate ideal. From this point of view it seems as if you might not dare to make reflection itself anything thorough-going, to think for the sake of thinking, or to be considerate for the sake of mere considerateness. Conscience, which inhibits instincts by reflecting upon them, thus in the end often, with us, tends to inhibit even itself as the instinct to reflect; and in consequence you will often meet, as in our own very community, with people—sometimes very noble women, sometimes very laborious clergymen, sometimes saintly laymen of devoted practical life—who are by nature essentially and fatally thoughtful people, but who nevertheless pass their lives in thoughtfully limiting and restraining their own disposition to think, in so far as such thinking would involve a criticism of sacred things, or an inquiry into too central recesses of our nature.

But now the French mind, less primarily and fatally scrupulous than our own, not only loves life with fearlessness, but also fears not to think critically, when the time and the taste for thinking chance to come—to think without any scruples as to the extent to which this considerateness may be allowed to go. One sees this essentially fearless tendency in every page of Guyau. To think is an ideal: well then, let this ideal have its way, just as if it were a part of your primal love of life. Nothing is so sacred that you may not name it, bring it out to the light, scrutinize it, define it. One's considerateness becomes frankly quite free from scruples. But as Guyau himself maintains, in defending one of the most subtle of his own ethical principles, this very willingness to make thought and self-possession an ideal may be the best way to escape from that primarily paralyzing tendency which we have just seen to be, in our own cases, the first consequence of reflection.

The man of instinct acts unscrupulously because he has not yet learned to think. When he begins to think, if he thinks after the frequent fashion of our own race, he becomes conscious of his instincts. This consciousness, in the first place, involves a sort of paralysis of instincts. To see why you acted is to see through the illusions of instinct. For each instinct is but a part of your life, and as such is now seen to be opposed to some other part of life. Knowledge brings this inner disharmony to light. You lose your naïve belief in each element of instinct as you reflect upon its blindness, and upon the false hopes that it involved. It hoped to realize the end of life. But life is larger than any desire, and every individual desire is seen as in war with others. This resulting paralysis may, as is the case with the conscientious people of whom I have just spoken, extend itself to include the very exercise of your own reflective powers. Even reflection is seen, as an instinct, to oppose other instincts. You learn to fear life, and consequently to fear even the life of thinking. But now go further. Make thinking itself your ideal, and comprehension for its own sake your goal. What is your result? To comprehend life wholly would mean simply the conscious and deliberate judgment of every instinct and desire in its relation to the whole of life. In such judgment your very guiding principle would be the ideal of a rational and comprehensible harmony of your life. You would still find the individual instinct paralyzed in so far as it was at war with the unity of life; but you would get before yourself the ideal of bringing desires into unity with one another and with life's plan; and this ideal would itself be the beginning of a new life, still subject to the laws of your nature, but organized by the pervading motive which your reason determined. Let reason have her perfect work, and she will suggest to you new and positive plans of life. You will no longer fear life, because you will see the plan of a way out of the conflicts which have aroused your fears.

To sum up so far, the merely scrupulous join to their other instincts the instinct to reflect. This reflection discovers the conflicts of their own nature. This discovery is paralyzing. Moreover, it reacts upon their very reflective instinct, and makes them fear to think. They remain permanently in a state of thoughtful inner discord, scrupulous and yet unwilling to scruple.* In such a state of mind our own racial temperament forces some of us to live. But there is the other way, more easily followed by many who are less fatally doomed to be scrupulous. It is the way of first finding out how to think, and of then letting thought run absolutely free, with a general sense that no scruples need hinder any instinct from winning its rightful place. But thoughtfulness, thus given its freedom, may, in happy cases, transcend the stage in which it merely discovers inner conflicts. It may come to conceive the ideal of a complete and now positive harmony of reasonable life. This ideal will be beyond criticism, because, when once formed, it proves to be the very basis and presupposition of all criticism of life. The evil about desires and primary instincts is that they are out of harmony with one another. This disharmony is what reflection first shows us. What we want is a way out of the disharmony, and when once thought, allowed to grow freely, learns to define this want, thought has won an ideal that henceforth justifies the most unscrupulous use of our insight, because whatever steadfastly means to make for harmony can never itself be in essential conflict with any of the interests of the life that it means to harmonize.

---

* For a classic instance of the resulting possibilities, the reader is referred to the experiences of John Bunyan, as recorded in an early essay of the present volume.

I have stated, and already in very much the way of
Guyau himself, an ideal of the work of thinking which has
especially good chances of being illustrated in the work-
ings of the French mind. The French mind is apparently
able to win the true freedom of the reason more easily than
our own, just because the Frenchman carries into the realm
of thought that gracious readiness to let himself go which
is at once his glory, and his danger. In baser form this
unscrupulousness of critical thinking appears, in modern
French literature, in certain well-known and cynical out-
growths with which Guyau's whole tendency is strongly
contrasted. But it is the privilege of those who love life to
show their love in many guises. The Frenchman who
loves discipline, order, loyalty, and his family, can express all
this devotion with a gracious gaiety unknown to those who
have scrupulously to consider every love before they quite
know whether it is righteous. On the contrary, our own
conscientiousness is itself often the parent of many forms
of anarchy and confusedness. Thus many of the more unhappy incidents that accompany our modern English and
American movement—a movement admirable on the whole
—in favor of an improvement of the destiny of women—
many, I say, of the accompanying and unhappy incidents of
this movement appear to be due to a form of conscientiousness which leads certain sensitive women to feel deep
scruples as to whether, after all, one is doing perfectly right
to remain a woman at all, since that is only an accident of
blind nature, and not one's moral choice. Well, much
safer, in a way, is the position of natures that are not primarily and insistently scrupulous, and that love to let
themselves go, if only their love chances to be for discipline, for order, for loyalty, for the family, and for reason as
being simply the noblest of one's instincts. And this, I
say, is essentially the position of the better natures that to-
day represent French philosophy—and in particular of a

nature like Guyau's. The result is a spirit of altogether enviable freedom—of freedom disciplined, critical, rigidly devoted to law, yet still of joyous freedom—a spirit which breathes through all our author's work, and which constitutes the chief charm of Guyau's whole manner and method, whatever may be his problem. He is a man who fears nothing, who shrinks from no topic, however delicate, and who still never runs the risk of feeling any morbid interest— who would comprehend all, and to that end first doubt all, but who nevertheless loves construction, duty, and the ideal. In many, one must say in most liberal thinkers who write in English, one feels, in their stern polemic, or else in their anxious defense of their rights, in their very consciousness of their merits, how with a great price they obtained this liberty. But Guyau was free-born. And in this respect, as I have said, he is only one culminating point in the recent French philosophical movement, which, in all of its best work, is characterized by this union of the spirit of thorough criticism with the graciously gay French love of life.

This union of the critical spirit with the love of life I mentioned above as the first condition of extensive and successful philosophizing. The second condition, also mentioned above, is the union of a considerable range of intellectual vision with a keen eye for the unity of things. Now the French mind, wherever it has philosophized, has always shown great skill in swift, exactly statable, and highly unifying generalizations. The defects of French philosophy have often been determined in former periods of its history by the one-sidedness of the individual French thinker's view of his world. The Cartesian doctrine, the *Système de la Nature*, and the Positive Philosophy of Comte, are all of them cases of this one-sidedness and relative superficiality of thought. Vast regions of life, accessible to his day and generation, still lie below the horizon of the man whose thought would encompass the whole knowable world. His very exactness is often but one aspect of his superficiality. He analyzes so skilfully, because he analyzes but a very little. He states so exactly, because he has found out so few things to state. The German thinker, on the other hand, has often been confused by the wealth of the life that he has discovered. His generalizations have been vast and many-sided, but so obscure that either, like Kant, he spends years in elaborating many and various thoughts as wonderful as they are, in certain regions, mutually inconsistent, or he is driven, like Hegel, to invent a barbarous tongue in order to conceal rather than to reveal his deep but too manifold meaning. The classic German philosophy of former generations is a realm of many-sided, but to the student baffling paradoxes—a labyrinth, where one wanders long before one even conceives the goal. French philosophy, as it has been developed in former times, is too often like a relatively bare room, full of electric lights, that shine with brilliancy upon a few diagrams, which pretend to be a picture of the universe. A similar one-sidedness has held in case of much of the more orthodox and official French thinking, where freedom gave place to discipline, and that was taught which officially ought to be declared true. Yet in the midst of all these defects, the French have at least always stood out for clearness, and have insisted that when you see the truth, you at all events see, whereas the German thinker has too often, in the past, baffled the untrained student by at least seeming to imply that if you want to see, you must use some wholly new sort of intuition, and must lay aside once for all your eyes.

I have thus spoken, and of course here one-sidedly enough, not of the value, but of the defects of the older sorts of philosophizing in France and in Germany. The strength that in both countries has gone beside these contrasting forms of human weakness, I have not here to define. Enough it is to say that despite this past history, the present day no longer justifies the old contrast. The French philosophical movement since 1870 has, on the whole, been nowise lacking in many-sidedness, and nowise disposed to the older superficiality. In fact, of late years, it is to France rather oftener than to Germany that you must go in order to enjoy the treasures of genuine many-sidedness and of truly philosophical liberality. For contemporary philosophical Germany suffers from one heavy burden from which France now appears to be free. I refer to the burden of academic officialism. In vain does that undertake to be free thought which may not use methods, or announce opinions, which a current university tradition declares to be opposed to the *Zeitgeist*, or to involve the appeal to an *ueberwundener Standpunkt*—that bogie of German scientific superstitions. And one cannot read current German philosophy, even in its best representatives, without feeling more or less of the burden of these current academic superstitions. Scherer, in his history of German Literature, has compared Germany's repeatedly exhibited tendency to turn her back upon the ideals of her own past to Siegfried's magic forgetfulness of Brynhild. Yet even Siegfried, in the days after he drank the cup of forgetfulness, did not boast that his old love for Brynhild was nothing but an *ueberwundener Standpunkt*. And there is often something pathetic in to-day's brutally outspoken neglect, in Germany, of the former ideal struggles of a philosophy whose work was indeed imperfect enough, but whose problems survive despite all the efforts of contemporary students to ignore or independently to struggle with them, as if they were not old stories, or as if philosophy, even according to their own confession, did not live in the history of philosophy.

On the other hand, the modern French movement, whatever else may be said of it, is free from superstitions, both religious and scientific. It is peculiarly many-sided and liberal. If it is not yet very richly constructive, it at least does not fear construction. Its representative magazine, the Revue Philosophique, was for years the world's best philosophical periodical. The most manifold interests get here a hearing, the spirit of the mere school is at a minimum, the relations of philosophy to all human interests, scientific, ethical, and practical, receive the best representation possible under existing circumstances. The spirit shown is at once docile and original, at once discreet and hopeful, at once constructive and historical.

And now of this modern movement Guyau himself is an admirable representative in just these respects. His outlook is wide, his desire to get his world into unity is strong. He began under the influence of Plato and Kant, he early experienced to the full the significance of the English schools, he remained always closely in touch with current psychological investigation. He was interested in ethics and in metaphysics, in æsthetics and in educational theory. He shared and expressed the modern interest in sociological problems. His general view of life is a sort of transformed Kantian, or even Fichtean ethical idealism, stated in a modern psychological terminology, and modified but never wholly overcome by its ingenious combination with a belief in modern naturalism, and by his acceptance of a somewhat conventional view of the process of evolution. His exquisite intellectual sensitiveness kept his mind open to influences of the most varied sort. He speculated with equal interest upon anthropological problems, such as the origin of religion, and upon confessedly transcendent problems, such as immortality. For him the first duty of the modern man is to live in every wise sense, to live openmindedly, many-sidedly, and considerately, and then to set down as he can the meaning of life.

I mentioned before, as the third prerequisite of philosophical success, a combination of a cautious sense of human fallibility with a courageous willingness to take your risks, and even to make your blunders. It is customary for people to condemn philosophy because it risks error in dealing, as it does, with transcendent problems. As if common sense did not risk error at every moment, and as if common sense did not, at every moment, deal, and very practically too, with all sorts of transcendent problems— with right and wrong, with truth and error, with appearances and with realities, with life and all the issues of life. The philosopher is not in the position of being able to avoid the risk of error by merely ceasing his beloved speculations. He knows, having once been awakened, that he deals with the problem of the meaning of life, and that he dealt with that problem, in a practical way, before he was awakened, from the very moment when first he performed his least act. He knows that if he ceased to think, he would not therefore cease to err, but that he would only err more blindly. For the essence of error lies after all in the falsity of your mental attitudes, of your inner deeds. All thought is action, as Guyau himself loved to say ; and all action implies thought. When one thinks, one merely finds out the meaning of one's acts. But the meaning was there before one reflected. And all error in the end is practical, just as all practice is liable to the penalties of error.

One would not then avoid error, nor yet its consequences, temporal or eternal, if one ceased to think of the deeper problems of life. The philosopher, unable, as fallible man, to avoid the risk of error, merely seeks clearness. Where others blindly go right or blindly err, he aims to make out what he can of the difference between true living and false living. Since life is his object, he ought to fear reflection, which aims to give life unity, as little as he fears life itself. But, on the other hand, nobody knows better than the philosopher what risks he takes when he thinks, and nobody ought more frankly to confess, or more frequently to remember, his fallibility.

And now the modern French movement, influenced as it is by the spirit of recent empirical science, is at once constructive and sceptical. Guyau himself can never be ranked amongst the system-makers, and is in nowise as constructive a thinker as his step-father Fouillée. He was in fact too cautious, with all his facility, to construct extensively until he had gathered together his materials. There are signs that had he lived longer he would have become more systematic. As it is, one goes to him not for a system, but for far-reaching and ingenious ideas, which he never had time to weave into one whole. These ideas, as I said before, relate indeed to a few persistently central problems. And they certainly are in nowise disconnected ideas. But before Guyau could have become responsible for a systematic doctrine he would have needed to devote time to some fundamental matters which, to judge by the topic of one of his latest papers, on the Origin of the Ideas of Time and Space, he was just reaching when death cut short his task.

II.

I have thus far very inadequately treated Guyau merely as a representative of a few of the general tendencies of the modern movement of French philosophy since 1870. I must now ask you to consider a little more closely the man himself.

One who was no special student of philosophy could easily take delight in Guyau's books for the sake of the author's personality. Our thinker's temperament continually and directly gets expression in his work. His style has that quality which is, once more, one of a Frenchman's not exclusive, but peculiarly frequent privileges—the quality of being full of sentiment, of personal experience, and of the frankest confession, without ever seeming to approach

what we ourselves fear as mere sentimentality, or scorn as
" gush." The man's whole personal bearing towards his
world embodies itself before you as plainly as if he were
present speaking his words ; the author never seems to note
or consciously to control this fact ; yet this childlike simplicity of confession is as free from awkwardness as from
posing. Every confession meets the author's purpose, but
meets it without premeditation, without any painful or suspicious self-consciousness. The person who speaks to you
in these books is obviously an invalid, who has suffered
much. He is accordingly self-observant, a professional
introspective psychologist. Yet he is never morbid in his
introspection, never takes himself too seriously, and never
even likes to boast, like some invalids, of the dangers he
has passed, although in one eloquent passage he has indeed
occasion to mention them. His enjoyment of the beautiful,
both in nature and in art, is manifold and intense. In the
intervals of his invalidism he gives himself over to long-
continued physical exercise, finds great fascination in
mountain-climbing, and makes frequent use in his discourse
of metaphors drawn from life amongst mountains. His
sensory life is very wealthy and complex, and he notes the
fact. He cannot see, for instance, why the prevalent æsthetic prejudice declares that we get an experience of the
truly beautiful only through the senses of sight and hearing. To him all sensations that appeal deeply and richly to
the general feeling of life within us, of life in its wholeness,
will be beautiful in so far as they heighten rather than de-
press this feeling of life. And what sensations may not,
under given conditions, possess this character. " I shall
always remember," says Guyau,* " the wonderfully grateful
sensation, that, in the heat of a violent fever, was produced
in me by the touch of ice upon my brow. To express very

* Problèmes d'Æsthétique Contemporaine, p. 61.

feebly the impression that I received, I can only compare it to the pleasure that the ear experiences in finding again the perfect chord after a long series of dissonances; but this simple sensation of freshness was far deeper, more grateful, and altogether more æsthetic than the passing accord of a few notes exciting the ear; it made me witness, as it were, a gradual resurrection of the whole interior harmony; I felt in me a sort of moral and physical pacification that was infinitely sweet." Nor is our author limited to the experiences of illness when he wishes to illustrate such extraordinary æsthetic effects: "One summer day," he says,* "after a tramp in the Pyrenees which had been continued to the maximum of fatigue, I met a shepherd, and asked him for milk. He produced, from his hut, beneath which a brook passed, a vessel of milk that had been plunged into the water, and kept at a temperature almost ice-cold. In drinking this fresh milk, into which all the mountain had mixed its perfume, and whose every draught gave me new life, I certainly experienced a series of sensations that are ill-defined by the word *agreeable*. It was, so to speak, a pastoral symphony, tasted instead of heard."

The rich life of sensation of which such passages, which are frequent, are only a hint, is in our author's case, however, first of all supplemented by a generous wealth of the more humane emotions. Guyau is evidently an admirable lover, and was so, we are told, from his earliest childhood. Fouillée tells us that Guyau's youth began with a Platonic faith that love is the soul of the universe, and with a metaphysical doctrine worked out upon this basis—the world being conceived as a collection of beings, conscious and unconscious, who somehow worked together in the bonds of a not always conscious but universal love, towards the common end. Fouillée also calls attention to one of Guy-

---

* Problèmes d'Æsthétique Contemporaine, p. 63.

au's own passages of childhood reminiscence: " I remember," says Guyau, " my long despair the day when, for the first time, it came home to me that death could be an extinction of love, a separation of hearts, an eternally mutual coldness; that the cemetery with its stony tombs and its four walls could be the truth ; that 'twixt to-day and to-morrow the beings who constituted my moral being could be taken away, or that I could be taken away, and that we should never be restored to one another. There are certain cruelties that you do not believe in, because they go too far beyond you. You say, ' It is impossible,' because within you feel : " How could I do that ? "

This humane tenderness of an affectionate nature remains with Guyau to the end—never paraded, always well controlled, but always ready to find such expression as was consistent with the thinker's clearness and honesty. The delights of a happy home-life are frankly confessed as the climax of his own private and earthly interests. He finds no better office for a man than to love and to be loved. He was himself husband and father, and writes as from his own home, in which, first of all, he is minded to be gay. To be sure, love is not only a gay but a grave thing ; for the shadow of death is constantly present to the invalid. Moreover, to think about the universe means, for this natural lover, to try to love the universe ; and in face of the mystery of evil, this sort of love is a grave passion. As Guyau himself expresses the matter :* " The higher metaphysical emotion, like the higher æsthetic emotion, is never clear of a certain sadness. The day comes, when, in all hearts, grave and even painful chords will awaken, will demand at times to vibrate as they once vibrated in the privileged hearts of such as Heraclitus and Jeremiah. The metaphysical sentiment cannot exist without something of sadness, as

---

* L'Irreligion de l'Avenir, p. 337.

is the case with the sublime that we feel ourselves incapable of ever grasping, or with doubt itself, or with that intellectual, moral, or physical ill, which always mingles with all our joys, and which this doubt echoes in our own consciousness. From this point of view, one may say that there is a measure of suffering in every deep philosophy, as in every deep religion. . . . One day," our author continues, " as I was seated at my desk at work, my love came to me, full of concern : ' How sad your brow !' she said. ' What troubles you ? Tears, alas ! Have I caused you grief ?' ' Ah, no, what grief have you ever caused me ? I am weeping at a thought—nothing more—yes, at a thought, in the air, abstract—at a thought concerning the world, concerning the fate of things and of creatures. Is there not in the universe enough misery to justify a tear that seems without an object, just as there is enough of joy to explain a smile that seems to spring from nowhere ?' Every man may weep or smile thus, not for himself, not even for his own, but for the great Whole where he lives. And it befits man —this conscious solidarity wherein he lives with all beings —this impersonal pain or joy that he is capable of feeling. This faculty of impersonalizing one's self, so to speak, is what will remain most lasting in the religions and in the philosophies, for it is hereby that they are most interior to our natures. To sympathize with all nature, to seek its secret, to want to contribute to its betterment, to leave thus one's egoism, in order to live the universal life—that is what man will always do merely because he is a man, because he thinks and feels."

Over against this warmth of natural experience, this rich life of sensory and emotional tenderness, there stand, in our thinker, two very marked characteristics. The one is a love of order—a love very freely and simply expressed, but very potent. This man has the invalid's fondness for regimen. Joys and griefs have to be well-ordered. He loves experience; but he must not experiment upon his frail constitution. Once, to be sure, he narrates, very modestly, how for a while he tried a quasi-Buddhistic experiment upon the art of attaining Nirvâna. The method lay in reducing his nourishment to a few cups of milk instead of the usual meals, in leading a life of abstraction from all worldly concerns, and in devoting his mind to "abstract meditation and æsthetic contemplation." After a prolonged period of such discipline the experimenter reached a stage that was "not a dream," but that was certainly very remote, he says, from ordinary life. Life now obtained "something ethereal which is not without charm, although without savor, and without color." But erelong he was now led to observe that if he had left earth, he was after all no nearer heaven. There was painlessness, but no clearer insight. Thought, even the most abstract, began to lose its outlines; and so, after some stay in the shadow realms on the very confines of peace, where even the last desires were ceasing, our philosopher deliberately returned to earth, observing, as he says, that in the Pyrenees the best paths are those which have been worn by the heavy feet of the asses. As in the mountains, so, he here says, in life, and even for the philosopher, the best rule as to the general conduct of one's earthly business is the mountaineer's motto: "Follow the asses." They do not understand mountain scenery, nor the heavens above; but here on earth they somehow know the road.

Apart from this one excess of severity in regimen, our author shows us, amidst all his complexity of thought and of sentiment, his love for simplicity and clearness of living. And now the other trait, which, as I said above, joins with this love of order to characterize our thinker's attitude, and to offset the natural warmth of his sentiments —is a very strongly practical sense for the application of doctrine to business. Guyau thinks for the world; and it is his practical skill that goes far to make him acceptable to the partisans of the modern spirit as such, both in France and elsewhere. He descends readily from the highest problems to the plainest questions of the day. His book called Education and Heredity, published posthumously, and known to our own public through an English translation, is an example of this practical disposition. From an introductory study of the deepest questions of psychology, Guyau passes, in this work, to a detailed discussion of the contemporary problems of both physical and mental training in the schools of France. In another book, that upon the future of religion, Guyau interrupts extremely subtle and profound philosophical inquiries to introduce a vigorous, delicately written, but extremely practical chapter upon the relations of religious belief and unbelief to the fecundity of races, with especial relation to the recent course of events in France. These easy transitions from theory to practice, from central issues to the plain of daily life, are characteristic and noteworthy. They help to complete the picture of this vigorous and suffering, gay and serious, tender and thoughtful, cool and sensitive, common-sense and speculative, essentially manifold personality. You will not be surprised to learn that Guyau published a volume of poems—Vers d'un Philosophe—poems that, so far as I know them, seem as frank and simple as were all of the author's other confessions.

III.

The philosophical doctrine that resulted from the work of this life passed through stages which Fouillée has authoritatively summarized. First there was the youthful, quasi-Platonic metaphysical hypothesis, never, as you will see, wholly abandoned, of the world as a community of beings, conscious and unconscious, engaged in working out an ideal upon the basis of an universal law of love. This hypothesis was obviously the direct result of Fouillée's own

influence upon his step-son's mind. A little later, the study
of the Utilitarian moralists culminated in a careful examination of the doctrine of evolution. Guyau came under
Spencer's influence, absorbed the naturalism of the day,
and accepted the physical doctrine of evolution, a doctrine
to which he henceforth remained true, although, like many
other modern thinkers, he reserved the right to study independently the probable metaphysical meaning of the process of evolution itself. But the current interpretation of
the doctrine, in so far as it was applied to the problems of
ethics by Spencer and by others, seemed to him from the first
unsatisfactory. His own ethical views never lost touch
with the Kantian influences that had so early moulded his
mind. He was, in his essential features, still an ethical
idealist, i. e., a man disposed to interpret the universe as a
realm whose significance lies in the ethical ideals that its
processes realize. Yet he had meanwhile become converted,
despite this fact, to the current modern naturalism. He
was deeply impressed by the apparent indifference of nature
to the ideals, and by the equally obvious isolation and in-
significance of man's place in nature. From the physical
side, it now appeared to him only too plain that our morality, our beauty, our ideals in general, are an affair of the
race, not of the universe. Unable to overcome, for the
time, this conflict between nature and the ideals, our philosopher resolved to define, at all events, the moral world,
and proceeded to his brilliant essay called Esquisse d'une
Morale Sans Obligation ni Sanction, where the view of our
moral nature already indicated in the introduction to this
paper is developed. Man is now defined as a being whose
manifold and inherited instincts determine all his natural
conduct, and whose intelligence means simply, at the start,
a bringing of his instincts into the light of consciousness.
There is no intelligence apart from some sort of action.
To know is simply to be aware of what you are doing.

But, to be sure, since our various instincts conflict, we no sooner bring them to the light of consciousness than we find ourselves naturally disposed to various and conflicting sorts of action, egoistic and altruistic, passionate and prudent, pleasure-giving and pain-producing. The first result of consciousness is therefore, as we saw, a tendency to a certain paralysis of conduct, a considerable inhibition of our instincts, because we have found them out. The problem of ethics is to find some fashion of viewing ourselves that shall relieve us of this sceptical paralysis of instinct by consciousness. Older ethical writers have sought to solve this problem by appealing to the idea of our obligation to God or to some form of higher law. But the modern man, in order to be ethical, must find his law within himself, and mvst not even, like Kant, seek for it in some supernatural aspect of his own being. Hence the new ethical doctrine must teach us a "Morale sans Obligation." To do right must come to mean for us simply doing what we ourselves most truly desire to do. But just so, once more, former writers have sought to give the moral law an external sanction, to tell us to do right in order that we may be made happy, by Providence, or by the rewards of our fellow men. Yet, in Guyau's view, true morality must be relieved of all such external sanction. Right must mean for me my own will, chastened and dignified, no doubt, by insight, but still my own very will, and not the will of another.

Well, the solution of the problem thus set for the ethical teacher, Guyau finds in a very originally stated form of a doctrine which many others have in recent times taught, and which is, after all, the Kantian ethic, much as Fichte restated it, but then translated into a terminology more in accord with the spirit of modern naturalism. What everybody wants, after all, is life—intense life, broad life, deep life. For this fullness of life instinct blindly gropes. This, too, our reason, even at the moment when consciousness,

bringing to light the one-sidedness of the individual instinct, paralyzes the instinct by detecting its conflict with
the rest of our nature—this fullness of life our reason even
then desires. For reason, like every state of intelligence,
is simply the coming to consciousness of some mode of action. When life as a whole comes into the light of consciousness, this means simply that we no longer blindly
desire life as a whole, but are aware that we desire life.
Not otherwise can we become conscious of our life. For all
knowing is simply doing lighted up by consciousness. All
ideas involve acts. When you learn to see, what you see,
within yourself, is simply your own mode of activity. Accordingly, to know life as a whole is consciously to love
life as a whole. If the single instinct, now become a conscious desire, wars with the whole of life, our interest in
life's wholeness now consciously demands that the rebellious special desire be subordinated, that our wants take on
the form of wholeness, that life be harmonized, and that
the desire for more life, for more harmonious extended, and
intense life, become the law of our being, ruling over special
desires, putting them down if need be, giving life a plan,
fulfilling the end of the Self in its wholeness. Such a
consciousness is that of our so-called reason. It invents
no supernatural mysteries. It simply counsels harmony
of growth. To be sure, I am not now harmonious. Yes,
but I can become so. *I can, and therefore I ought.* This
consciousness of the power to make the love of life in its
wholeness victorious over special and subordinate aims is,
as Guyau maintains, the true form of the moral consciousness.

For the rest this moral consciousness is theoretically
defensible only because it consents to be more than merely
theoretical. Kant's error lay in appealing to pure reason,
without noting that the pure reason, viewed merely as an
abstract source of law, would be empty. Action is prelimi-

nary to theory, and survives mere theory. The truth of
Kant's Categorical Imperative of the so-called pure reason
lies in the fact that the desire for life in its wholeness is
more fundamental than any special desires. To become
conscious that what one wants is life, in all its fullness,
intensity, and unity, is to become conscious of a categorical
imperative superior to all particular aims, such as the aim
of pleasure. Here then is at once the truth and the correc-
tion of Kant's view.

But this love of life has its social as well as its individual significance. The ordinary separation of the ego from
the rest of the world depends upon an essentially false
classification, which our blindness often makes, but which
nature ignores. Man's organism is already within itself, as
Guyau loves frequently to point out, a society, a combined
group of living cells, which coöperate in order to carry out
the end of all. And by nature, this cell-colony which constitutes for each one of us our organism, is linked in the
most manifold and real ways to the other organisms about
us. One cannot *first* live for himself, and *then* for others.
To live his own life is to recognize his organic relationship
to his fellows. My desire to love is as much a part of my
own inner life-interest as is my desire to eat. If I want to
live largely, intensely, and in unity, I want to live a life
that cannot be conceived alone. I want to *love* largely, intensely, harmoniously. Were pleasure my goal, I could
ask, how much pleasure will loving acts give me personally. But if I want just to live, for life's sake, I can no
longer separate my own life from the common life. The
richest interior life, as for instance the life of thought, is at
the same time the life that is most obviously social. I cannot think alone. I can only think with others. If I want
to live the thinker's life, I must then make it part of my
aim that there should be other thinkers in my world, my
equals, whose ideas are as valuable to me as my own, and

whose mental advantage is as much a part of my goal as is my own intellectual growth. All communication is social, if you will altruistic. It is done for the sake of those to whom I speak. But it is also done for my own sake, since utterly uncommunicative thought quickly comes to mean nothing. To think is already to speak interiorly to some conceived companion. Thus life and action exist only through their fecundity. Mere egoism is self-mutilation. Life is expansive, goes beyond itself, lives in social relations, is best for me within, when it is best expressed for those without. Or again, I live best when I do work. But work means the production of fruit that my social fellows enjoy.

In such fashions, which could be indefinitely illustrated, Guyau undertakes to give his ethics of life, or, as many would prefer to say, of self-realization, an essentially sociological turn. The more our philosopher proceeded in his work, the more his formulas became, in fact, sociological. His posthumous book on Education and Heredity is conceived in this sociological spirit. The problem of the intense and harmonious life is to be solved, for the individual as for the race, for the philosopher as for the educator, by laying stress upon the fact that man is born for the richer experiences of companionship, and can solve the problem of his own destiny only by recognizing to the full his solidarity with all men. Only he who loves most lives most. Hence no egoistic consciousness can be successful in the pursuit of its true aim, which, consciously or unconsciously, is life in its fullness.

The charm of these ideas, as Guyau presents them, lies in the originality, not of their essential contents, but of their form, and of the manner of their presentation. Such truths get a new meaning whenever they come as the embodiment of the more personal experience of a man of original temper. The book now before us is the work of a man of twenty-nine. The union of vigor with simplicity, of vitality with clearness, of naturalism with idealism, of youth with mature thoughtfulness, are thoroughly characteristic of the author's position and quality. As Guyau now, in 1885, turned from morals to his wider philosophical interests, he saw immediately before him, amongst the countless tasks which awakened his ambition, three that he had time in some measure to accomplish before his death. One of these was the topic of a posthumous work, namely, that on Education and Heredity, already mentioned. Another was the problem of Æsthetics, which, in Guyau's mind, is closely associated with that of morals, for if the ethical ideal is the attainment of the fullness of life, the æsthetic pleasure is, according to Guyau, the enjoyment, through sympathy, of the contemplation or the presence of life. In his own words : " To live a full and strong life is already æsthetic ; to live an intellectual and moral life, is beauty carried to its maximum, and therein also is the supreme delight." The beautiful is " a perception or an action that stimulates in us life in all its three forms at once (sensibility, intelligence, and will), and produces pleasure by the swift consciousness of this general stimulation." In consequence, the beautiful is such because, on the one hand, it awakens in us " the deepest sensations of our nature," while on the other hand it appeals " to the most moral sentiments and the loftiest ideas of the mind." The study of æsthetics has thus for Guyau an extremely practical aspect. And the sociological importance of the beautiful is, in his eyes, rendered all the greater, not only by this close relation of the beautiful (as that which appeals to our deepest sense of life) to the moral (as that which depends upon making life an ideal)—not only by this relation—but also by the fact that in modern times the beautiful must more and more be depended upon to take that inspiring place as the moral awakener of men which in the past has been taken by dogmatic religion.

The third problem which Guyau had still time to treat, he dealt with in his very remarkable book L'Irreligion de l'Avenir—another of his "sociological studies," and his strongest work.

The title of this book easily misleads any one who has not come to know our thinker's childlike simplicity, and transparent honesty of speech. One may well doubt whether he is right in maintaining, as he does, that his own view is essentially irreligious, or that the future to which he looks forward is, even in his own account of its destiny, in any proper sense a future of "irreligion." The matter is largely one of words. But Guyau loves frankness so much that he had rather lay stress in his title upon his differences with tradition, than arouse false expectations by an appearance of conformity. These are matters that every man must decide for himself. If Guyau's opinions, as here expressed, were my own, I should unhesitatingly call them religious, for the reason that I should then see in them, as he himself sees, the fulfillment, in reasonable form, of what the religious instinct of humanity has been seeking. For the rest this volume breathes everywhere that spirit of spiritual unconventionality which, as I must confess, seems to me one of the first qualities that the philosopher ought to cultivate in relations with the universe. To love law, is not to love convention as such. To accept convention in one's daily life amongst men is, within certain limits, the ordinary business of the loyal citizen. But your relations with the universe, with the truth, with the absolutely ideal, are simply not conventional. And that is precisely why some of us, even if we love both the name and the universal cause of religion, may find outward and personal conformity to the mere accidents of current religious convention personally repugnant, and distinctly depressing to our best concerns, so that, however much we sympathize, still outwardly such amongst us must stubbornly decline to conform. For with God—even when he appears to your insight through the thin and transparently fragile veil of every human thought and relation—with God as he is in himself, you have, in a certain sense, to be alone, especially if you reflectively and independently think out for yourself what you take to be your relation to him. Consequently it is in one way with God as it is with death, and with love. These exist for all men ; yet into each man's life they come as in some sense incommunicably his own. Of course you may tell this or that about them if you will. Speech is free. Thought has, as thought, no secrets. The way to the truth is open to all, and is to be publicly heralded and discussed. But your own sight of the truth when you see it—nobody else has or can have just that. You and your truth, at the moment of insight—you are alone together, in one harmony of appreciation not elsewhere attained in the universe. And now, this being so, one has a right to be sensitive as to the essentially lonely freedom of this one's union with the truth. It is a marriage. If any given conventional mingling with others who are or who take themselves to be in presence of that truth, chances to jar on one's private sensibilities, not because one fails to love one's fellows, but because one does not love the note they strike, one has here an absolute right to one's private taste. The world has a right to your service, but never to your religious conformity. That is due to God alone, and you can only express it in your personal way. If a given outward and worldly conformity chances to inspire you, you are welcome to it. But then that is merely your temporal accident. In the eternal world there are countless worshippers and servants, but there are no conventional religious ties. Such worldly ties are the mere trappings, and the suits of the religious insight, which, in itself, passeth show.

Now in these last words I have spoken of course for myself, and not for Guyau. His religious, or, as he would say, in his simple fashion, his irreligious insight, is not that of a metaphysical idealist, but rather that of a merely ethical idealist. He takes nature, to the end, much more seriously than, in our philosophy, some of us are disposed to do. But the sense in which I find myself agreeing with the tone of Guyau's book, even on its negative side, is determined for me by this spiritual unconventionality which has led him to choose his title. By irreligion he means, after all, little but unconventionality in one's religion. In the future, he holds, men will differ as widely as now in opinion, they will never give over speculating upon the eternal problems, and they will love the ideals and consciously fulfill the harmony of life better than we do. But they will lay aside both the authority of dogma and the forms of conventional religion. They will reason together, live together, observe together, but every man will, in the end, aim to see the truth with his own eyes. That men can learn to live in this way without losing the very aims which the religious consciousness in the past has pursued— this is Guyau's thesis. He defends it by a series of brilliant analyses, full of learning, ingenuity, criticism, kindliness, and hope.

First comes a briefly sketched theory of the religious history of humanity. The motive for the development of the religious consciousness was primarily dependent upon the psychological nature of the social consciousness· of man. Having in an especially clear and vivid fashion the idea of human fellow-beings, man, as a social creature, was peculiarly predisposed to use this central idea of his consciousness as a means of interpreting nature. Hence he easily saw comrades, enemies, and masters all about him. The world of spirits, and later the gods, consisted of the members of an enlarged society, of a society formed in the image of human society. Not so much anthropomorphism as "sociomorphism" is the principle that determines the contents and the growth of religious faiths. In time, civilized man, just as he learns to live in orderly and organized political bodies, learns to conceive his gods as in orderly and organized relations to himself. The constitution of his ideal religious state gets definitely conceived, just as his own political constitutions come gradually to his consciousness. The result is a series of highly determinate and elaborate social relations to the gods—relations which are expressed in myth, in cultus, and at length in dogma. The religious world is the world of a mythical social order.

But this elaborate sociological structure, viewed in the light of a larger knowledge of nature and of man, appears in every case, first as an accidental product of given historical conditions, which produce one set of conceptions in one region and another in another—and then as a product not of the scientific study of nature, but of the sociological imagination of man. Hence, in the long-run, every determinate mythology, rite, and dogma, must be doomed; and for the truth one must turn to science and to speculation.

Science, when we appeal to her for light, shows us not the ultimate, but only the partial truths. She does reveal to us that apparent indifference of nature before mentioned. But hereby science only whets our appetite to know the final truths, which science as such cannot, at least at present, hope to bring within the range of experience.

There remains speculation. Speculation involves risk of error at every step, but, on the other hand, speculation is the expression, in theoretical terms, of that very love of life, boundless and ideal, which we have already seen to be the soul of morality. As a limitless expansion, guided by reason, but incapable of being cut off at any point by any rational interest, is what the self, as it becomes conscious, sets before itself as the practical business of life, so a constant striving to pierce behind the veil, and to find out the mysteries of truth, is the inevitable theoretical business of the awakened mind. We cannot yet know. We must hope to know. This is the way in which theory expresses what our practical consciousness puts in the form of the principle : We are not yet fully living ; but we must hope and strive to live more and more intense, and organized, extended, and harmonious lives. Consequently, while Guyau apparently does not expect that exact science will at any definable time replace our speculation, he does believe that, so long as exact science is incomplete, men may and must speculate, and that therefore the decay of faith will never involve the cessation of philosophy. The eternal, the ideal, will always be, next to life itself, our strongest interest.

Our actual speculations must of course be guided by probability. The task of the philosopher, in reviewing theories, is to find which of the theories proposed is the most consistent, both with experience, and with itself. With ready skill Guyau reviews a number of the best known of the world's metaphysical hypotheses. Dualistic theism discontents him ; the optimistic pantheism of Spinoza and the pessimistic pantheism of Schopenhauer and von Hartmann are alike rejected as inadequate expressions, both of the place of evil in the world and of the facts of evolution. A metaphysic that in the present day is to be plausible in the light of experience, and in view of the demands of our thought, must take account both of the doctrine of evolution, and of the sociological constitution of those regions of reality best known to us men. The religions have been wrong in their dogmatic sociomorphism, which has filled the universe with arbitrarily imagined social structures. They have probably not been wrong in conceiving of the universe as substantially, after all, a social order, where, as in our own case, beings develop from unconscious isolation to conscious and social unity and harmony of life. A theory, closely related to that of Fouillée, and intimately related to Guyau's own sociological interests, is thus propounded as the most likely interpretation of the universe. The world is one of evolution from unconscious to conscious will, with a growing solidarity of interest amongst the members of any groups that thus evolve. The apparent indifference of nature is very possibly illusory. The universe is doubtless full of life, and the sociological rather than the mechanical view of the nature of being has the better chance of being true.

Meanwhile, as we are now, every man of us, loving life, wants immortality. Have we any right to hope for such a fortune ? Once come to regard the universe, as Guyau now does, in the light that makes probable a deep sympathy between the inmost nature of things and our own highest interests, and then your naturalism will no longer exclude the hope that immortality, if not already in the possession of the present humanity, will be obtained by the future race as the result of further evolution. In the closing chapter of the work now before us, and with a literary skill that makes this eloquent peroration the very climax of our author's artistic efforts, this dying invalid, joyous in the face of death, sets down the speculations which occur to him concerning the last great mystery. One cannot prove immortality; but does our knowledge of nature tend to exclude its possibility ? Here the sociological view of man's nature comes to our philosopher's aid. Man could not survive merely by virtue of the survival of a soul-substance. Man must survive as a conscious being. But then consciousness is social. One lives in one's common life with others. Why is it not possible that, if sufficient social unity, sufficient quasi-telepathic interrelationship came to be established amongst minds, one individual, in the course of human evolution, could come actually to live as consciously, as genuinely, in the midst of the very mental life of those whom he loves, as in what is now called his own mental life? At present, when our friends die, their memory remains, love holds them, and they seem to live on, because they live for us, in our love. Suppose that the group of mental states that now constitute my memory of my friend became as warm, as full of movement and spontaneity, as independently active, as are now the states of mind of my living friend. Suppose that this spontaneity went so far as to establish a continuity of memory between this living image of my friend and his real past. Would not my friend then live on in my love? And if many loved him so, if in social intercourse all their loving images united into one, might not, upon some higher plane of evolution, love hold its own forever, and the beloved survive, not as voiceless memories, but as speaking comrades, sustained in life by the activities of other organisms than used to be theirs, but genuinely alive, in precisely whatever was most ideal and lovable about them? These are indeed bold speculations, and Guyau fully knows the fact. But, reasons Guyau, we stand, as we study some of the newer psychological oddities, upon the borderland of mysteries hitherto undreamed of as to the relation of mind and mind. And so we have still our right to hope.

As for death as it is, one, by facing it frequently, may get quite used to it, says Guyau. "Death, for the rest," so he concludes—" death for the philosopher, that friend of every unknown, offers still the attraction of something that is yet to be known. It is, after birth, the most mysterious novelty of the individual's life. Death has its secret, its enigma, and one keeps the vague hope that it will solve that enigma by one last irony even as it crushes you, that the dying, as the old faith had it, prophesy, and their eyes only close because dazzled by a flash of light. Our last sorrow remains—our last curiosity!"

26

In this paper I have not desired to criticise, but to portray. I beg to introduce to you in this way one to whose immortality, if his brilliant conjecture be right, you may perchance joyously contribute, by finding him a very gracious, ingenious, and abiding friend.

THE END.

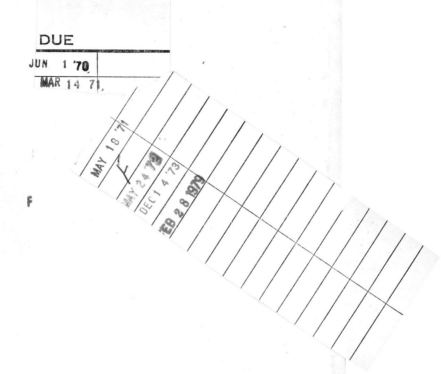

F